'This book is propelled by a brilliant intuition: by comparing two non-Western countries (Ghana and Thailand) with each other, instead of the usual and futile comparisons with Western models, the authors have uncovered some true secrets of the "wealth of nations" or lack of it. It helps that they know both countries so well.'
Edward Luttwak

'Once in a while a work of scholarship comes along which is well researched, insightful and readable. This book by the Thompson father-and-son team is one such. It is highly recommended to all those interested in development, comparative politics and international affairs.'
MR Sukhumbhand Paribatra, Deputy Foreign Minister, Thailand

'A superb book that, by focusing narrowly on two countries which the authors have studied so thoroughly, offers considerable insight into the broader question of how countries grow and build political and civil society. A book for anyone interested in development and a must-read that is made only more compelling for the father–son team that wrote it.'
Andrew Cockburn, author of *Out of the Ashes: The Resurrection of Saddam Hussein*

'In lucid and expressive prose, this study evidences a deep understanding of both societies.'
Professor Kusuma Snitwongse, Director, Institute of Security and International Studies, Chulalongkorn University, Bangkok

'Smart, witty and vivid, this engaging study of two very different societies navigating the rapids of development is an illuminating analysis and a joy to read.'
Ronald Steel, Bancroft Prize and the National Book Critics Circle award winner, author of *Walter Lippmann and the American Century* and *In Love with Night: The American Romance with Robert Kennedy*

The Baobab
and
the Mango Tree

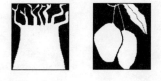

LESSONS ABOUT DEVELOPMENT
African and Asian Contrasts

Nicholas Thompson
&
Scott Thompson

White Lotus
BANGKOK

Zed Books
LONDON & NEW YORK

The Baobab and the Mango Tree was first published in 2000
by
Zed Books Ltd., 7 Cynthia Street, London N1 9JF, UK and
Room 400, 175 Fifth Avenue, New York, NY 10010, USA

and in Burma, Cambodia, Laos and Thailand by
White Lotus Co. Ltd, GPO Box 1141, Bangkok 10501, Thailand

Distributed in the USA exclusively by St Martin's Press, Inc.,
175 Fifth Avenue, New York, NY 10010, USA.

Cover design by Andrew Corbett
Designed and set in 9.6/13 pt Palatino, with Comic Sans display
by Long House, Cumbria, UK
Printed and bound in the United Kingdom
by Biddles Ltd, Guildford and King's Lynn

A catalogue record for this book
is available from the British Library

US CIP has been applied for

In Burma, Cambodia, Laos and Thailand
ISBN Pb 974 7534 49 5

ISBN   Hb 1 85649 809 3
        Pb 1 85649 810 7

Contents

Figures 185

Endnotes 188

Index 206

❧

Boxes

Foreword
&
Acknowledgements

This book is the outcome of a train of reflection launched by an email about soccer sent from son in Bangkok to father in Washington DC. 'Why is the style of soccer so different in Thailand from in Ghana?' And then, soon after: 'Why are these two countries so different? Dad, what on earth has happened since you first came here?'

Thirty-five years ago the elder of us set out to explore a new and vital world by wending his way through Africa. He ended up writing a dissertation, and eventually a book, about Ghana in its continental and world context. It hardly seemed, even by the time that effort was concluded, that Africa would head in a direction that would lead to a world so poor and far from freedom; but it did, and he started to turn east. From then until now he has examined the swift-rising stars of Southeast Asia.

The younger partner set out in 1998, one year after graduation, on a *wanderjahr* in both Africa and Asia and returned haunted with a family of queries: why did Africa fall so soon into a downward trajectory and why didn't anybody foretell it? Why did Asia's tigers leap ahead economically so astonishingly far – and why at the same time have they had to suffer such tremendous social and environmental costs?

Both authors have studied both nations – indeed one of us has written about them since before the other was born – but we come from markedly different perspectives. The younger of us was in grade school when the Berlin Wall came down, has accumulated none of the typical scholarly or popular fashions surrounding these two countries, and is part of a generation acutely aware of the price of wealth and the quest for its accumulation. The elder of us has lived in both Ghana and Thailand during violent changes in power, has been teaching students about international development for thirty years, and comes from a generation defined by the Cold War and the contest between communism and democratic capitalism. Despite these differences and many others, we see international development and its challenges in similar ways and hope that the contrast in our backgrounds has broadened, not muddled, the analysis.

The timing seems right for a comparison of such different places. After five decades of remarkable growth, Thailand came crashing down in 1997, sparking a crisis that spiralled out of control and swept over all Southeast Asia. At the same time, after a generation of economic downturn and paralysis, Ghana was finally showing the patient results of a decade of good housekeeping. Thus we not only have the good and the bad – but the bad and the good. Social science never expresses itself in plain black and white categories; and recent events in our two bellwether countries show the possibilities for catastrophe always inherent in success – and the possibilities of redemption where hope has been all but lost. As we write, there are new lessons for reconstruction coming from Thailand, which has finally begun to recover from its meltdown; and a looming benchmark of democracy for Ghana, as it prepares for a crucial political transition.

We have written this book for people interested in how the developing world can cut a middle path between the impoverished dysfunctionality of Ghana and the rich, yet horribly polluted and more elaborately dysfunctional well-being of Thailand. The roads that the developing world's women and men are choosing are of paramount importance for the four-fifths of the world's people who live in developing nations – but also, in not so long a run, for everyone else. As the Asian economic crisis of 1997 showed us, countries are interlinked. When one goes down, others collapse with it. Moreover, the current situation, with brutal inequality in resource and income distribution, is morally untenable and an incipient international security nightmare: all the wealth gripped by a few hands, with sophisticated weapons and technology everywhere. But if every nation drives down the same road to development as Thailand (or the United States) we risk homogenization along with global environmental implosion, even if for a generation we can all sputter around in smog-ridden luxury. And if every country continues to develop, or rather de-develop, the way that Ghana did over a painful generation, within a century we all will be starving in an environment compromised by failure, not Faustian overachievement.

Inevitably, and most pleasantly, many people are involved in an undertaking like this one, since any book is always a web not of isolated study and insights only but of generosities and obligations. In Ghana, the Oheneba of Ashanti, Dr Osei Tutu Poku, once a student and now our teacher, helped us in Kumasi and welcomed us to Ghana. We also received tremendous help from Michael Alandu, Nasser Adam, George Ayittey, Bright Boakye, Rasheed, William Azure, John Kwadzo Avuletey, Prince Adam Hamidu and all the folks at the YMCA on Castle Road in Accra. Gilchrist Olympio deserves special thanks for welcoming Nicholas into his home, three decades after he last saw Scott and, ironically, just as he was being accused of fomenting an armed attack across the Ghana/Togo border. We also thank Kwame Pianim and Nana Akufo-Addo for their insightful help to both of us.

In Bangkok both of us literally began our Thai adventures, even though almost thirty years apart, with the bounteous hospitality and insight of MR Rampi Kasemsri and our foremost friend and teacher in Thailand, ML Dr Birabongse Kasemsri. Last year we asked him if we could dedicate this work to him, but out of his usual modesty, and in view of his position as the King's principal private secretary, he declined. His untimely death as we go to press impels us to honour and remember him for his friendship and his encouragement to both of us over 31 years. Dr Bunyaraks Ninsananda has so exhausting and exhaustive a range and pace of ideas that were we able to take in a tenth of the help he proffered, our book would be a masterpiece and double its present length. On all our visits to Thailand we have had the continuing help and collegial support of Dr Kusuma Snitwongse, as well as that of senior *farang*[1] William Klausner, both of whom read our work and made essential corrections and comments. We thank also Dr Darmp Sukontasap and Dr Suchit Bunbongkorn. Dr Thanat Khoman, Southeast Asia's elder statesman, always prodded us to think out our views with Gallic logic and Thai intuition. His current successor, Dr Surin Pitsuwan, we equally thank for his insight, as we do Deputy Foreign Minister and old friend MR Sukhumbhand Paribatra. HE Amaret Sila-on and Pornvit Sila-on gave of their time, ideas and hospitality, as did Dr Suvit Yodmani and Khunying Songsuda Yodmani.

Others have given of their time and particular knowledge. Professor David Abernethy and Dr Ronald Bird read the manuscript carefully and made centrally important comments for which we are over-whelmingly grateful. Daniel Arnold, Danielle Goldman, Roger Pasquier, Ken Weisbrode, Michael Wang, Greg Wright, Zach Lum, Josh Rosen-blum, Sebastian and Pamela Einfer and many others also assisted us. We thank Aaron Padilla for his friendship as well as insights over the course of three months, and thirty bus trips, in West Africa. General John Galvin made available the funds for Scott's most recent research trip to Ghana. Jonathan Tay did a great deal of editing and without the inspiration, persistence, encyclopaedic knowledge and friendship of Timothy Dickinson we would never have completed this work. The book is dedicated to Rob West, Scott's mentor and beloved colleague – and a development economist whose ideas and nuanced views are extremely important to our analysis – who died in his prime, leaving a host of grieving, grateful students around the world; and to John Kwadzo Avuletey, Nicholas's closest friend in Ghana, who died suddenly at age thirty only two months after Nicholas last visited that country.

We split the work down the middle – alternately drafting and editing chapters and trading ideas back and forth – through the dura-tion of a Virginia summer and a Washington fall. The errors, alas, are ours.

Nicholas Thompson
Scott Thompson

Amissville, Virginia

CHAPTER 1

Introduction

Just over forty years ago Kwame Nkrumah, Ghana's founding Prime Minister and one of Africa's grandest political and ideological leaders, rose in the polo grounds of Accra to toast Ghana's independence: 'At long last the battle has ended! ... We are prepared to make a nation that will be respected by any nation in the world.'[2] When he spoke, his country was richer than Thailand and the future looked bright both for Ghana and for its continent. Asia[3] was mired in oligarchic violence and revolution amidst abject poverty. In China, the Great Leap Forward would soon strew thirty million corpses behind the worst famine that the world has ever seen. In Thailand, factional military feuding overcame constitutional politics as Marshal Sarit, a harsh if ultimately canny strongman, pushed his way into power. Nkrumah had won three parliamentary elections under British supervision, and over-flowed with energy and forceful ideas. Ghana and Africa seemed to be on their way to prosperity and real liberty. 'We shall achieve in a decade what ... took others a century', Nkrumah exulted, 'and we shall not rest content until we demolish these miserable colonial structures and erect in their place a veritable paradise!'[4]

Within a decade, Ghana's long blunder into poverty was in-escapably apparent. The colonial structures had indeed been destroyed but nothing had blossomed from their ashes, and Nkrumah's dream of a united Africa led by a prosperous Ghana had consumed itself. Ten years after his overthrow, Ghana was still sliding, and it would take another decade for the tide to begin to turn. Today, Ghana is moving forward toward wealth and freedom and could well become the leader of a renewed Africa. A bursting population and thirty years of failed policies and continental turmoil have guaranteed, however, that

Ghana will be no richer, citizen for citizen, on its fiftieth anniversary than it was at independence. Kwame Nkrumah, whose dream is still remembered, would not be pleased.

Seven thousand miles due east, and despite the economic crisis of 1997, luxury stores line the streets of Bangkok, paupers have become princes and cars are now clogging roads where shoes were rare four decades before. Marshal Sarit left office burdened with gold, but at least he left his country freer to advance than when he arrived. Thailand is no paradise, but it has undeniably sprung forward. To compare life in it today to life in it forty years ago is to compare pulling a rickshaw with driving a Volvo.

The Antinomies of Ghana and Thailand

There are astonishing differences between soccer played in the streets of Accra and the same game in Bangkok. In Accra, you must attack the ball and try to stop the man dribbling; he's not going to pass the ball to another player unless he's stuck. The game revolves around skilful, beautiful passes and clever shots. In Thailand, when playing defence, one never attacks the man with the ball because he is always looking for a pass. Thai players are preoccupied with the practical and, as one of us can attest, for someone just arriving from Africa, playing soccer in the Bangkok streets is like trying to walk around with two left shoes on.

These are two very different societies: Africa versus Asia, capitalism versus Nkrumahism, corruption versus cronyism, dramatically different attitudes toward ethnicity, results and authority. Thailand was never a European colony; Ghana was. Ghanaians are volubly confident; the Thais are cautious and unassuming. Forty years ago, Kwame Nkrumah exulted in extraordinary terms: 'Seek ye first the political kingdom and all else will come to you.'[5] Thai leaders since Sarit have persistently placed economic goals at the top of the agenda and Thai newspapers put the kingdom's actual economic standing on the front page, above the fold – right where Ghanaian newspapers used to put Nkrumah.

Ideal Types

Despite their differences, for forty years both countries have been leaders, albeit with highly contrasting styles. This is certainly not a comparison between pure success and abject failure. It is, much more, a study of what the world can learn from two very different but important ideal types. Ghana was the first black African state to receive independence from a colonial power. In the long, depressing anticlimax after Nkrumah, Ghana became the exemplar of the collapse of development plans, programmes and ambitions as the great visions of the 1960s diminished into the miasma of the 1970s and the pioneer republic became a tragic kleptocracy. By the early 1980s, to paraphrase Richard Hodder-Williams, Ghana was a serious sovereignty only by courtesy of the outside world's designation of it as such. It had become a 'case study of all that could go wrong with an African state'.[6] Yet in the past decade Ghana has again become a model, rescued from near-bankruptcy by one of the IMF's first structural adjustment programmes in the early 1980s. Unlike so many of its other applications elsewhere, the IMF's medicine worked: in March 1998, fifteen years after Ghana hit nadir and the IMF came in, Ghana's President Jerry Rawlings stood beside President Clinton in Accra, toasting the beginning of the longest-ever visit by a President of the United States to Africa. In the same polo grounds (now Independence Square) which Nkrumah had consecrated to the pursuit of freedom forty years before, Clinton heralded the continental example set by Ghana and Rawlings. Ironically but appropriately, Clinton's message was much the same as that of Vice President Richard Nixon, who had hailed Ghana at the state's independence ceremonies in 1957. 'It is time for Americans to put a new Africa on our map,' said Clinton.[7] America may do that. And, if there's truly hope for Africa, as we think there is, its heart is probably in Ghana – the one country in its region to escape bloodshed, the one country to have balanced ethnicity; the one country where no one goes to bed at night worrying about thieves and machetes.

The kingdom of Thailand shares with the United States the distinction of being one of the few countries with a significant natural resource and agricultural base to develop rapidly, and it was one of the first to be examined under the now universal lens of growth versus development.[8] It was the first country to learn how to play off the

United States's role as a world power and its willingness to give away the barn and the family mule to help stop the spread of communism. And in the 1990s it was apparent that the Kingdom had somehow done something right. No economy had ever attained the rate of growth that Thailand displayed between 1985 and 1995. The World Bank produced a study, *The Thai Macro-economic Miracle*, that ironically enough barely preceded the catastrophe of summer 1997, even as it made the point that what had happened in Thailand up to that point was – and still is – truly miraculous.

But Thailand has also been an ideal type in the negative sense. Few countries have so quickly turned their forests into asphalt, and not without cause is Bangkok known as 'the whorehouse of the world'.[9] Thailand is also a piranha tank of culture war – the collision of historical values and those carried by globalization. As Sinith Sittirak has written about the fate of traditional Thailand, 'development is part of that Westernizing process of excluding difference by imposing sameness (a global consumer culture or monoculture)'.[10] To many thoughtful people, before 'development' rural Thai were doing quite well and had no need of the pomp and affluence now splattered across the country. This same battle between development and tradition is being fought, on different scales, in almost every developing country in the world today, including Ghana.[11] It only reflects, with a new starkness, the impact of modernity in the developed world, its maelstrom of challenges and values: abortion on demand, moves toward race and gender equality, homosexual liberation, virtual communities. Perhaps to compare life in Thailand today with life there forty years ago is to compare pulling a rickshaw and driving a Volvo with a half-finished bottle of whisky in your hand.

A SKETCH OF THAI HISTORY

The Thai people emigrated from what is now southern China early in the second millennium AD and established kingdoms in Sukothai, Ayuddhya and Bangkok in the thirteenth, fourteenth and eighteenth centuries respectively. Wars with Khmer, Burmese and Vietnamese teetered back and forth until the early nineteenth century, when the present Chakri dynasty began its almost uninterrupted expansion and consolidation of core territory.

In the fourth and fifth reigns of the Chakri kings, from the mid-nineteeenth to the early twentieth century, Mongkut and Chulalongkorn undertook a remarkably wide-ranging modernization of the feudal structure in a very brief period, introducing modern administrative practices along with modern medicine and education. The boundaries of provinces were established, often as a game against French geographers; governors were appointed; hospitals and schools were set up; and a systematic attempt to minimize the power of the nobility continued. It was to be king, country and *sanggha* (the Buddhist brotherhood), and nothing in between. Modernization came as a result of the growing power of the throne.

The immediate successors of Mongkut and Chulalongkorn were mediocre and uninspired epigones. In 1932, fed up with stifling administrative practice and economic stagnation, a group of mostly military 'promoters' overthrew the absolute monarchy and established a nominally constitutional regime, invigorated by truly startling, if usually bloodless, *coups d'état*. Thailand's revised monarchy was very weak but in 1946 King Bhumibol came to the throne after the death – officially the murder[12] – of his young and popular elder brother, and reigns today. Bhumibol has arguably been the most successful monarch of the century anywhere. He rekindled the lustre of his dynasty, helped to unite the country against communist and anarchical foes, and gave the nation continuity amidst great changes.

In 1957 the sternest leader of the modern Thai period, Sarit Thannarat, seized political power and initiated the process of reform – and the ensuing rapid economic development – that continued until the meltdown of 1997. Military leaders initially directed the expanding polity, but from 1973 until 1992 democratic aspirants seesawed in and out of power.

Generals would take control until the repression became too much for the people to endure; then democratic leaders would resume office until the anarchy became too much for the military to countenance. Eventually, it seems, the democrats won, and the norms of democracy have deepened their roots in Thai culture. In 1992 a blustery bid by the army to retain power brought bloodshed and some realization that the Kingdom's economic gains depended on more transparency, democracy and public participation – a lesson insufficiently grasped, however.

The great meltdown of July 1997 stemmed from the convergence of dramatically rapid economic growth, corruption in the political-economic system, and the coming to power of unusually venal and foolish (civilian) leaders. But within a year a new government had brought purpose and motivation to the well-articulated national renewal. Numerous obstacles remain but a tradition has been established which weaves reform into the pattern of economic growth.

Thai Leaders mentioned frequently in this book
Rama (King) V, Chulalongkorn, *1868–1910*
Rama IX, Bhumibol Adulyadej, *1946 – present*

Prime Ministers
Field Marshal Sarit Thannarat, *1958–63*
Field Marshal Thanom Kittichachorn, *1957, 1963–73*
Judge Sanya Thammasak, *1973–5*
MR Seni Pramoj, *1975, 1976*
MR Kukrit Pramoj, *1975–6*
Thanin Kraivixien, *1976–7*
General Kriangsak Chomanand, *1977-80*
General Prem Tinsullanond, *1980–8*
General Chatichai Choonhaven, *1988–91*
Anand Panyarachun, *1991–2, May–September 1992*
General Suchinda Kraprayoon, *1992*
Chuan Leekpai, *1992–5, 1997-present*
Banharn Silpa-archa, *1995–6*
General Chavalit Yongchaiyudh, *1996–7*

But What's the Difference?

It is our thesis that three primary if not exclusive differences separate these two countries and the histories of their development. The first is a difference in historical trajectory from their ancient civilizations through the age of imperialism and the Cold War. The second is a difference in leadership. The third is a difference between open and closed societies.

We will discuss the issue of historical trajectory throughout the book but primarily in the first chapter. Our argument is that the undeniable impact of colonialism upon Africa did not manifest in the mode ascribed to it by most analysts. The critique evolved in recent years, mainly by the left, has it that colonialism clapped Africa in irons, forcing entire multiplex nations into crude subordination as primary producers servicing European consumption, stifling education and splitting the continent along irrational borders. These analyses are all to an extent true, but it was the timing of the transition out of colonialism that can now be seen to have been the most important factor. The sudden end of European rule and the nature of the transition to independence led to a political system which almost inevitably empowered charismatic, not necessarily qualified, leaders who devised economic models with as much potential as zeppelins loaded to the brim with concrete. These leaders, suddenly aware of their lack of deep authority on 'the morning after', fell tragically soon; their failure to offset the disintegration of their legitimacy under the administrative and economic disasters which followed upon independence was only too apparent. Colonialism in Africa, along with the continent's prior centuries of tortured relations with the rest of the world – involved as an object, not a participant – also led to a backlash against the West and a zero-sum view of international relations that had dire long-run consequences.

The failure of African leadership, however, extends well beyond what can be explained away as a reaction to colonialism and the transition to independence. African leaders after independence were absolutely awful but their successors have been even worse. In 1970, they hit rock bottom. Then they started digging. Now Africa is cursed by a political culture of change-by-coup that virtually prohibits competence. Young men who think about political power in Africa join the military and learn to kill instead of joining the public sector and learning to manage. Few citizens not connected to power have any faith that governments exist to serve them, or that a politician can handle anything more demanding than his own image.

By open society, we mean not only a civil society but also open economies, open attitudes toward foreign affairs and, most importantly, a view of the world that is not reducible to a zero sum. Aristotle says that tyrants only need to fear when their subjects begin to trust one another, and most African regimes seem to have set the crushing of this trust as their top priority. African leaders have consistently clamped down on their people, prohibiting everything from earning money[13] to engaging in foreign trade, knowing their legal or their property rights, voting in fair elections or importing foreign technology. African governments have never trusted markets, civil organization or foreigners, and the outcome has been predictable. Ghana has also shunned immigrants and the rest of the world: while Thailand has spent forty years creatively milking wealthy nations like the United States,[14] Ghana has tried to go it on her own.[15] The Thai culture of understatement and moderation has proved a naturally hospitable matrix for the restraint which modern politics requires before the half-formed ideas, ill-discerned possibilities and ever-revised plans which drive a complex economy can work. At the beginning of his reign, Kwame Nkrumah wrote that 'capitalism is too complicated a system for a newly independent state'.[16] Quite obviously, Nkrumah had his pants on backwards.

The temptation to spin this last argument about open societies into an argument for strict free-market economics is strong: at the end of the millennium, every society that had tried to direct its economy had failed. With the gigantic exception of China, all the successes were overtly market economies and you don't have to be Milton Friedman to argue that China has been a success only to the extent that it has marketized. However, the free-market or bust argument fails. First, no nation has really got it right. Human beings have created a terrible crisis for their environment, and great traditional cultures and values have been lost as the world has become globalized and homogenized. Our chapter on the meaning of development argues that the price of coming out of poverty is going to be paid in another kind of poverty down the road – and free markets have not come up with a solution.

The state still has a large role to play in stimulating markets, facilitating scarce investment and providing proper incentives. Completely free markets often lead to political and economic concentration and, with that, ironically and destructively, to a vast reduction in the freedom that originally let the leopard out of the bag. History isn't over and turbocapitalism, to use Edward Luttwak's phrase, hasn't won. Planned societies, however, have clearly lost.

A BRIEF SKETCH OF GHANAIAN HISTORY

Like those of most other countries in Africa, the borders of Ghana were drawn arbitrarily. The Gold Coast was a slaving outpost turned into an anti-slavery patrol station by the British: only in the later nineteenth century did the British seriously determine to move inland, laying out the west and northern frontiers. The most powerful counterforce to their expansion, the Ashanti living upcountry around Kumasi, held them off for half a century, even beheading a British governor in 1824. In due course, though, British rifles and steam-supported power broke the great kingdom.

African participation in both world wars heightened the demand for greater self-governance. Successive reforms increased the suffrage and extended autonomy, but it took riots in 1948 in a period of weak governance to convince the war-spent British that the cost of continued control was not worth it. In 1954 independence was conceded, to take effect three years later.

In 1957, Kwame Nkrumah, leader of the independence movement, became black Africa's first Prime Minister. Posing initially as a friend of the West, he soon revealed an affinity for authoritarian socialism that required or rationalized aligning his country with the Soviet bloc. Somewhat contradictorily, he also gave priority to the development of a united Africa to the neglect of his own country, and over and over was caught interfering in the sovereign affairs of neighbours and other countries across the continent.

Yet he truly had founded a nation, albeit one he found embarrassingly small for his ambitions. While he was flying around Asia playing the role of the unsolicited, unwanted and useless international peace broker and hero, a group of soldiers and policemen dramatically seized power, transferring it in 1969 to a democratically elected Kofi Busia, a sociologist turned politician who had long opposed Nkrumah.

Busia ran the country for two years before being overthrown by another military coup, this one inspired by a lack of perks given to the military and by a devaluation of Ghana's currency. The leader of the coup, I. K. Acheampong, an incompetent tyrant, was overthrown in 1978 after taking his country almost to the point of no return.

In 1979 Jerry John Rawlings, a flight lieutenant, led a coup and gained power – though within a few months he would give it up under dubious circumstances to a democratically elected coalition. Two years later Rawlings overthrew the democrats and has been in power ever since, holding internationally approved, ethnically divisive and universally doubted elections in 1992 and 1996. In nineteen years Rawlings has got Ghana back on track and, despite his very shaky record on human rights, he clearly has figured how to do a few things right. He also has helped steer Ghana out of tragedies that have all but destroyed almost all of its neighbouring countries – from Sierra Leone, Liberia and Ivory Coast to Togo and Nigeria.

In 2000 Ghana will have elections again. Rawlings will have the option of choosing between holding on to power, as so many of the brutal leaders of Africa have done in the past, or honestly and quietly leaving the public eye to live in the country he probably saved but can still quite easily destroy. Most likely, he'll go – and Ghana could show the way to a new Africa: one of the first countries to make the transition from tyranny to democracy and, we hope, the first country to show that double-digit economic growth is possible west of the Mekong.

Ghanaian Presidents who come up frequently in this book
Kwame Nkrumah Prime Minister then President, *1957–66*
General Ankrah, Major Afrifa, *et al.* (National Liberation Council), *1966–9*
Dr K L Busia, *1969–72*
General Ignatius Acheampong, *1972–8*
General Fred Akuffo, *1978–9*
Flt Lieut Jerry Rawlings, *1979, 1981–2000*

The Baobab

The sum of these theses, and the central point that we will make in this book, is reflected in our title: *The Baobab and the Mango Tree*. In *The Little Prince*, Antoine de Saint-Exupéry tells of a prince, alone on a tiny planet, desperately trying to keep it free of baobab trees. If a baobab tree were to take root, it would swallow his little world. The state in Ghana, as in the rest of Africa, has been a baobab tree. Its role hasn't been to help people, but simply to swallow, to consume, to obstruct, to stick its branches aggressively in the air and thrust its roots through the ground, sucking up every available resource. What primitive accumulation means for the bourgeoisie in Marxist theory, it is for the power élites in African practice. Like Kwame Nkrumah or Ignatius Acheampong, Ghana's chief kleptocrat from 1972 until 1978, the baobab tree concedes nothing and is unwilling to let anything else take root and bloom. Worst of all, so like the brutal regimes that have disfigured Africa for two generations, baobab trees are damned hard to uproot.[17]

The baobab tree also has little interest in development. Some observers have suggested that, in the mouths of leaders, 'development' is either a euphemism for telling Western donors what they wish to hear or a means of providing outright disinformation; it certainly does not even periodically correspond to the noble goals laid out. Professor Jean-François Bayart is not just practising Gallic cynicism, but articulating a plain truth, when he observes that 'far from being a threat to the regime, economic stagnation and hardship have made [the traditional] method of regulating political society easier'.[18] Thailand may have been corrupt and even careless at times, but at no point was the government consciously and intentionally acting against the interests of the people or of development. In Africa, for at least four decades, the role of the state has simply been to entrench itself while sucking the people dry. The baobab tree in *The Little Prince* does better if there's nothing else in the soil.

The Mango Tree

The image of the mango tree comes from an old Sanskrit romance, *The Story of Mahajanaka*, which King Bhumibol himself translated and modified in 1988.[19] It takes place in a royal park shadowed by two mango trees, one heavy with fruit, one bare. Once the king himself has tasted the rich fruit, everyone can pick a mango, tear off a branch, or even uproot the tree itself. If too many mangos are eaten, of course, the trees will not reproduce and everything will die. Once the damage has begun, only the most modern machinery and methods can repair it.

There are three lessons that the king spells out: perseverance, self-restraint and a focus on the long term. Stealing is okay, but not if it leads to destruction in the long term. King Mahajanaka 'practised perseverance without the desire for reward which resulted in his gaining a throne and bringing prosperity and wealth to the city of Mithila by the strength of his qualities'. And lest it still be unclear, the subtle variant spellings of words used to express perseverance are translated for us. 'Perseverance is an essential thing: had we not persevered … we would not be on the throne', he so very accurately concludes, in what could well be the central epitaph of his great and long reign. Another implicit conclusion is that, had he reigned baobab-fashion like most leaders in Africa, and eaten all of the mangos, the grove would just as surely have died. Interestingly, the king only published his book on the eve of the meltdown – just as his government was summoning the most modern machinery, and drawing on the rest of the world for ideas and solutions, to repair the damage of the all-too-rapid destruction of the mango trees.

King Bhumibol has used the ancient story to illustrate a central principle that illuminates not just his own ascent from obscure prisoner-king to beloved ruler, but his kingdom's success in bursting through every growth barrier that has confronted it: perseverance. But the story equally illustrates the interplay of good policy, luck and greed: the fertile land provided fine mango trees, but inept stewardship led to their stripping, and only wise and persevering conduct will reconstitute the health of the trees. In this construction we find the metaphor not just for Thailand but for rapidly growing developing countries.

What is Development?

Beyond this analysis of Ghana and Thailand lie three major questions that we will try to answer, looping our answers around a study of these two countries, the United States and the rest of the developing world. The first question is simply: what is development? There isn't one simple model that all developing countries should strive to emulate but there are certainly some things that are better than others and there are ways that decisions should be made and ways that they shouldn't. In Chapter 5 we will look at what development really entails and at some of the more important economic theories guiding developmental economics. As we will stress, modernization is not development, though the two are interlinked. In Chapter 6 we will look at three central issues for development: environmental devastation, the role of women in society and income inequality.

Economic Growth and Political Development

The second question we confront is that of the relationship between economic growth and political development. We come back to this again and again, particularly in Chapters 6 and 8 where we focus on the debate over Asian values. The question has been misstated in a generation of heavy tomes. As early as the Social Science Research Council's prestigious series thirty years ago, there were attempts to show the virtues of one over the other, but it was never quite clear which of the two was preferred or what the correlation between them was. The ambiguity isn't surprising because the evidence is mixed. An authoritarian but gentle regime in Thailand made decisions quickly, kept unions down in the 1960s and unquestionably made Thai exports more internationally competitive, to the short-term gain of a few and the long-term benefit of many. Yet the Thai boom collapsed. Indeed, the origin of the greatest economic crisis anywhere since the American-European depression of the 1930s can be traced to Thai financial viscosity emanating from the corrupt political sector. The authoritarianism may have helped Thailand grow, but the lack of transparency also led to its collapse. It used to be part of the conventional wisdom that foreign investment followed authoritarian government ('Philippine stock shot up on Wall Street', a big investor told one of us, the day Marcos proclaimed martial law). But that was a long time ago. These days investors are unwilling to put money into a country that can conceal half of its foreign exchange losses because of political corruption. The global information economy is all-consuming and it depends on transparency.

In Ghana, the evidence is also mixed: the country certainly did require a strongman to seize the moment in 1982 and put Ghana on a growth track. But the country hasn't boomed, precisely because of the lingering perception that Jerry Rawlings is just another African 'big man'. Internationally, the evidence is just as mixed: for every Botswana, democratic and booming, there is a Singapore, authoritarian and booming, and an India, democratic and drowning. But the evidence, in totality, is that there is indeed a relationship between political freedom and economic growth. They don't necessarily lead to one another and political freedom can also be destructive, but the general correlation is importantly and clearly there.

Second Chances

The great development economist Robert West asked, 'Do countries get a second chance?' We will return again and again to this question, and its corollary: how does a country pick itself up when it is down? This is the central topic of Chapter 9 and the third question that we will be dealing with throughout the book. Countries are not entirely like people; they seldom die and, at least in theory, a state can always rejuvenate, even reconstitute, itself, where people usually just dwindle away in later life.[20] Brazil and Argentina seem to have made a living for economists promoting this notion, flying up, sliding down and then flying back up. Samuel Huntington warned us in 1968 that decay accompanied development, but few paid heed.[21]

Second chances are important. It is difficult for countries to get out of the syndrome of bad government, bad banking, corruption, and indifference to popular needs. New leaders want the privileges the last ones enjoyed plus a little bit more. Most of the population has been beaten down and ceases to believe that government matters, can be changed or is worth fixing. In the end, the cycle repeats itself; while countries may have a second chance, it is a hard-fought one. The roots of the baobab tree are very hard to pull up.

The question of second chances can also be boiled down to the issue of momentum. Once momentum starts in the wrong direction, it is very hard to stop, turn around and start moving back in the right direction. Ghana's President Rawlings has said he is going to give up power; he has said that he will never make another political arrest; and he has said that he welcomes foreign investment. Yet his people are still scared that he is going to stay in power. People are constantly afraid to voice their opinions and foreign investors will probably not flood into the country until after Rawlings has packed his bags and left Osu Castle in his limousine for good. Everyone assumes that the future is going to be like the past and that, when he gets desperate to hold onto power, Rawlings will destroy almost everything he has built.

In fact, second chances are in some ways implicit in the stories of the baobab and the mango. In *The Little Prince* there is no hope for a second chance once the tree has set its roots. The entire planet gets swallowed up by the single tree and nothing else has a chance to thrive, just as no one with ideas counter to Kwame Nkrumah (or almost any other leader in Africa) was given a chance to see if her ideas could work. In *The Story of Mahajanaka*, the whole point is that the opportunity to have a second chance comes through perseverance. If the government of Thailand can't figure out the solution to a problem, surely the ingenious Thai people can. After all, in Thailand – as in open societies and mango groves – many trees are much better than one colossus. And enlightened policies can lead to their nurturance, sustenance and, where needed, their regrowth.

The baobab and the mango: one leads to certain destruction; the other leads to a qualified success, if you do everything else right, too.

PART I

CHAPTER 2

Historical Trajectories

If you refilled the Suez Canal and sealed the Straits of Gibraltar, Africa would be part of Europe and they both would be part of Asia. With a couple of extra water bottles, thick tyres and luck, you could ride a bicycle straight from Paris to Cape Town and then back up and over to Beijing.

Of course this isn't true in any more than one geographical sense; sand could never make Africa part of Europe for reasons both geographical and cultural, the former greatly influencing the latter. The Sahara has cut off Africa south of that great desert from the rest of the world: the people who live in Senegal in northern West Africa are closer ethnically, physiologically and culturally to the inhabitants of Mozambique four thousand miles southeast than they are to the Berbers living just north in Morocco. The countries in Africa south of the Sahara developed with roughly similar social structures, were colonized and received independence at about the same time and have followed very similar political and economic trajectories to this day. The same can be said of Asia only very loosely, for there is more of variance both in history and in present situation among the countries even of Southeast Asia than there is among the states of sub-Saharan Africa.[22] To go from Burma or Cambodia to Singapore or Thailand is to encounter a greater disparity in both economics and attitude than one meets in any similar transition in Africa.[23]

In this chapter we consider five different ways in which the historical trajectories of these two great regions have affected their present situations. First we examine cultural capital – and the endemic power of ancient civilization. Second comes geography and the ways that nature herself has shaped development. Third, ethnic patterns and the reasons for the ethnic make-up of both Thailand and Ghana. Fourth, the impact that Africa's relationship with her colonizers has had on the continent's economic, political and social make-up. Last, we ask how luck has played its part in the reactions of two continents to the scattered, frenetic nature of world events – without forgetting that, as Pasteur said, 'fortune favours the prepared mind'.

Cultural Capital

It is common to hear East Asia's successes, as contrasted to Africa's gridlocked agony, attributed to 'civilization', to 'culture' and to 'history'. Mankind may have originated in Africa but, the argument goes, Asia's civilizations were more organized for longer periods, far more developed, and thus contributed more to our world today.[24] Writing in 1922, Lord Lugard – who has the dubious distinction of being the creator of modern Nigeria[25] – stated this supposition with conviction:

> Africa has been justly termed 'the Dark Continent', for the secrets of its peoples, its lakes, and mountains and rivers, have remained undisclosed not merely to modern civilization, but through all the ages of which history has any record. There are many regions in Asia … in which modern explorers have claimed to make discoveries. But all these countries were the seats of ancient civilizations, some of them highly developed, and exploration was concerned rather with piecing together chapters of past history than in discovery.[26]

While such historians as Basil Davidson have shown the strength and robustness of African traditional society and its most differentiated kingdoms – Buganda in what is now Uganda or Ashanti in what is now central Ghana[27] – there is little doubt that the Asian empires of the ninth to the fourteenth century – Angkor Wat, Pagan, Borobodur and the plinth regions of three Chinese dynasties – were as advanced, if not more so, than any other civilizations on earth at the time. Indeed, Kwame Nkrumah's decision to change the name of his country from Gold Coast to Ghana, the name of an ancient empire in the region now encompassed by Mali, was an admission that the new state needed a stronger historical anchor.[28] The boundaries of Ghana, after all, do not overlap for even an inch with that ancient empire.

But the gap is not nearly as great as many historians argue. Thailand may have derived from India a common religious heritage, a script that it modified, and kingly traditions vibrant to this day, but this issued in no literary tradition.[29] The early modernizers were Chinese and Western traders and tutors, of whom wise kings chose to make good use. It is hard to argue that Thai dance and other art forms exceed in their aesthetic contribution what can be found in West Africa: consider, for example, the monumental importance of Benin and Yoruba sculpture, which was also a substantial influence on Cubism. It is said that when André Derain was shown a Yoruba mask for the first time, he was 'speechless' and 'stunned' and soon brought it over to show his friends Picasso and Matisse.[30] In turn, Picasso and Matisse would weave this art form all through their own work and use this ancient new-discovered power to change the eyes of a century. African drumming and rhythms are the fibre from which jazz is woven, surely the most important American artistic creation of the twentieth century – indeed, its magnificent leap into New World autonomy makes it very arguably the only original American art form.

So there is a gap, albeit a small one, but would even that count in itself? China may have been a great cradle of civilization but its hundreds of millions of peasants were no better off in the past half-millennium than their counterparts in the least historically developed parts of Africa. Cambodia, home of the world's greatest civilization at the time of Angkor Wat (a city, in its thirteenth-century heyday, at least forty times as large as the teeming London of Henry III, and incomparably more magnificent), has probably suffered more in the past quarter-century than any other nation on earth. Saddam Hussein is the most notorious despot in the world and yet he presides over a land once the matrix of great civilizations. The Tswana, unself-pitying masters only of the Kalahari desert, have grown faster over the past twenty years than any other nation, although no one has even tried to find a triumphant ancient civilization underlying the modern miracle of Botswana. If it is this gap, or crack, that separates Asian triumph from African stasis, why did it not yawn so in the 1960s when, surely, the temples of Angkor Wat were even more magnificent than they are today, or were when Pol Pot swept into Phnom Penh to deliver the new Cambodia in the blood of a quarter of his countrymen?

There are just too many contradictions to let that elusive variable 'civilization' assume much import. The argument has been more effectively posed in reverse. Reading Gunnar Myrdal's milestone three-volume *Asian Drama*[31] one senses history's burdens rather than its opportunities. At the time of his writing, neither India – his main interest – nor China had much prosperity to show for their glorious histories and two billion remarkable people.[32] Thinking back a generation to the impressions people like Tom Mboya, Leopold Senghor, Chinua Achebe and Julius Nyerere were making on the world stage, the presumption of excellence in fact worked in Africa's favour. At the very least, as it was sometimes cynically observed in those days, Africans had so much less to unlearn.

Note: In the dialogue that follows – pursuing the point raised above – Taylor and Tara are fictional characters.

Taylor: You can't claim that one civilization is better than another.

Tara: Why not? If you can claim that one person did more for civilization, that Aristotle did more than Mobutu for example, you can claim that one civilization did more than another. A civilization is just an aggregation of all of its people and surroundings.

Taylor: But who's going to make these judgments? And what values are they going to be based on? Yours?

Tara: I'm not saying that European history is superior. Remember what Gandhi said when asked about European civilization? 'I think it would be a good idea.' But I am saying that, at different times, different civilizations have contributed the most to the world and left the most for posterity. For a while it was the Europeans. It has also been the Chinese, the Khmer, the Mayans, the Egyptians. It's really worldwide.

Taylor: But never the Africans. I still say that the only fair way to deal with this problem is to call everyone equal – or at least to say we don't know how to discuss superiority.

Tara: Look, if all civilizations and cultures are equal, was the
         Confederacy equal to the Union during the Civil War? Was the
         Third Reich equal to Churchill's England?

Taylor: People who win wars write history and define which culture was
         better. We think that the Union was superior because it won.
         If the Confederacy had won, their heirs would have educated
         us and we would have learned at age eight that Abe Lincoln
         butchered kittens in churches.

Geography

A Victorian rhyme warns of the Nigerian swamps: 'Beware and take
care of the Bight of Benin, whence one comes out, where forty went in'.
Short of Antarctica, Africa is the hardest continent for human beings to
survive on. It can be argued rather convincingly that the African
miasma of the past generation is predominantly a function of
uncooperative geography. Africa's rivers are fragmented by rapids,
waterfalls and shoals; the Niger and the Congo were unnavigable at
certain points for many years, effectively stopping the most natural
mode of transportation and route for trade. As Adam Smith pointed
out in 1776 – and economists still echo him today – seaborne trade has
always been less expensive than trade by land.[33] Throughout the
world, this is reflected in the astonishing fact that two out of every
three people on the planet live within 50 miles of the ocean.[34] Alas, the
coast of Africa is remarkably tight-drawn around the vast continent
behind it: natural harbours are conspicuously few.

Moreover, the elements impose themselves. The rain patterns in
Africa are more unpredictable than anywhere else on earth. The sun
beats down over the entire continent, fostering a climate very
favourable to parasites and malaria-carrying mosquitoes and not so
favourable for humans, their cattle or their crops. Spend a few days in
almost any part of Africa and you'll quickly learn why, particularly
without water readily available, afternoon naps are rather popular.
The simplest movements are barely possible when water isn't

available and the sun is pounding down upon you. Thomas Sowell points out that the kinds of provincialism that pervaded Africa stemmed from 'the geographic barriers to mobility' that limited cultural and technological interchange with more advanced societies.[35] On the other hand, the booming cities of Southeast Asia are (or are near to) natural harbours and have been nodes of exchange for centuries. Since the nineteenth century they have been the natural magnets and dynamizing marketplaces for the tides of Chinese emigrants who made Singapore and Hong Kong history's two most successful port cities, and remade Guangchou, Manila, Xiamen and Bangkok into thriving entrepôts not far behind them.

Southeast Asia is fertile. Southeast Asia is lush. Bangkok is the southern point of a rough triangle of rich lands running several hundred miles, its strong rivers irrigating swelling rice fields and affording safe navigation. The north and northeast are defined by the mighty Mekong, which provides a concourse for trade and the interchange of peoples for hundreds of miles. The Thai people, once harnessed – almost literally – by strong kings, could expand into and settle a geographic unit with somewhat natural frontiers. Once challenged from outside, the successor kings could move social organization into the provinces and villages to collect taxes and provide services, in that order, for the protection and expansion of the kingdom. Whatever else it was, Thailand had become a coherent collectivity by the nineteenth century, even though connectedness between ruler and ruled outside the greater Bangkok quadrant was slight until the mid-twentieth century. Geography had poised the kingdom for economic take-off.

Perhaps the most thorough study on the impact of geography was carried out by Jeffrey Sachs at the Harvard Institute for International Development. Sachs regressed dozens of variables against economic growth rates in an attempt to establish some quantitative sense of why some countries have done so much better than others. He concluded that economic growth from 1965 to 1990 was dependent on four variables. The first of these was initial conditions: just as fat people can lose weight more rapidly than thin people, if you are poor at the start, you are more likely to be able to grow quickly. A general orientation toward free trade helped, as did fiscal prudence and the absence of corruption. Third, population and demography played a role, as can easily be seen in Ghana or in any other country whose population doubles every twenty years. Fourth, physical geography matters in several ways:

> Landlocked countries grew more slowly than coastal economies [being entirely landlocked was found to subtract roughly 0.7 percentage points from a country's annual growth]. And tropical countries grew 1.3 percentage points more slowly each year than those in the Temperate Zone, even after allowing for other differences. This seems to reflect the cost of poor health and unproductive farming.[36]

But while most of Africa has been severely disadvantaged by Mother Nature, Ghana draws one of the luckier tickets. As Sowell writes, West Africa has the advantage of its 'more fertile soil, ample rainfall, and the Niger River system'.[37] Small wonder that it was here that 'some of the larger African kingdoms arose'.[38] Ghana, for example, has a very advantageous climate, particularly by African standards, yielding lush woodlands and rainforests as well as fairly good soil, of which there remains for this generation enough into which to expand. Unlike, say, the Central African Republic or Mali, Ghana could feed itself. The north of Ghana can be as dry as neighbouring Burkina Faso stretching into the Sahel, but the central rainforests and the surrounding lands are as lush as anything that can be found in Africa. This is one more reason why Ghana has done better than so many of its wretched neighbours.

The Politics of Ethnicity

You don't have to be the Dalai Lama or the UN High Commissioner for Refugees to realize that there are ethnic problems in Asia. But these are on a different scale from those in Africa. That continent has been torn apart by ethnicity more than any other, and the reasons for Africa's ethnic chaos and Asia's relative stability are critical for our analysis.

For one thing, by far the largest ethnic group in the world, the Han Chinese, so overwhelmingly dominates, in numbers and policies, the strategic mass of East Asia – and increasingly the groups at the edge of their country – that the dominant model contradicts Africa's from the start. Korea and Japan are among the most homogeneous countries on earth and are both certainly more homogeneous than any state in Africa by several orders, except the booming Botswana and the now nearly non-existent Somalia.[39] The principal countries of Southeast Asia all have a dominant ethnic group large enough at least to be capable of economically and politically absorbing smaller ethnic groups. The (Malay) Javanese overwhelm their archipelago even if there are pockets of ethnic war and now religion-based pillage. Filipino (Malay) linguistic groups are sufficiently well balanced to make deference necessary among them, always allowing a bit more equality to the centrally located Tagalogs. Malaysia is a different case: the Chinese there were threateningly numerous and successful enough to become the target of lethal Malay-led riots in 1969. But the Chinese role was critical enough for future growth to compel the Malay majority to construct a workable contract, the innovative New Economic Policy, to prevent the complete destruction of the state, even as the majority Malay demanded and got a guaranteed share of the growing economy.[40] In Thailand the central Thai had geography – their affluent and underpopulated plain – working to their advantage. Their less-favoured ethnic cousins, the Lao of Issan, on the southern bank of the Mekong, were easily brought into the kingdom. In the north, ethnically distinct groups were overwhelmed by the vastness of the Thai economic juggernaut during the 1970s and 1980s and ethnic revolt was suppressed, stifled and dodged.

In Africa few states are either ethnically homogeneous or have a strong enough central ethnic group to pull the rest into their magnetic field. The Ashanti kings of central Ghana, the region's dominant ethnic group, consistently failed to bring the coastal peoples under their domain. Even Uganda, with the most impressive traditional kingdom included within it, quickly turned on the once-dominant Baganda as soon as the British had left. Frederick Mutesa II, who was President of Uganda as well as King of the great traditional Baganda monarchy, lost in the power struggle with Milton Obote, the Prime Minister, and was sent off with his crown to an undignified death in London's East End.

The lack of dominant ethnic groups in Africa is in a large part due to the short, arbitrary history of its states. Asian nations rest on old foundations and in each there has been enough time for one ethnicity to conquer the others. In Japan the ruling ethnic group was in control of the nation from the start: the present incumbent claims that 126 emperors have ruled before him. In Korea ethnic battles have been averted for hundreds of years, despite regional hostilities even within the two constituent parts. In Africa the British, the French, the Belgians and the Germans arrived in the late nineteenth century, hacked up the continent into almost random slices at conferences five thousand miles away, and put real borders around people who had never had politically enforced frontiers. The Ewe people of western Togo are of the same ethnicity as the Ewes of eastern Ghana but they are divided – sometimes within old villages – by a quite serious frontier between them and forced to live in separate countries that even have separate official languages (English in Ghana, French in Togo). Africa's borders were based less on where they made the most sense for the Africans and more on the machinations of European politicians with ulterior and often petty motives – from this or that explorer's desire to be knighted to German Chancellor Bismarck's need to create a colonial crisis every seven years when his military budget came up for approval. There was also, of course, the African version of the Great Game of the late nineteenth century: the competition between France and Britain to fill the white spaces on the map, in which Africa's role was as a strategic space behind the crumbling Porte and the ever-crucial routes to the East.[41] Africa mattered to Europe but the Africans didn't.

Perhaps more importantly, the colonizers only knew how to govern by the rules of the nation state. They began to treat the leaders of different ethnic groups, who had previously held little legitimacy, as the equivalent of European princes. And ethnic identities that had barely existed before were cemented by issuing birth certificates and tribal identity cards. Chieftains without tribes had power pressed on them even if they had to invent kingdoms to get their share of roads and hospitals. African power and standing were differently conceived: the Europeans did not bother to learn how. They only saw posturing (how different from Buckingham Palace) so they changed the rules and Africans suffered. It is telling that a standard textbook, Lévy-Bruhl's *Les Formes élementaires de la Pensée*, was translated for British officials as 'How Natives Think'.

In Asia the story was different. In Malaya, the British ruled indirectly through the sultans, establishing the legitimacy for a later rotating kingship and laying the foundations for a truly workable republican and parliamentary kingdom. They put down a long-running insurgency with the intimate cooperation of their Malay subjects and encouraged the development of the economy through the exploitation of natural resources in such a way that Malaya at independence was the world's richest major colony. French rule consolidated the sense of Vietnamese nationhood, while Dutch rule in its 'Netherlands Indies' created a large administrative entity around Java, enabling the élite to keep the periphery under its domination from independence to the present day. The remains of an ancient civilization around Borabadur did not hurt in the creation of an Indonesian *imaginaire*, to use Professor Chaianan's term for Thailand.[42] As always, the battered nation of Burma sticks out like a sore thumb: under colonialism, the country was run by the British as the last outpost of rule from India and thus faced all the bad stuff of colonialism – the indignity of the occupation, the condescension, the destruction of the traditional power structure – and none of the good.

The end results have been predictable. In Africa, ethnic rivalry is nearly everywhere not so much the main game as the only game, even though this is seldom admitted outright to Westerners. A Cameroonian student in a class that one of us taught on the Third World admonished his fellow students against the use of the term 'tribe' because of its colonial connotations of divide and rule, and because it seemed to detract from the notion that Africans were wholly engaged in *nation* building. When asked at a later date in the same class what would be the reaction in his native village if he brought back a prospective wife of a different ethnicity he instinctively and naturally replied that 'everyone in my tribe, not just my family, would reject her … I could never do that to my tribe'. 'Tribe' is natural among Africans and the term is used naturally – as long as 'Europeans' (i.e. whites) are not present.

Jean-François Bayart felicitously describes this situation as 'the shadow theater of ethnicity'.[43] Ethnicity in Africa is always there, but never there. Or, as one Ghanaian told us: 'It doesn't matter; except when you get to the nitty gritty.'[44] In the first Nigerian coup, Ibo officers killed the prime ministers of the non-Ibo regions and knocked off the Hausa Federal Prime Minister and his mentor[45] for good measure, then wondered why everyone turned on them in a ruinous civil war. Today in Ghana the question is whether a non-Ewe has a chance of advancement or a chance of gaining any sort of meaningful government contract. President Rawlings is half-Ewe (his father was a Scot) and most of the people in his entourage are Ewe. Nkrumah, a nation builder who hated ethnic division, predictably came from a small group, the Nzima, and had an incentive to build a greater, non-ethnic Ghana (but note that his bodyguards were all Nzima). Since Nkrumah, the politics of ethnicity has dominated – and so harsh had Nkrumah been toward the recalcitrant Ashanti that he got no real support from them, the largest group in Ghana. Even when it comes to soccer, ethnicity doesn't disappear.[46] When Ghana was eliminated from the 1998 Africa Cup of Nations soccer tournament, people celebrated in the streets of Kumasi, Ghana's Ashanti stronghold. They saw the failure of their 'national' soccer team, in which there were very few Ashanti players, as a setback to the national government and as a failure of the ethnic groups in power, who seem not to pay the Ashanti any heed.[47] And if people aren't going to root for their soccer team, are they really going to be concerned with national economic development? If people don't care about the state, is the government really going to try to help them?

So ethnicity is a divisive issue in Africa, far more than in Asia – with the outstanding exception of Burma, which resembles in its repression and division almost the worst of Africa.

The Impact of Colonialism

In his book *The Africans* a long-time Africa correspondent, David Lamb, suggests that 'colonialists set the scenario for disaster and the Africans have been doing their best to fulfil it.'[48] He is right. But colonialists aren't responsible for Africa's miasma in the ways that conventional wisdom, particularly in the politically correct version, would have it.

What did colonialism do for or against Ghana? The degradation of the independence years makes it easy to forget that a generation ago one saw the monuments of British imperialism standing proudly. Achimoto school, later college, was the Eton of British West Africa, the place where Jerry Rawlings escaped from a brutal childhood. What became the University of Ghana had a superb physical plant and all

THE POLITICS OF ETHNICITY IN RWANDA

The nomadic Tutsi arrived in Rwanda several hundred years ago, where they found Hutu farmers and Twa pygmies. The Tutsi, tall and with angular facial features, were clearly different from the much shorter Hutu; nonetheless, they chose to assimilate instead of building their own separate state. Gradually, the Tutsi came to worship the same God as the Hutu and to speak the same language; eventually, the distinction between Hutu and Tutsi depended more on class than on ethnicity.

In the mid-nineteenth century the Tutsi King first began to discriminate on ethnic lines and, when the whites arrived, solidified the division by declaring the Tutsi to be superior to the Hutus.[49] The colonial government and the Catholic Church soon enough aligned themselves with the Tutsi power structure, while in the 1930s the Belgians issued identity cards that solidified racial distinctions. As Gérard Prunier wrote in his *The Rwanda Crisis – History of a Genocide*: 'Thus through the actions, both intellectual and material, of the white foreigners, myths had been synthesized into a new reality.'[50]

This was the origin of the ethnic rivalry, competition and, ultimately, hatred and genocide that have dominated Rwanda for the past decade. Clearly things are not the fault of the colonizers alone; just as clearly, the colonizers helped to get the ball rolling in what became an irreversibly catastrophic direction.

the right ideals. Roads, hospitals and the whole Western judicial tradition were fitted into place.

But the real legacy of colonialism wasn't the infrastructure. It was the fear and resentment of the outside world that Ghana developed; the imposition of the jarring ethnic juxtaposition we discussed in the previous section; and the political problems, amounting to vacuum, created by the sudden departure of the colonial power, which we will discuss presently. The colonizers were sanctimonious and condescending; they treated most Ghanaians so poorly that, since independence, Ghana has seemed consciously to be trying to spite the

West – and mainly injuring its own interests in the process. The economic trajectory that most African states have followed since independence has been shaped, largely and disastrously, by the reaction to colonialism. Africa has been isolationist, hostile to immigrants and international business, reluctant to accept foreign advice: all self-destructive attitudes, all predictably ruinous – and all, unfortunately, understandable.

The worst consequence of colonialism was that the colonialists' departure allowed, perhaps even forced, adaptations to the state that figuratively metastasized into the baobab tree. First of all, to recapitulate, Africa was isolationist largely in reaction to colonialism, and only in an isolationist society can government grab the rest of the nation by the throat as Kwame Nkrumah and so many other African leaders did. Second, because the borders of Africa were so politically real and humanly unreal, and the situation at independence so confused, the first wave of leaders had to consolidate power quickly, buying friends and talking 'fine lines' quite reminiscent of the colonialists. They stuck their fingers into every possible pie while cutting off the fingers of anyone who challenged them. Furthermore, lacking experience of the most ordinary running of government, leaders like Nkrumah built walls around themselves to prevent criticism and challenge. And, as we will discuss in more detail in the next chapter, the struggles for independence had been so short that the leaders who emerged were not the Nelson Mandela types who emerge from long, terrible, reality-testing contests; instead they were mostly charismatic but shallow figures like Nkrumah or Sékou Touré of Guinea.

As Lamb said, the colonialists set the scenario for disaster. Just as importantly, the influence of colonialism wasn't uniform; its inheritance varied enormously. There were many successor élites and populations that bore no animus toward their former rulers. In Ivory Coast, for example, far more Frenchmen came to live after independence than when the country was a colony. The first nationalist élite in the Gold Coast[51] had come up through British-devised, increasingly representative institutions before independence, and were much closer to the colonialists. Indeed, it was held against J. B. Danquah, the first Gold Coast nationalist leader, that he maintained such congenial ties. The same was true for the Ashanti royal house, whose leaders have – since not long after one of them put a British governor's head on a spike –

enjoyed the warmest ties with their fellow members of a master class.

Secondly, the absence of a colonial tradition is no guarantee in itself that there is no reason for popular resentment of internal leaders or outside advisers. Benedict Anderson has referred to the pattern of Chakri expansion in Thailand throughout the past century and a half as 'internal colonialism'.[52] As the authors' distant Indian ancestors will tell us, the same applies to the United States. Over and over, Thai and outsiders attribute Thailand's successes to the absence of colonialism. But the argument does not stand scrutiny. Both Liberian and Ethiopian leaders and educators in the past attributed their countries' extreme – and relative – backwardness to the absence of the *benefits* of colonialism.

In the end, colonialism, like the geography that did so much to drive it, has contributed to Africa's problems, but it hasn't been the only factor. Colonialism planted the seed for the baobab tree, and perhaps the harsh climate helped it grow. But surely, as in Botswana, it could have been uprooted, not fertilized and watered, had the right decisions been made at the right times. Even before diamonds were mined in that country, the leadership was laying the groundwork, through dedicated leadership, for the astonishing efflorescence of the state.

Taylor: Africa is poor because of colonialism.

Tara: No, Africa is poor because of Africans.

Taylor: The colonialists came in, scrawled arbitrary borders on the map and turned entire economies into exporting zones for cheap sale to Europe. Look at the borders of Ghana: they were drawn by some bloated, ruddy-faced British gent, sipping tea to cure his hangover while drooling muffin crumbs on the floor, desperately hoping to be knighted and mumbling about 'African culture'.

Tara: The colonialists came into a society that was basically anarchic. They may have drawn the borders a little wrong, but they had to do something. They laid the basis of the modern state. And the failures of the following generations weren't their fault. Independent Ghana could have got rich off its cocoa. And, by the way, Britain introduced cocoa to Ghana. Here's a joke. How do you develop a small company in West Africa? Take a large European company and let Africans run it.

Taylor: But Ghana *didn't* get rich, because the British set them up for failure and then never came to their aid when needed. And Africa wasn't anarchic: there were great societies; the colonialists just didn't understand them and didn't know how to classify them. Then, when the colonialists departed, they left nothing behind. In Guinea, when Sékou Touré took his first tour of Government House, he found nothing. Even the bathrooms had been stripped. Plus the country was producing nothing. Not a match. Not a pin.

Tara: Colonialism wasn't perfect, but it did have a positive civilizing effect. All of these regions were still participating in the slave trade – to exploit themselves and to sell to the whites – and there were civil wars going on throughout the continent. The real problem is culture. Africans just don't want to succeed; they just don't care.

Taylor: First, your history's wrong; second your cultural analysis is wrong; and, third, even if you were right, the cultural problems were caused by colonialism too. Have you ever read Fanon, or even Naipaul? The problem with colonialism is that it demoralizes people. It taught three whole generations that they were subservient; a brilliant Nigerian diplomat told me that he couldn't go into a classroom or a dinner party where whites were present – even *today* – without having to work through feelings of inferiority. Small wonder three whole generations grew up with the ambition to drive the colonizers out – and think of nothing after that.

Tara: It also showed the natives how a modern economy runs, it showed the people who lived in Ghana how they could build roads and how they could do better if they used things like telephones. You know that when Zaïre got its independence, there were over 10,000 miles of functioning all-weather roads. Guess how many there are in Congo today?

Taylor: Just tell me.

Tara: Virtually none, outside the principal cities. Those that remain are still only passable by four-wheel drive vehicles. The jungle has swallowed the rest. This made it easier for Mobutu to keep his rivals apart, and Kabila really hasn't done much to help.

Taylor: And, if there hadn't been Europeans, there would have been no need for Mobutu, or even for the tribal conflict that is chewing Zaïre – Congo – up. No matter how you deal with it, the problem of Africa today is the problem of geography and the problem of ethnicity. The borders are false and the people who live inside of them are going to be fighting with each other until the borders can go back to a more natural state.[53]

But Can Trust Ever Return?

One other point must be drawn from the lessons of colonialism: that the West has never really known, or been able to admit, what it was doing in Africa. Today, almost everyone accepts that colonialism's prime objects were to play petty strategic games and to earn profit. Back then, no one said that. Everyone said, and seemed to believe, that they were actually doing Africa a service. This may have been true of many of the people who actually went to live – and die – in Africa, but it certainly was not true of the leaders back home. One person who saw this was the Asantahene, who said to a British emissary who came to him elaborately explaining that the British Empire had nothing but the good of the Ashanti at heart:

That cannot be your motive. As regards industry and the arts, you are superior to us. But we have relations with other people, the Kong, who are as little civilised in relation to us as we are to you.

Yet there is not a single one of my subjects, even amongst the poorest, who would be willing to leave his home to civilize the Kong. So how do you hope to convince me that you have left the prosperity of England for such an absurd motive?[54]

One has to be careful when thinking about policy relationships between the West and Africa. If everything billed as acts of goodwill in the past was actually done with exploitation or at least manipulation at heart, why should Africans, or anyone for that matter, trust Western initiatives today?

Luck

Last comes the question of luck in the shaping of historical trajectories. Time worked steadily for Thailand. Marshal Sarit, the unpromising leader who came to power in 1957, was smart enough to hear the hoofbeats of history. He saw the scope and depth of the American move into Southeast Asia before the massive wave engulfed almost the whole region along with America itself. And while Thailand's titular ally, the Republic of Vietnam, foundered in the war that followed, ultimately Thailand came out in every sense ahead.[55] Just as it could be said that Japan won the Cold War, it can more accurately be said that Thailand won the Vietnam War. The Kingdom was poised to take advantage of the great build-up. The United States for its own reasons poured in infrastructure, laying out the basic highway grid that unified the largest region – Issan – with the central Thai, permitting the Thai to nail down their rule and legitimacy over that vast, poor countryside. Some of the great Thai fortunes were made on the backs of the American build-up; the entire top military prospered and became bound to the Americans for a long time to come. While Africans were lining up to plunder Ghana's glory, Thailand was building up solid foundations of economic growth and international protection because it had an indispensable asset: real enemies.

The Thai saw time running out, with the region falling to hostile forces fully capable of engulfing them. This created a need to be useful to, and cut deals with, the only power with which they felt comfortable, the United States. It wasn't difficult. When Field Marshal Thanom Kittikachorn, Sarit's protégé and then successor for over a decade, was asked to name the most admirable person among the world leaders he had met, he replied without hesitation: Dwight David Eisenhower, a man so Thai himself in his collegial and soft-spoken approach.[56]

Even the war's outcome worked for Thailand. It was Bangkok's accurate – if sometimes nervous – judgement that America could be trusted, that their situation was different from that of the Vietnamese. Moreover, the Thai economy was poised for take-off. The benefits lost from US military spending were beginning to be outclassed by growing agricultural exports and even small industrial enterprises. Thai diplomacy whipped into place following the American reconciliation with China and quickly and deftly moved to exploit Chinese–Vietnamese hostility: not just the relief on its eastern border afforded by the Chinese attack on northeast Vietnam, but China's need to deny Vietnam further success. Once Deng Xiaoping regained power, he suspended Chinese aid and countenance to the Communist Party of Thailand. By 1980, Thailand had squeezed every drop of benefit possible from a world politics in motion.

So, for Thailand, the Vietnam War lasted just long enough but not too long, and regional instability made this somewhat strained monarchy an island of stability in which America had a growing stake. By the time of the 1985 Plaza Accords, when Japan was battered into revaluing the yen and pushing Foreign Direct Investment (FDI) beyond its borders by the bale, Thailand had put down its insurgency, launched into 9–14 per cent annual economic growth, and moved into a quasi-democratic mode that suited most élites and provided sufficient outlet for most other potential pressures. At the decade's end, the effervescent General Chatichai Choonhaven, hero of the cavalry and one of the most popular Thai politicians ever, became Prime Minister and declared that the goal of foreign policy was to turn Vietnam's battlefields into marketplaces. Strategic luck was now apparent over the whole regional map, and Thailand was coming into its own just in time to grab onto its neighbours' coat tails.

For Ghana luck ran almost in reverse. The Ghanaian élite thought that they were going to have twenty years' headstart as black Africa's first independent nation; others would come along, but none was scheduled for independence in 1954 when the Gold Coast was confirmed for 1957. But in 1956 the British and French faltered at Suez and the world began to notice that the sand was spilling from the colonial hourglass. Soon Nigeria was to be independent in 1960, and the die was cast. In late 1959 the Belgians, their nerve broken by rioting (catalyzed by a conference in Accra), announced that they would leave the Congo in six months, even though the vast country had only eight college graduates. As recently as 1958 the francophone African territories had voted – with the sole exception of Guinea – to stay in the French Union, and therefore to be domestically autonomous only. Now they had to realize that Harold Macmillan's 'Winds of Change' were sweeping them into the vortex of independence too. In 1960 all but the hardest nuts were cracked: the remaining eleven francophone states, Congo and Nigeria claimed their seats at the United Nations. London rushed to set dates for East Africa and to find a way out of its 'kith and kin' dilemma in the Federation of Rhodesia and Nyasaland – now Zimbabwe, Zambia, and Malawi. Ghana had expected to lead the way, and to an extent at some levels it still did, but continental momentum brushed aside the already archaic Ghanaian example. Soon South African exiles, in flight from a real industrial behemoth, were mocking Ghanaian pretensions to continental leadership. While Ghana had thought it had time to establish the patterns of pre-eminence which Nkrumah deemed his due, the reverse was true; the reality principle never intruded enough to save him from his messianic delusions.

History. Geography. Ethnicity. Imperialism. Luck. None is paramount or uncontested, but all five factors have worked to nurture the baobab tree and to temper the cutting of the mango grove.

CHAPTER 3

Leadership

'We succeeded because we had no leaders,' Thailand's great Foreign Minister Thanat Khoman once said thoughtfully.[57] Not the whole truth, but an important one. Most societies have leaders; few have industrial development. If being inspired by or under the dominion of a leader were the most important factor in development, the streets of Accra would be lined with gold and China's peasants would all be sleeping in velvet beds.

In this chapter we follow these two lines of thought, analyzing the impact of historical circumstance upon leadership and how much individual leaders were able to accomplish or destroy. Leadership is certainly a necessary explanatory factor of the Ghanaian–Thai differential, and at times even seems a sufficient one. Kwame Nkrumah was the most notable leader in black Africa for more than a decade. He had an international following, and to this day is something of a cult figure in the country that drove him into exile.[58] But well before the fall he seemed to have made every mistake a leader could, and had driven his country in short order to bankruptcy.

Bad Leaders

Weisbrode and Thompson, in an earlier study, examined all the Third World states with economies that had declined between 1971 and 1991. They found that, with only two partial exceptions, all had leaders who usurped functions, squashed opposition, and in general fought to gather all influence to themselves, and to block all other avenues to power.[59] Ideology mattered little. In 1971 Zambia, under that reflexively leftist African, Kenneth Kaunda, enjoyed the same *per capita* income (PCI) as Zaire under the grotesquely military-authoritarian Mobutu: about $390. Twenty years later, despite billions of aid and investment, Zambia and Zaïre (soon to become the Democratic Republic of Congo) still had PCIs of approximately $390. Bad leadership transcends ideology. Even today, Zaïre has a new – old – name, a new leader, a new revolutionary attitude and the same quality of leadership along with the same abysmal PCI and a new civil war, Africa's greatest violence ever.

No one is universally wise. Even if the world produced such paragons, the law of comparative advantage would apply as much in politics as in economics: even a philosopher-king can't do all and decide all. But if all competing power centres are squeezed out, decisions float up to the top or await completion, sometimes until death provides a solution. As the Akan proverb goes, *Ti Koro nko agyina* – 'One man alone is insufficient for the full deliberation of an undertaking.'[60]

There comes a point of badness where the word leader becomes meaningless and the manifest function need not be the real one: a chairman of the board who is an embezzler is likely to be an embezzler far more than a chairman of the board. Nevertheless, while one man alone may not be enough for full deliberation, the right man or woman can certainly help a good deal, particularly if he realizes the truth of the Akan proverb and collaborates with the right support and information networks. Singapore's Senior Minister, the one-time Prime Minister Lee Kuan Yew, surely got as close to the role of platonic philosopher-king as any post-war leader, particularly if we are to judge by material results: if the United States had grown at the same rate as Singapore since the latter's unwanted compulsory independence in 1965, the PCI of Americans would today average three hundred thousand dollars, and more equally distributed too. Lee Kuan Yew did not demand that he control everything: he wanted extraordinary national success, but no more than great personal power. He was also smart enough to see that the two were not identical – nor even, beyond a certain point, harmonious. He always let a distinguished and weighty cadre of bankers and industrialists hold the reins of the economy. The extraordinary Central Provident Fund, one of the most innovative social security networks ever devised, did not spring full-funded from Harry Lee's head, after all. One didn't cross him, but he earned that honourable formidability which did not grow from the barrel of a gun.

Africa stands out in the past generation for failed and, at times, catastrophic leadership. If we ignore such remaining communist tyrannies as North Korea, virtually all the truly barrel-bottom leaders of the Third World cast themselves upon Africa's shores: Amin, Obote, Mengistu, Abacha, Mobutu – the line will go on to the crack of doom if we don't look out. Southeast Asia, although it has offered examples far more chilling than Africa's of relatively 'principled' tyranny as distinct from kleptocracy (Pol Pot, the House of Kim) has come up with no such truly classic examples of plain moral anarchy. In Africa over the last forty years, 'road system' or 'power grid' are to be read only in a Pickwickian sense, but 'presidential palace' or 'secret police' meet the standards of the developed world.

The great author Chinua Achebe puts the point forcefully, if with slight exaggeration, in his famous words about his home country, which read just as well if you substitute 'Africa' for 'Nigeria':

> The trouble with Nigeria is simply and squarely a failure of leadership. There is nothing basically wrong with the Nigerian character. There is nothing wrong with the Nigerian land or climate or water or air or anything else. The Nigerian problem is the unwillingness or inability of its leaders to rise to the responsibility, to the challenge of personal example which are the hallmarks of true leadership.[61]

Bad African Leaders

In most of Africa, the leaders who inherited the post-colonial settlement were outstanding political organizers, men who could drum up mass street support and galvanize the urban populace. They were not equipped, or even imaginatively prepared, for the level of economic management that their horizonless visions of political power entailed. Their first goal seemed always to be to consolidate a fantasy of personal supremacy, not to promote vulgar prosperity – the business, surely, of clerks and mammy entrepreneurs. The need to consolidate political power most likely came in a large part, as we argue elsewhere, from the false borders created by colonialism and the weak centralized structures left behind.

Furthermore, the struggle against colonialism was relatively brief and theatrical, in the limelight of the capital; it did little to illuminate or indeed to sieve out the character and capacity of those who took over. 'How many lives did you lose in your struggle, sir?' Ben Gurion asked one African leader at the UN. 'Twenty? Oh! And you are building a nation on twenty dead?'[62] What comes cheap is rarely adequately assessed or truly valued; the often theatrical leaders of short struggles are very unlike the grim survivor types thrown up by the big wars. Sékou Touré of Guinea[63] made a fine ideologist in his Left Bank publications and was brave enough, if not very reflective, in saying 'Non' to the French in 1958, but he didn't lead a real struggle. He couldn't have, lacking the strength or true commitment. Sadly, once ensconced behind thugs loyal to him alone in a presidential palace (not very presidential in any republican sense, but truly a palace) he proved to be as terrible (in both senses) a leader as any in Africa. His true colours showed when he hanged his most distinguished diplomat, Aschkar Marof, a man of innumerable useful friendships throughout Europe and America, on suspicion of involvement in a failed coup, although Marof had actually turned himself in to Touré when the coup began. If you know that you aren't truly strong, you must destroy everybody else who ever might be. Thus Ghana was casually damned to the tender mercies of Nkrumah, whereas South Africa, after decades of struggle, earned the right to be led by Nelson Mandela.

Moreover, as Thomas Sowell has wisely observed, African leaders brought back from the West 'not the practical or scientific knowledge and skills behind the wealth and power of the West, but rather the social theories and moral speculations of European and American intellectuals'.[64] Even those bringing more practical skills back, like Dr Hastings Banda, assimilated to the political role rather than expanding their medical or scientific interests and influence. Until his dotage, Houphouet-Boigny might at least have brought his practical experience in French government (though, thankfully, without importing the politics of the Fourth Republic in which he served as a minister) to Ivory Coast. The élites who came back may have brought skills – but when given positions of power, as George Ayittey has said, 'their brains just turned to fufu'.[65]

Kwame Nkrumah

It is worth considering just how bad a standard Nkrumah set, not just for Ghana but for Africa as a whole. There is no doubt that he had the impulse and urge to greatness – for himself, for Ghana, and for Africa (and there is no doubt that releasing Ghana from colonialism was a tremendous accomplishment). Political leaders always do: visit the White House early in any new administration and then double that enthusiasm. Indeed, the gap in Accra between aspiration and operation, even at the most obvious levels, needs careful measurement to be believable (as it often does in the White House, too). In 1959 Nkrumah stated that the goal of Ghana's foreign policy must be to 'promote and maintain peace and security among the nations of the world,'[66] a lofty goal for such a small country, but something that he honestly believed was possible. Such honest belief, alas, when so distant from reality, can only rest on dishonest assessment.

Nkrumah's great goal was a 'union government' for Africa. A well-known British journalist wrote that 'union is not only a political ideal, but an economic necessity', without which Ghana's economy could never expand. 'It is fair to say that a lesser man than Nkrumah would have been sorely tempted to chuck revolutionary ideals for a generation on the grounds that for the time being the human material is not there. But this option would be unreal: in this game one gains or loses ground and can never stand still.'[67] Wise words indeed – but in the ensuing year Ghana's trade with its neighbours was halved as Nkrumah trained subversives to overthrow fellow post-colonialists in the crazed dream of subjecting a continent.

Nkrumah met with encouragement at every turn long after his vanity, ideological duplicity and disingenuousness had marked him as a danger. There is a tendency for officials, journalists, political intellectuals, and even bankers with short memories to take anyone in power seriously. Bureaucrats, national or international, are trained to accept authority, to accept even the preposterous, for either 'there isn't any alternative', or 'the man has certain redeeming qualities', or, simplest of all, 'it is an internal matter'. The scribbling set deserves its share of blame. Sir Arthur Lewis, the distinguished West Indian economist, saw it as early as 1964:

Western democrats have abandoned the African; even long-standing friends of Africa hesitate to speak out for fear of offending those now in power. As for our political scientists, they fall over themselves to demonstrate that democracy is suitable only for Europeans and North Americans, and in the sacred names of 'charisma', 'modernisation', and 'national unity', call upon us to admire any demagogue who, aided by a loud voice and a bunch of hooligans, captures the state and suppresses his rivals.[68]

Sir Arthur might have added that for every scholar who comes to Third World political science out of an interest in democracy there are ten who come out of an interest in power – and an impatience with the cautions that skewer rival disciplines such as economics. Nkrumah certainly had power, due in no small part to his substantial political skills. Gilchrist Olympio, one of the first people to conceptualize the problem of leadership in Africa,[69] has said of Nkrumah and his rival Kofi Busia, who would serve two bumbling years as Prime Minister in the early 1970s, 'Busia was one hundred times as smart as Nkrumah, but Nkrumah could still tie knots around him politically.'[70]

In the end, Nkrumah's delusions and ego brought a double tragedy to Africa. Part I was manifest in the state of Ghana when its first leader was finally forced out. Part II was the way in which the undoubted energies and ideals which Nkrumah so clearly mustered and represented in the beginning were later betrayed by himself and by others who followed his example. As Ghanaian presidential candidate Nana Akufo-Addo says sadly, 'Nkrumah gave us something in the beginning. He gave us pride and a feeling that we could do it ourselves.'[71] If he had stepped down in 1961, or if his later politics hadn't been dominated by ego and a parodic simulacrum of communism, perhaps everything in Ghana would have turned out differently.[72]

Coups Are Like Sex

After the generation of 'independence heroes' of the Nkrumah school died off or had been overthrown, Africa began to institutionalize, if you can institutionalize lawlessness, a political culture of 'change by coup'. Once one army leader had done it, his brother generals over the frontier or one rank down, former classmates and boozing pals were visited by similar thoughts. The first coup toppled and slew Sylvanus Olympio of Togo, one of the most remarkable leaders Africa has had.[73] Since then, 'gunfire at the palace' seems to have become Africa's supranational anthem.

In 1966 one of the present authors invited two leaders of the first Ghanaian coup, General Afrifa and Colonel Kotei, as he then was, to his bungalow to meet two American scholars of Africa. After Kotei had recounted the fears and uncertainties of plotting and executing a seizure of power, the learned Carl Rosberg put the question to Afrifa directly: 'You have made a coup, you are reforming the country, and you promise to turn the government over to an elected government in the near future. What's to guarantee that you won't undertake another coup, if it fails to live up to its promises?'

'A coup is like sex,' Afrifa responded. 'The first time you're very nervous. After that [it's] easy and fun ... if a new government is corrupt or dictatorial, we'll overthrow it with ease.' Afrifa was no fool, but couldn't have foreseen that two coups down the road the new ruler would execute him – at the age of 36 – along with Colonel Kotei.

Yet it shouldn't have surprised Afrifa that Jerry Rawlings had come to the same conclusion about coups. His return to power was carried out seemingly without effort and with minimal bloodshed (at least during the actual coup; little fighting then, plenty of murder afterwards). Moreover, Rawlings had executed all of the other leaders the first time around. He didn't have to worry about the African equivalent of an elder statesman coming back for seconds.

Matters have reached the point that, in many parts of Africa, young men who want to be political leaders don't work in business or the public service; they join the army.[74] This has led to absurd and tragic outbursts of power-drunkenness across the continent. In Zambia in 1997 a young rogue soldier with no support, calling himself 'Captain Solo', tried to overthrow the government almost single-handedly and was rebuked. In Burkina Faso the current President, Blaise Compaoré, came to power in 1983 by shooting his close friend, partner and certainly the most popular and best leader that the country ever had, Thomas Sankara, who had changed the named of his country from 'Upper Volta' to 'Burkina Faso' or 'land of the good-natured people'. The working of the 'militarist international' is probably best illustrated by the back-to-back coups attempted against Julius Nyerere, Milton Obote and Jomo Kenyatta in 1964, only put down by British intervention: their leaders, after all, had trained together in British staff colleges. Nothing gave the coup leaders in Ghana in 1966 more glowing encouragement than the Nigerian coup just ten weeks earlier. Revolution by the old-boy network:[75] 'revolution' for power; rarely for change.

The Demonstration Effect

Another reason for Africa's terrible failures in self-government is that bad leadership reinforces itself. The continent's kleptocrats and adventurers gather annually at the Organization of African Unity, encountering only their own look-alikes as role models. No one has set an example. If just one major country in Africa had been able to break out of, or through, the cycle which seemingly has ensnared every nation, it might well have been able to bring the rest of the continent with it. Even the most highly regarded leader – Julius Nyerere of Tanzania – presided over such economic catastrophes that no confrère, however admiring, was going to emulate a particle of his policy. To his credit, Nyerere was the first African leader to speak out against the autocracies that had become all but universal on the continent[76] – a flawed stance in itself, however, for his own prisons were full of political opponents. Kenneth Adelman described the great man's commitment as 'human rights for others'. The most astonishing economic miracle of Africa, Botswana, was too small to be much of a model – and unfashionable until recently by virtue of its inability to join the 'front-line states' in the struggle against South Africa's apartheid regime. Christopher Clapham rightly notes that for at least the first two decades after independence, 'even the most muted criticism of the internal autocracy of other African states was virtually nonexistent'.[77]

Consider Jerry Rawlings today. Rawlings is no Mandela; in fact his regime is arguably more than a little corrupt and brutal – an undertow of corruption had gripped the state by the millennium. Nor is he the brightest kid in the sandbox, although he got more marks for honesty than certain Western politicians when he said, as Ghana lurched into structural reform in the early 1980s, that he didn't understand all those economic theories – 'blah blah blah' was his widely quoted verdict, in which many concur. But compared with his peer group – including the late Sani Abacha, Daniel arap Moi and Gnassibe Eyadema – he stands out. At least when Ghana's condition had become desperate he had the courage to change course. When Clinton went to Africa he started out by acclaiming Rawlings, not because Rawlings is a great democrat, but because he has at least given up shooting people at whim.

The case of Rawlings is also instructive about what may be the most ruinous element of leadership on the darkened continent: how expectations make the cycle brutally hard to escape. Even today, to many people in Ghana their country's principal problem is the profound reluctance nationwide to work or invest for lack of confidence that Rawlings will ever give up power – or, indeed, that he will not simply revert to tyranny, loot the country and leave it in ruins. Such doubts naturally engender a form of defensive driving in which the vehicle simply does not move. After all, coups are like sex and, if Rawlings ever leaves office, the most constitutional of successors will only have to recall the flight lieutenant's own way with the older generals.

Rawlings first seized power over twenty years ago, shooting the surviving former heads of state to underline his new authority and eliminate threats to his rule. After briefly returning power to elected civilians, he brought off another coup. In the years immediately following, Rawlings liquidated several inconvenient judges, jailed many of his opponents and threw himself into the role of a stereotypical African 'Big Man', which casts an interesting light on his current staunchly constitutionalist utterances: 'My time is up. I want to obey the Constitution.'[78] (Of course, he may have lost the last two elections, in which he was never the less declared to be elected President: what is the constitution between friends?)

Not everyone believes him, and the doubters include many Ghanaians. Leaders have pledged exactly the same thing in Togo, in Nigeria, and in nearly every country in Africa – yet almost never have they followed through. But it is clear that Rawlings is indeed different from the leaders of Togo and Nigeria. On the most obvious levels, until the late 1990s he was never accused of personal corruption – although then the problem became vast; he doesn't require that his photograph be hung throughout Ghana; he doesn't travel in giant motorcades. More profoundly, he has indeed made progress toward freeing his country and getting it back on the right economic track; and even an unmistakable political opponent, Dr Edward Mahama, has conceded that 'he has been an evolutionary leader'.[79]

This legacy will be cemented if he proves capable of ensuring a peaceful and honest transition for either of the two leading candidates, Ashanti John Kuffour or John Atta Mills, the president's chosen successor and current vice-president. Following Senegal's peaceful and democratic transition in 1999, this could have a powerful impact on the continent.

The African Military

Another reason for the failure of African leadership is the character of the people – very often, the category of people – who have assumed power. In Africa, Ghana being a prime example, the military has never regained a sense of limits since its taste of blood in 1966. Its thieving possesses an almost Homeric quality, combined with the self-deceiving pretence that it is actually the nation's high-minded trustee. As Bayart put it, 'War's great advantage over simple delinquency is that it legitimizes in the name of justice and the revolution the use of arms to get access to the resources of the state.'[81]

Professor Mullins has made the perceptive observation that the Third World military, in general, contrasts heavily with the traditional military of Europe in the state formation phase.[82] The Connétable's role, after all, was to bring home riches and the control of turf from over the mountains, across the river or even beyond the seas. Louis XIV thus set out to employ his army in the expansion of France to its 'natural frontiers' and largely succeeded. The military, particularly in Africa, came to independence with set borders, for reasons we have already discussed, and had nowhere to use its guns, for a long time, except internally. And that it did, enriching itself and impoverishing many countries. Thailand is less the exception for having had soldier-statesmen than because the whole notion of the military is different in its history and culture. Thailand's army has been around for centuries at about the same level. Ghana's armies, and the armies of most of Africa, were suddenly given positions of immense power almost overnight. They had never really fought in a war that they cared about and they had no sense of duty to the state, much less to the Crown.

Not surprisingly, the most brutal leaders in Africa have come from military backgrounds. Of all Ghana's appalling years, probably the worst lie between January 1972, when Colonel Acheampong seized power from an elected if unpopular government, and July 1978 when he in turn was overthrown. Acheampong capitalized on the well-earned unpopularity of Professor Busia's regime. The cedi had been devalued, labour was unhappy, and the government had systematic-ally hollowed out all the rest of its traditional support structures. But it had an elected term of office. Moreover, with the price of cocoa rising, economic relief was on the horizon. But Acheampong moved and initially made half the right noises, summoning some of the most distinguished Ghanaians as ministers and advisers. The recruits included the old and skilful veterans Komla Gbedemah and Joe Appiah, among the most popular and respected of all Ghana's civilian elder statesmen. Within months they saw that they had no role; in any case, the colonel's 'National Redemption Council' soon replaced civilian ministers with military officers.

There was no programme and no attempt to formulate one; as the Russian analyst Youry Petchinkine put it, it was all 'demagoguery; slogans and promises do not mean government action'.[83] 'Self-sufficiency' for the country's economy only meant more import substi-tution, of course and Acheampong's revaluation of the cedi only meant substantially more opportunities for corruption. Acheampong had no compass except an unmistakable thirst for power and money. The scope of his corruption was only hinted at in the evidence presented before his execution – that he had shortly before bought three houses in London, several in Kumasi, and transferred 'large sums in hard currency to Swiss bank accounts'.[84]

In contrast, Thailand has never produced even a Latin American or African-style praetorian strongman. With some qualifications, it can be said that Thai military leaders have governed with some sense of fitness, resting on their sense of the passivity of their people, at least until recently. The exceptions tend to prove the rule. Suchinda so

JERRY JOHN RAWLINGS:
MILITARY MAN OR CIVILIAN?

Jerry Rawlings's mother was a prostitute and his father a Scot who left Ghana and could never serve as a parent. Rawlings's childhood was brutal but he was able to pull himself up and became a very charismatic flight lieutenant. The rest is history. At the time of his coup, J. J. Rawlings was referred to by many as 'Junior Jesus' as he fought, or at least was perceived to be fighting, against corruption.

In the beginning, there was no doubt that Rawlings was a military man: he acted just like a typical African despot. But in 1992 he very noisily took off his uniform and organized democratic elections which he unsurprisingly swept; slightly more surprisingly, particularly given the evidence to the contrary, the elections were sanctioned by the international community.[85] The dose was repeated in 1996, although local dissent, at least, was louder.

Today Rawlings would like everyone to believe that he is just like a normal civilian President. But there are doubts. As Kwame Pianim has said: 'He's like a leopard saying he is a lamb just because he has hidden his spots.'[86]

Pianim has reason to be angry. He might be the strongest opposition candidate for President but he cannot run for office because under Ghana's current constitution anyone convicted of plotting a coup against the government (and Pianim spent ten years in prison on just such a charge) is ineligible. (Rawlings, who came to power twice through coups, is of course exempted. 'Treason doth never prosper: what's the reason? Why, if it prosper, none dare call it treason.')

And as the moment of truth approached, the Ghanaian government approached bankruptcy, mostly because corruption was mounting – or being suctioned up, perhaps, from the top. The universities were closed in late 1999 over disputes over who paid, and the government was often not paying for goods received: the privatized companies handed out to favourites were not paying their dues back to government – they were not favourites for nothing – and mismanagement was mounting. It was widely believed that Rawlings and Nana Konadu, his wife, were increasingly on the take. The fish, it was everywhere said, 'rots from the head'.

enraged a populace provoked beyond passivity less than two years after his coup that in 1992 the King was called on for only the second time in his reign to throw the Crown's power into the scales. Phibul's legitimacy rested on his primacy among the original 'promoters' who overthrew the absolute monarchy in 1932. The single great strongman, Sarit, however light-fingered and imperious, could communicate his commitment to the development of the kingdom; his wisdom in restoring the influence of the throne – the apparent limitations upon himself being much less than the real legitimization that accrued to him thereby – and his quick results made him popular enough not to need excuses or legitimization. And, but for a single execution in 1981, after a general officer was shot in cold blood during a coup attempt, Thai coups have been almost pirouettes. If the First Army wished to change the structure of command, there wasn't much point in resistance and so little was attempted. When the young Turks attempted to put their own man in power – the so-called April Fool's Day coup of 1981 – General – and Prime Minister – Prem needed only to escort the royal family to Korat for the movement to implode.

Leadership in the Middle

Beyond the plain brutes at the top of the pyramid, another problem with leadership in Africa has been the inability to develop we-groups, groups of leaders who will make sacrifices for the country in crisis, will fight for it, and will accept sacrifices among the separate component groups, whatever these be, in order to advance the interests of the country. These 'we groups' must transcend ethnicity.

Through such adjustments and balances countries can and do change. Most dramatically, after the 1969 riots Malaysia's Malay, Chinese and Indian leaders got together and realized they all had more to lose by not working out a better deal for the country's majority ethnic group, the Malays. Under a complicated but sensible scheme, the Chinese leaders agreed, without having to accept cuts in their existing businesses, to incorporate 'Bumis' in the enlarging economy. Everybody won. Without the agreement, the Chinese, who were giving up the degree of control they had over the country's economy thitherto, were certain to lose more lives and to exist in a business framework where expansion was impossible and where nationhood withered.

Professor Ranis, a World Bank consultant, tells of his work with the Mexican government after its debt crisis of the early 1980s. The leaders of different sectors gathered with the leaders of the republic and accepted their share of the necessary sacrifices. He compared this unfavourably with the tendency in the Philippines, during the Aquino period, for all the sectoral leaders to try to sustain their own advantage.[87] But one can see enormous improvement on this score in the Ramos presidency. Cajoling, encouraging, rewarding, Ramos made competing groups see that they had more to gain even by sacrificing than by zero-sum competition at the national expense. Senior bureaucrats began to talk of the disappearance of their turf consciousness, as the glittering Thai upper apparat had done for decades, moving from department to department as needs of the nation arose.

A we-group has always existed in Thailand in the modern period, although its locus has shifted and in recent years evolved and enlarged to incorporate new groups, like the Chinese. True, in the 1930s there was a period of more than latent anti-Chinese legislation and social dictatorship; in a joke that persists, every Thai hates every Chinese – except his mother and grandfather.[88] But the bottom line was still that a Chinese taking on a Thai name, or modifying his name in the Thai direction, and sending his children to Thai schools, could readily expect to become 'Thai'. The Hakka Taipan of Thailand, Banthoon Lamsam, is the grandson of the family founder – and married the very Thai granddaughter of the former Prime Minister, Field Marshal Thanom, and Thanpuying Chamkol Kittikachorn. More recently the expansion of the élite has been in the direction of class, as more and more leaders emerge from non-traditional sources – marginal universities, poor provinces, even NGOs.

The special case of Thailand is surely to a significant degree a function of a continuing and, until recently, self-perpetuating central élite that has had enormous self-esteem, self-confidence and the will to rule, and has delivered the goods in sufficient measure to stay in power. True, 1932, the year of the overthrow of the absolute monarchy, marks an important break with tradition (although, significantly, the anniversary is barely noted these days in Bangkok). Until then, sons and grandsons of the great kings Mongkut and

Chulalongkorn had ruled most ministries tightly, allied with wealthy families like the Bunnag and Snitwongse. Yet the 'promoters' who seized power in 1932, and who with their linear descendants continued to rule most of the time until the 1990s, never ceased to depend on this same remarkable élite. Prince Wan at the Foreign Ministry in the 1950s, and another grandson of King Mongkut, Prince Dhani, who wielded a powerful cultural influence throughout the Kingdom, kept the old élite's image well burnished even under the foulest years of military oppression after the Second World War. One of the most talented great-grandsons of a king, MR[89] Chatumonkol Sonakul, insisted in 1996 that 'titles and social standing don't matter in Thailand ... what matters is having power and money, after which everybody clings to you'.[90] But when this brilliant one-time permanent secretary of the Ministry of Finance became governor of the Bank of Thailand in 1998, one knew it was not so simple. He had an allure that included the glory of the Chakri name.[91] The children of the current King are discussed incessantly and candidly, even at the risk of stiff *lèse majesté* penalties, while the best of them – the popular, indeed venerated, Princess Royal – is elevated beyond elevation: but they are of the blood and have enormous privileges and allure at all times. Monarchy is back in fashion.

But Thailand continues to evolve. The class basis of the ruling élite has changed, widening mightily in recent years. Under Prime Minister Chavalit, Saranrom Palace was in 1997 overseen by Foreign Minister Prachuab, who came down from a poor northeastern village to Bangkok and drove a *tuktuk*[92] to pay for his education at Thammasat University. Later he made a fortune in the Middle East, several far cries from the playing fields of such former Foreign Ministers as Prince Wan – or even of Thanat Khoman, in so many respects the classic mandarin.

Talent

Perhaps the unique operating advantage of this we-group was its capacity, with barely visible subtlety, to block the coming to power of any single, truly destructive leader out of tune with immediate realities. Dictatorship, in the sense of military rule, was inescapable, but the individual 'dictators' governed rather lightly as these things go in the Third World – certainly by the standards of Burma or Vietnam.

Indeed arguably the trio in power in Bangkok in the early 1970s was not driven out by the reaction to its barely visible highhandedness but caved in to the dry rot of its own permissiveness. It had educated a wholly new candidate class for élite status, too great for the economy to absorb at once, leaving plenty of unemployed young graduates to throng the streets. The press was fairly free and researchers – like one of the present authors – were able to ask embarrassing questions wherever they ventured, with no fear of imprisonment (in contrast to what the same researcher experienced in Ghana, even under a pro-Western regime – not, alas, that this last is any guarantee in itself, as a hundred zealously pro-Western or at least pro-Pentagon juntas in Latin America reminded us).

Along the way Thailand found a number of other talented leaders for its first and second echelons, proving at every crucial juncture that the society had developed mechanisms to encourage them to emerge and play their part. No society has unbounded talent, and so the question is whether it uses what it has as best it can. Nothing replaces political power, but Thailand is unique in the Third World in the respect it accords its experts. Permanent secretaries of the important ministries are respected and deferred to as in few other societies. The governor of the Bank of Thailand is – revealingly – considered the *senior* bureaucrat, which is why such attention has rightly been given to 'what went wrong' at the Bank prior to the 1997 meltdown. But the society knew how to remedy its defects. We have seen that Prime Minister Chuan appointed as governor one of the cleverest, most talented, wittiest, most prophetic and self-confident civil servants we have ever met in the Third World: MR Chatumonkol Sonakul, who had predicted with devastating accuracy[93] the pattern of events from early 1996 onwards. The King and Prime Ministers have a current and detailed knowledge of the stable of expertise. Indeed in the 1980s the palace frequently intervened to ensure the promotion of those whom they judged the most talented.

General Chatichai, who barely escaped execution in 1957 – as the rich and popular son of the leader of the clique overthrown by Marshal Sarit – rebuilt his base in diplomacy and was able to seize the moment in the 1980s, when he famously asserted that Thailand would turn the Indochinese battlefields into marketplaces. And when he formed a party and became Prime Minister he did far more for Thailand's relations with its once-hostile neighbours and for the grandly growing Thai economy than he did for his corrupt ministers, some of whom earned the amusing euphemism from the coup group that replaced them: 'the unusually rich'. He worked in tandem during the 1980s with Air Chief Marshal Siddhi Savetsila, a wise strategist who guided the kingdom's foreign policy in the most treacherous times – when Vietnamese divisions were near its eastern boundary, and the only thing protecting Thailand from one last push by General Giap's army, the wags wagged, was Bangkok's traffic.[94] But Marshal Sid had also been allied with the clique whom Marshal Sarit had deposed; Sarit's group was wise enough to let him grow in power, too.

In Ghana, talent has had little value. Alex Quaison-Sackey had been president of the UN General Assembly but because of his distant association with Nkrumah he was banished to Cape Coast, his home district, after a brief stint in jail following the 1966 coup. He died relatively young, his great talent wasted. Kofi Annan left Ghana to find a fit outlet for his talents. Kwame Pianim, probably Ghana's best economist, is banned from running for office. Today there is little hope of building a group, in part because it is much harder to get one started after forty years of factional fighting, but also because of the divisive role that ethnicity has always played in Ghanaian politics.

Lak Thai and King Bhumibol

Thailand has a history of strong monarchs. Rama IV, King Mongkut, not only began the modernization of the kingdom; he began its modern diplomacy. In the Archives of the United States one may read his remarkable and, its own way, prophetic letter to Abraham Lincoln offering the services of Thai battle elephants for the war for the union; Lincoln's reply shows a respect for the king's canny offer, turning it down diplomatically on the basis of the advice of veterinarians. Even looking back to the twentieth Thai king in a previous seventeenth-century dynasty one finds a clear impulse to greatness. King Pra Naret Rachathirait, according to a contemporary Dutch observer,

> often had pieces of flesh sliced off from those (even among mandarins) who committed the smallest mistakes and had them eat their own flesh before his very eyes.... He always said, This is the

way you Siamese must be ruled because you are obstinate people of abominable nature and in a rotten state. But I shall do these things to you until I make you a respected nation. You are as the grass on the fertile field; the shorter you are mowed, the more beautifully you grow. I will have the gold strewn in the streets and let it lie there for months. Whoever looks at this gold with greed will die.[95]

Words Idi Amin might have used – without, perhaps, the dream of greatness. Van Vliet notes that, since Pra's reign, 'the Siamese kings have never been subject to any other prince of this world'.[96]

Small wonder, then, that *Lak Thai*, meant to imply Thai greatness (though the term has no specific denotation), should surface from time to time as a controlled aspiration. In this light it is no surprise that the Kingdom has produced one historically great leader in the present period. Although monarchy almost made a comeback in the aftermath of the Soviet break-up, it is fair to say that it has generally been on the defensive since the First World War. In Thailand it goes from strength to strength. But the best observers will always note they talk about *this* King, not monarchy. With the passing of King Hussain, no monarch in the world is as powerful in his own country as King Bhumibol. He started from a menaced and puppet-like position, without influence or prospects – only the prestige of a throne in a country that had always, like so many others, had kings, but not had one *in-country* for over a decade. When he finally had a chance truly to reign, in 1957, it had been over fifty years since his country had had an effective monarch. At his accession the ruling clique symbolically tormented him to keep him in line. Phibul began systematically replacing royal pictures with his own.[97] His emergence as the powerful reparative leader he became was at least half his own work. For it was also the smart move of the Sarit group, which saw his usefulness – and, in fact, literally valued his expertise.[98] Unlike the lesser men they replaced, they saw the legitimacy the king could add to their development efforts, as well as their programmes for extracting support from outlying areas like Issan.

A revealing anecdote of Air Chief Marshal Siddhi Savetsila's shows royal regalia didn't get in the way of royal adaptivity. When the Vietnamese divisions were near Thailand's eastern borders in 1979, and probing inward, the security of the Kingdom was in serious doubt for the first time since early Chakri days. Marshal Sid, however, although possessing an MIT degree from before his days as a partisan with the US-backed Free Thai, did not speak the royal, Khmer-based, language which is required at Chitrlada Palace and which has served to maintain the distance of the throne and the power of the nobility and court from the whole world elsewhere. But the King was needed, immediately, to advise, to broadcast, possibly to go into the threatened area to demonstrate the commitment of the country at its highest level. When the King discerned that Marshal Sid's inhibition in discussing the emergency was his own lack of facility in the royal dialect, he immediately and disarmingly switched to demotic Thai. In effect, His Majesty was saying, a joke's a joke: but this is *survival*! A monarch adaptive enough to see that not only his throne was at stake but the Kingdom as well, and to adjust accordingly, speaks volumes. Those not familiar with the intensity of royal pre-eminence in the Kingdom will have difficulty discerning the analytical importance of this episode. Consider: the Thai people even have difficulty *articulating the name* of the king; generally, they point up high to the sky to denote the eminence of their reference. And in the royal presence people – *distinguished* people – routinely fall to the ground.

But the value this monarch has added to Thai development during his reign makes too long a story for us here. For all intents and purposes – with a minor exception – he has not left the Kingdom for a generation, tending to problems where he has judged that he can best make his mark, and allowing the pattern of these interventions to evolve into a distinctive role. More than anything he has adressed the economic problems of the poor Thai: when the governing élite was at its worst, seemingly looking only to the interests of their own rich fellows, it became obvious that the palace was the last resort of the worst-off. Forest people in 1997, for example, losing their access to land, appealed to the throne and gained dispensation. The King uses his influence carefully, but the simple fact is that no longer would any Thai dare even to contemplate going directly against the wishes of their monarch: opposition to the order of things, of which the King is lynchpin, comes through the most circumnavigated routes. His influence has even included foreign policy, official and unofficial – he was, alas, the primary instrument through which Burmese admission to the Association of Southeast Asian Nations (ASEAN) was accomplished.[99] Western eminences like David Rockefeller routinely have audiences with him during their visits to Thailand, and the consequence is that the foundations they influence set up academic programmes, medical chairs and whole schools in the Kingdom. It is not too much to say that his influence has been magical – except that, in fact, it can be explained in anthropological and psychological terms.[100] To say that other countries cannot emulate or copy Thailand, having no royal line, is to miss the point. They can have leaders of stature who know when and how to assert, guide and reprimand. The late Karamanlis in Greece, or de Gaulle in France, are good examples. The fact that this king's grandfather, the great Chulalongkorn, ended public obeisance, only for it to be reasserted by popular consent today, shows how far he has come in resurrecting Chakri authority, however fleeting the bright star may be.[101] In 1973, just as King Bhumibol was coming into his prime, and when with the help of the Sarit group he had built a solid political base, quite literally, throughout the Kingdom, he performed his first great transformative act, putting the polity on a path toward political modernity. The trio that succeeded Sarit – Marshals Thanom and Prapat, and Narong (Thanom's son, Prapat's son-in-law) – were out of line with the aspirations of the growing middle class; their own educational investments had created too large a generation of graduates for the economy to absorb smoothly, providing masses with time on their hands for demonstrations. The military could have put down the mass demonstrations only with great bloodshed, and the King ultimately intervened, exiling the three, appointing a respected university professor as Prime Minister, and waiting for the air to clear so that elections could be prepared. The trio had laid the basis for the economic miracle but they failed to see the need for commensurate political reform, which the King, although deeply conservative, grasped sooner than they – and barely in time.

Similarly, in 1992, the assertive General Suchinda, who had seized power the year before, appointed himself Prime Minister against constitutional provisions, bringing hundreds of thousands of protesters onto the streets. This was no Tienanmen incident – indeed one of the highest of Thai opinion makers has insisted to one of the authors that there was no bloodshed, which is not true[102] – but the left played it for all it was worth. General Suchinda, in fact, was one of the brightest of the military leaders. Smart analysts have identified him as the only Thai leader who had the foresight, insight, intelligence, and seriousness of purpose to have been even remotely likely to take the steps necessary to prevent the meltdown that occurred five years later.

But on with our story. When Suchinda and the demonstrating masses were at equilibrium, the King – after letting all parties turn slowly, slowly, in the mud, for just long enough – sent for him, along with General Chamlong, a Buddhist reformer and hero of the streets. No observer anywhere in the world could have been unmoved by the television image of two headstrong men of power – power of the gun and power of the demonstrating masses – abject on the floor at Chitrlada Palace, competing to take the royal medicine administered by a mild, ascetic and gentle man. It is important to recall that Suchinda's generation of army officers had grown up seeing commanding generals treat the monarchs – including, up to 1957, the present monarch – as playthings. Bhumibol had earned his respect.[103]

So we have the usual position, that the King who tries to enjoy his kingship loses it,[104] while the ascetic one who works for it and knows its limits enlarges it. And we also have the reverse position, that the bully leader who tries to be a king lives in fear, gaining all the disadvantages of a throne – and none of the advantages. Thus, in Africa, leadership has largely reverted to the traditional king-by-divine-right. In Zimbabwe, racked by compounding economic disaster and a 25 per cent AIDS rate, all 53 ministers received a new Mercedes each and the President demanded a larger jet for his foreign journeys, of which he made forty in 1996–8.[105] At least he would not then have to commandeer – and displace passengers from – the national airline. But the equivalent of almost half a billion dollars that the government had its central bank print only meant yet worse inflation. What could be done about it? Reginald Matchaba-Hove, perhaps the country's most distinguished human rights advocate, puts it with characteristically brave bluntness: 'The President? He's like a king.' Nkrumah lost little time in ensuring that the deference paid him was higher than to the Asantahene, and though foreigners were embarrassed that he was everywhere addressed as *Osagyefo*, 'Saviour', with a straight face, Africans understood.

As Gnassibe Eyadema, President of Togo since 1966 and one of the worst blights ever to be cast upon Africa, said after stealing another so-called election, 'I am like the sea. I shall always be around.'

CHAPTER 4

Statecraft

No one makes it on her own. The choice and use of allies, partners and friends from outside is a key variable in the success or failure of a state, and profoundly affects the pace at which a state waxes and wanes. Partners can give you a helping hand or they can give you a quick kick to the abdomen. And when you're small and your partners are big, you obviously prefer the former.

Thailand made a virtue of necessity and learned how to balance its needs with important international friendships. Ghana decided that it wanted to take on the world headfirst and had the hubris to think that everyone was going to pay attention. It just ran into a brick wall. Parallels can be drawn on a larger scale. All of the Asian tigers helped each other, at the very least. Few countries of sub-Saharan Africa, Mandela's South Africa being an obvious exception and francophone states being partial exceptions, can really claim to have figured out how to work (and work with) the rest of the world.

Foreign policy for the most part has been an issue of leadership. After all, usually it has been the province of ruling élites; only recently – through the filter of 'public diplomacy', mostly in the industrial West – has it become a function of mass politics as well. Not surprisingly Thailand, with its fairly effective and accountable leadership, has done a far, far better job than disordered Ghana. Although Thailand made mistakes, especially in tying itself too closely to its American ally in economic matters recently, overall it got the benefit of tacking with one great partner. Loyalty and good policy paid off.

Ghana: Going Nowhere Between East and West

Ghana got the worst of all worlds during the Cold War era: tactically it played to the West in its early years, while laying the groundwork for a great tilt to the East in the early 1960s. The West thus came to distrust Ghana while Communist states had difficulty taking it seriously.[106] It continued to pay a price for the inability of its Eastern partners to deliver on their promises well into the 1980s, especially in the realm of industrial projects that either never reached fruition or never became efficient. Worse, to this day it suffers from the continued despairing fascination of so many of its educated élite with universally discredited policies fashionable a generation ago.[107] The break-up of the Soviet Union, let alone the collapse of the Ghanaian economy, seem never to have got in the way of the notionally Marxist dreams and fantasies of a key echelon of the Ghanaian élite.

There was substantial fascination with the experience of the Soviet Union in the Africa of the 1960s and it's not that hard to see why. Lenin had expressed his support for colonized people as early as 1917 and in Ghana even conservative politicians like Kofi Busia, Nkrumah's long-time opponent, sometimes admitted admiration for the Soviet experience.[108] Khrushchev's shoe-banging rant struck a chord with the somewhat resentful leaders of the newly decolonized states; even in the United States, it was still commonly thought that the Soviet Union had developed a system that would inevitably lead to greater economic productivity. No one knew how few clothes the emperor really had on and how unstable the Soviet system was, and people ignored the internal Tsarist colonization that had gone on within the USSR over the past century.[109] Only a generation after world depression and fascism, to the starry eyes of African leaders Russia looked as good a model of development as the capitalist West.

But even if attraction to the ideals of the East can seem slightly justified, there's no justification for Ghana's pre-Copernican vision of its place in the world. The sun doesn't move around the earth and the world didn't revolve around Ghana. A country must have a strategy proportional to the size and competence of the society. The underlying theoretical point of an early case study of African – indeed Ghanaian – statecraft was that not even the greatest of statesmen could much transcend the power, size and scope of the state.[110] Kwame Nkrumah tried to unite Africa, to reconcile China with both Russia and India, and to settle the Vietnam War – but his base was the inverse of his ego, and his international dreams died a bitter death.

The International Setting

Timing lies at the heart of politics. I do not go to church because the bell tells me to, said Gladstone, I go because it tells me that it is time. It was self-evident throughout Africa in the 1960s and 1970s, and indeed well into the 1980s, that the important winds were blowing from the East.[111] To be sure, African dictators usually had coteries of Westerners assuring them it was so: Geoffrey Bing, the Nunn-Mays, the brilliant Oxford don and Marxist Tom Hodgkin – all were in Nkrumah's court. But it was the leaders themselves who made the decisions and the judgements. Nkrumah was bedazzled by American power, as once he had been by imperial show in Britain, but he believed in the Red East and its destiny. He cast his lot with Moscow, more as an act of faith than as an operationally pertinent choice. The Ghanaian élite, while still sending its children to Britain and America, did not resist that intellectually fatuous judgement.

True, there were good reasons for this: the West had been the colonialists and the West was still unpleasantly close to apartheid-ruled South Africa, the scourge of the Organization of African Unity. But shrewd African leaders like Houphouet-Boigny saw through that one: Moscow's aid to the liberation of Southern Africa was largely rhetorical. The West was the party with leverage and hence the one through which solutions would come – and where the truly relevant anti-apartheid action commenced.[112] But Houphouet, and others like him, could not generalize their astute diplomatic hands and had to play them covertly.

Even if he didn't have a strategy, Nkrumah had a goal: he wanted to milk the West, toast the East and unite Africa under his command. It was, in the circumstances of the early years, at least rational to develop ties with the East, if nothing else to establish a marker among the competing superpowers. Nkrumah also saw that the financing for his initial dream of industrializing Ghana through the Volta River Project, a huge dam, could only come from the West. His pan-African strategy hinged on combining radical Guinea and Mali, as a nucleus of crystallization for all in a 'union government' – the leadership of which, he assumed, was nowhere in question. In fact, not even these first states had included deference to Ghana among their priorities.

The new state of Ghana inherited most of its early choices and at the beginning had to side with the United States in the Cold War. The British, however eager to leave, were there, and were as always playing to their senior American partner's wish for privileged access. There was even tactical guile: A. L. Adu, the head of the civil service at independence, argued that the new state was too fragile to withstand the Cold War competition between the American and Soviet embassies in Accra – especially the presence of intelligence *apparats*; Nkrumah went along with him. But the Americans had to be there.[113] Since even Nkrumah's advisers universally assured him that his ambitious development plans could only be realized with Western funds, he gave no hint of his intent, which was manifest, however, in his earlier writings.[114]

What followed was an exercise in disingenuousness with all its penalties – but few of its possible gains. Between 1959 and 1961 Nkrumah revealed his hand, until in Moscow in 1961 he had all but allied with the Marxists he so admired. Ironically, just as Trotsky had said that 'socialism in one country' was impossible – it could survive only in a world of socialism – Nkrumah believed that the grip of 'imperialism' had to be broken everywhere, and that all Africa had to develop itself on socialist principles on the Ghana model. For Ghana's neighbours, its principal trading partners, and the dominant powers in Africa, were overwhelmingly still the West and its friends. He was now on a collision course with his former partners and chief development funders. Soviets, Poles, Czechs, and their socialist rivals, the Chinese, were now rushing in to establish turnkey projects that would enable Nkrumah to make Ghana the first Soviet African state with everything from collective farms to heavy-handedly socialized state industries.

The records of the committee he established – CECEC, the Committee for Economic Cooperation with Eastern Countries – are sad and fascinating. CECEC was feared and powerful: but not powerful enough. And *faute de mieux*, it was staffed largely by Western-trained Ghanaian bureaucrats, some of whom took pleasure in CECEC's ongoing failure.

Thus the Ghanaian embassy in Tirana reported, against instructions to seek out areas for cooperation, that

> Unfortunately the quality of this country's products and the level of its university education are so low that [the]Ambassador found it impossible to advise our Government to send Ghanaian students.... In short ... Ghana is far ahead in all spheres of Development, and the Albanians rather have much to learn in our country....[115]

Western-oriented Ghanaians only had to wait for the dramatic openings to the East to collapse under their own ill-distributed weight. But the opportunity cost was great. Just about everything that could go wrong did so. Only a tiny smattering remains today of the gigantic inputs the socialist countries mounted to bring Ghana Eastward in the 1960s. But if most of their embassies and shops were closed when Nkrumah was overthrown in 1966, the Eastern bloc left behind a substantial Ghanaian élite sufficiently convinced that they were on the right track to delay any early effort to reconcile Ghana's real strengths with the self-important state. The intelligentsia, in what was perhaps their one true success, set out to sabotage the investment plans of Western firms. Not to put too fine a point on it, their curdled radicalism died hard. We might add, extending Max Planck's famous dictum, that people find it easier to die and to be replaced ideologically in the succession of generations than to change their minds.

But while Ghana's doomed flirtation with the East was to set any further attempts at foreign policy finesse back for years, there was a period of close friendship between Washington and Accra during the National Liberation Council (NLC) government's three years in office between 1966 and 1969. The men who overthrew Nkrumah were not commonplace officers. They had taken on not just a regime and its leader but a myth and its ideological buttressing.[116] They were strategists and they also knew how limited Ghana's options really were, which was unflattering to the average Ghanaian and even more so to the intellectual élite, who had forgotten everything and learned nothing. Thus the NLC quickly got rid of most Communist apparatchiks, took Western advice in the most sensitive areas, and in return gave Western intelligence agencies access to all the records of Eastern undertakings in the old regime.[117]

But after the NLC there never really was a coherent and strategic foreign policy. The country was on the road to economic ruin and nothing from outside could save it if it would not save itself. Accra, which had once been the 'diplomatic cockpit of Africa', was now just part of the Ouagadougou–Mogadishu axis of punishment postings for big-power diplomats who had put a foot wrong, or vanity postings for big contributors who needed a title to keep their cheque books open. Increasingly, Christopher Clapham's words became applicable to deteriorated Accra:[118] 'to travel from Washington to Ouagadougou, was to be confronted with a level of inequality that verged on the surreal'.[119] Until the election as Secretary General of the United Nations of Kofi Annan – who had made his name wholly outside Ghana – no one paid the slightest attention to Ghana anywhere outside its immediate neighbourhood. In the 32 years between Nkrumah's overthrow and Clinton's visit to Accra in 1998, the only time Ghana made the front pages was when Rawlings, upon first seizing power, lined up his three living predecessors before a firing squad.

Ghana had enjoyed real choices. An interesting counterfactual scenario for Ghana comes from Singapore, whose leader – as the smartest politician in the Malaysian federation – had expected a larger stage for his great talents than the city state of two million people could possibly afford him. Singapore's expulsion from Malaysia, Lee Kuan Yew's greatest life-trauma, entailed a completely different game. The only option was to make it the best-run, most efficient, fastest-growing economy in the region – a model, in fact, of what Nkrumah might have done for Ghana in seeking a broader stage. By the 1990s Singapore had a higher standard of living than the United States – indeed than *every country in the world*, save Luxembourg! – and an audience everywhere. Through self-discipline, the stability that attracted enormous foreign direct investment, and consistency in its foreign policy, it had become a state to which others paid attention. Its foreign reserves almost equalled those of all black Africa. Even as the retired 'senior minister' of the island republic, Lee was frequently referred to as the most successful leader of the past generation – certainly as the smartest.[120] One can be sure that Lee will not be over-thrown by an internal coup when he is off trying to solve some world crisis, as Nkrumah was on his voyage to Vietnam.

The degree to which Nkrumah was rebuffed from all directions, in contrast, for the obstinacy and sheer fatuity of his policy is indicated by the very nature of the Organization of African Unity, founded in 1963. Clapham comments that its charter, in direct reaction to Nkrumah's call for a 'union government', something in 'the realm of fantasy', was in consequence 'one of the purest statements of the elements of juridical statehood to be embodied in any international organization, stopping a very long way short even of the concessions to supranationality made in the Charter of the United Nations'.[121] At the second annual OAU Heads of State meeting in Cairo in July 1964, the most respected of Africa's leaders, Julius Nyerere, responded to Nkrumah's attack on the attempts to build an East African Federation – as falling selfishly short of total continental union – with sheer mockery and humiliating unseriousness:

> To cap this whole series of absurdities, after all the wonderful arguments against unity in East Africa, we are now told again, at this very rostrum, that those who are ready [for continental union, presumably under Nkrumah] should now go ahead and unite. Now we have the permission to go ahead …. If I were a cynic, I would say we of the United Republic of Tanganyika and Zanzibar are ready. I would ask Ghana to join our United Republic. But I am not a cynic.[122]

The Devil Outside

As Nkrumah's plan failed and the idea of unity imploded, he compounded his mistake by making a scapegoat of the West and burning the bridge he was standing on. This wasn't a new tactic: ideological crusaders often avoid their failures by blaming their problems on the perfidious large international forces of capitalism or communism. According to several economists it took Zambia a decade to realize that its increasingly desperate problems were remediable and not merely the work of outside conspirators. Get into the mind of Nkrumah by 1962, after the nearly successful assassination attempt made on him at Kulungugu, in northern Ghana. The forces of imperialism were 'out to get him' and any time he needed reassurance thereof he could call in Ambassador Rodionov from the Soviet Union (although even he had second thoughts toward the end) or his well-paid claque in the press and at the Kwame Nkrumah Ideological

Institute at Winneba. Then he could hear what he wanted to hear. After the coup that overthrew him, and riotous celebration in Ghana, Nkrumah tenderly cited a letter from the destructive President of Guinea, Sékou Touré:

> It is true, as you say, that this incident in Ghana is a plot by the imperialists, neo-colonialists and their agents in Africa. As these imperialist forces grow more militant and insidious, using traitors to the African cause against the freedom and independence of our people, we must strengthen our resolution and fight for the dignity of our people to the last man, and for the unity of Africa.[123]

When Sékou Touré died in 1982, people celebrated in the streets of Guinea's capital, Conakry,[124] and they weren't put there by the United States.

The crusader's mind is resistant to all useful information that is operationally pertinent, because his crusade transcends all other concerns. That a country should burn with him would seem only just to a crusader: 'the worse the better', in the Marxists' most apt phrase for the disasters that befell the twentieth century.

Region

There is a psychology to the way a region's politics reinforce or under-cut virtuous trends in rising polities. Books began appearing on the 'little tigers' – Taiwan, Singapore, Hong Kong and Korea – just as the biggest tiger of them all began to make its weight felt on the world scene: Beijing's possible emergence as the world's largest economy in the early third millennium focused many minds. It is worth noting, as some have argued, that the Southeast Asian tigers, in fact, had been the beneficiaries of the 'extraordinary forty-year sequestration from the global market of the greatest power in Asia'.[125] And as soon as these perceptions had spread, the world began to notice the rest of the region: Thailand was booming as no other; Indonesia was moving ahead, with its giant population, at 7 per cent growth a year; Fidel Ramos was beginning to work miracles in the Philippines. Vietnam, although a long, long way from wealth, was churning up some of the most remarkable growth statistics of any country in a long time. Wealth attracts wealth, which is why most OECD investment until the

1990s stayed within the OECD. There are simply no inducements big enough to bring large capital to countries that seem to wallow in poverty. Anyway, the diseconomies of scale usually forbid it: how could a major investor justify the opportunity cost of moving plant, engineers or even money to poor countries, however great the return on capital? Money flowed to Vietnam, for example, because it has a large demographic base, is in a fast-growing region, had the will to grow and has benefited from strategic factors. In Africa, until late in the 1990s, the only countries that had done reasonably well were north of the Sahara and in Southern Africa, too far away for there to be meaningful interaction with most of sub-Saharan Africa – and for there then to be productive competition. And no African country would have wanted to have anything to do with apartheid-controlled South Africa.

But consider what would have happened if Mobutu had set his sights upon the general betterment of his country, instead of subjecting it to ruin and plunder as his own private fiefdom. Had Zaïre, at the continent's strategic centre, with its nine contiguous neighbours, got rich, 'productive jealousy' might have inspired other countries to follow its example. Other African leaders would have tried to learn from him and eventually stories would have spread about how much healthier peasants in Northwest Zaire were than peasants in Southeast Ghana. In the latter country there would have been more debates about the direction that the government was going in. There might even have been demand for change. But, as history happened, no Africans wanted to be like Zaïre and they presumably don't wish to be like its successor, the (not particularly) Democratic Republic of Congo.

It's not as though there never has been useful competition and coalition building in Africa. Ghana and Ivory Coast share a border, many of the same resources and a historic competition that reached a remarkable climax when Nkrumah and his opposite number, Félix Houphouet-Boigny, made a bet over which country would develop faster over the next ten years. The degree of Houphouet's conservatism is well gauged by his remarkable article in *Foreign Affairs*, which came out just after Ghana's independence. His country, he said, preferred 'partnership' with France, despite the temptation of independence. For, he went on, 'the exercise of this power in a fashion consonant with national and human dignity is difficult ... we have won a place in the history of France and of the free world. We do not want to abandon this recent heritage by trying to go back to our origins.' There could have been no more antithetical sentiments than those driving Nkrumah and the African radicals. Of course Houphouet's capitalism won hands down in the 1960s and 1970s. Ivory Coast was the first developing country to borrow in the Eurodollar market and by the 1970s it was one of four African countries in the thousand-dollar-*per-capita* category. But the bizarre decisions that Houphouet made in his final years reversed his country's course so decisively that Ghana overtook it in the 1990s. Both countries, meantime, have also served as smuggling grounds for each other's goods, the direction depending on the net advantages prevailing and the corruption levels of the respective countries' marketing boards.

The Southeast Asian Advantage

By the 1990s Southeast Asia was officially a winner and everything it did seemed to turn to gold, all the way to the 1996 Asian–European summit, when every single EU head of government or state paid homage in Bangkok to the Asian miracle. It was just enough and just in time. Come the crash, Southeast Asia had already assumed enough importance in the world of finance – and in the minds of people everywhere – for the world to give due attention to its reparation. Never before had the leaders of the IMF flown secretly to middle-sized capitals to lay out the scale of impending doom: too late, but it showed how they would focus on getting these some-time winners back on track.

There are two reasons for the import of the regional factor. The first is that strong neighbours make for a strong country. A strong neighbour can transfer technology, trade is easy and, as long as there isn't a threat of war, the poor nation should continue to benefit from the rich. (This may not be the case historically in the example of the United States and Mexico, perhaps because the two countries share a common border and start from such disparate histories, although with the creation of NAFTA it is becoming so.) The classic example of this comes from East Asia where, without a doubt, one of the forces that pushed the rest of the region forward was the strength of Japan's economy – and until the 1980s Japan was for all intents and purposes denied access to her most logical trading partner, China. Her involvement in Southeast Asia became all the more necessary and salient. Thus while her investment in Thailand was of the order of $50 million annually in the early 1980s, it rose to over a billion dollars at its peak in 1990.

The second reason is the phenomenon that is sometimes called 'keeping up with the Joneses'. As Mark Twain said, 'no man can stand wealth, another man's that is'. The same is true of nations. Having rich neighbours makes a nation want to be rich itself. Thailand saw no reason it couldn't do what Malaysia, Singapore, Taiwan and, more distantly (but in some respects more relevantly), Japan were doing. It was shame at having fallen so far behind that gave the Philippines in the 1990s the motivation to revamp its economy and make the sacrifices and changes necessary for rapid economic growth. As Rafael Buenaventura, the well-known president of a major Philippine bank, told us in 1996, 'We were ashamed. It was a choice between being big fish in diminishing ponds or accepting a smaller – but richer – place in an expanding ocean.'[126]

The case of Thailand offers a different set of lessons from Ghana's. The Kingdom nominally allied itself with Japan in the Second World War but even at that point there were far-sighted diplomats and soldiers who saw the likely foolishness of that.[127] MR Seni Pramoj, then a diplomat in Washington and later Prime Minister, simply and brilliantly refused to deliver his government's declaration of war on the United States.[128] He then quietly helped the development of Seri Thai, the Free Thai movement, which included some of the Kingdom's greatest post-war strategic leaders – among them the sometime foreign minister Air Chief Marshal Siddhi Savetsila, who parachuted into Thailand with the OSS. That helped in the post-war settlements, but not enough. What led Washington to revalue Bangkok was its own strategic sense of the growing danger from China and communism worldwide. Therefore it prevented both Britain and France from exacting the degree of tribute they sought for Thailand's nibbling away at their colonial frontiers under Japanese protection. To this day the Thai express gratitude – a very important Thai value – for America's help. The memory remains constant and vivid.

At all points in the years following that great war Bangkok saw to it that it was ably represented in Washington and New York. When Thailand had its turn on the UN Security Council, its permanent representative, ML Birabongse Kasemsri, discharged his duties famously, becoming one of the foremost experts on the law of the sea and handling the question of Khmer representation brilliantly and successfully.[129] Not only that: he circulated within the commanding heights of New York society for reasons other than social prestige, bringing great benefits back to his country.[130] Even when it looked as if the United States would cut and run from Southeast Asia after its débâcle in Vietnam, the Thai had plans ready to provide for a shift of resources that would replace the income American troops and military subventions had provided. One of the brightest Thai economists of the present period, Bunyaraks Ninsananda, wrote a thesis in America on this precise contingency five years before it came to pass. Then, when the worst happened, the royal Thai government had alternatives prepared.

An astonishing contrast appears if we compare alliance building and regional diplomacy in Southeast Asia with the African experience. As early as 1963, the then Thai foreign minister Thanat Khoman was already conscious of the need to hedge Thai bets – *yiep rua song khaem* (to have a foot on either side of a boat to prevent capsizing) – for the long term, however loyally Thailand would side with the United States. Only the previous year Thanat had invigorated the American commitment to the Kingdom by gaining an understanding – the so-called Rusk–Thanat agreement – by which the US could move to protect Thailand under the umbrella of the Southeast Asian Treaty Organization (SEATO) with or without the agreement of the other signatories. But Thanat had a correct sixth sense of the tide of diplomacy. He was already busy looking to regional arrangements with like-minded neighbours who could strengthen the Thai hand in the struggle for mastery of Southeast Asia.

As it happened, his first efforts were premature; the 'Association for Southeast Asia' drowned in the seas of Indonesian *konfrontasi* with the newly enlarged Malaysia and Marcos's fatuous efforts in the Philippines to wrest Sabah from Malaysia. But by 1967 not only were those issues substantially reduced in magnitude, but the risk of the war in Indochina to Thailand had risen. The US was demanding more and more access to Thai turf, and higher levels of direct participation in the war. Thanat upped the ante. With the cooperation of the Malaysian and Indonesian foreign ministers and Carlos P. Romulo, foreign minister of the Philippines, he pulled off ASEAN: in 1967 surely the most successful regional association in the annals of Third World politics commenced, and its Thai sponsorship was never questioned. True, the Thai did not ask for or get the credit they deserved, not wishing, after all, to appear to undercut their American allies. For over thirty years ASEAN has gone from strength to strength, now incorporating all of the region, moving into the economic realm, and providing an arena – in the post-ministerial meetings – in which the US Secretary of State and other such worthies can hold consultations.

All this while, Nkrumah was attempting to build a nonsensical (from the point of view of available infrastructure and commitment elsewhere) 'union government' for the continent – and sabotaging such regional organizations as had a chance of obtaining results. [131]

Ironically, Ghana should have enjoyed diplomatic success, given the achievements of a highly trained corps chosen from the top of the civil service. That one of the first batch of eight, Alex Quaison-Sackey, became President of the UN General Assembly in 1965, and that one of the second batch of top civil servants became the first black African Secretary General of the United Nations, says it clearly.

But a foreign service can do little in the service of bad policy. All but one of the early group, although loyal to the political leadership, had grave misgivings as to whether Nkrumah's turn to the East would yield anything worthwhile. Thereafter they could only have a diplomacy of triage. Ten years later it was even worse: Ghana had descended into the worst part of the African politics of the belly where, as Bayart puts it, 'In the world of sinecures, foreign links are crucial, because they are the major conduits for the circulation of wealth.'[132]

But the Clinton visit to Accra in 1998 shows a modest overlap with Thailand with respect to the almost absolute principle of unequal foreign partnerships: tenacity bringing results. Once Rawlings had determined the necessity of accepting the IMF's structural adjustment programme he stuck to it – except during election run-ups when he had tacitly to bribe the population to make sure he ended up back in office. As we have seen elsewhere, he understood the necessity of building new support structures for the programme, including even permitting multi-party elections. Soon, indeed, he could be offered up as a model for other failed states. There were fifteen years of excruciating belt-tightening but they came after a generation of national self-indulgence. In any event, the alternative to that pain was the far greater pain of total economic collapse, perhaps the status of failed state. That Rawlings's policies bore some fruit, starting in 1998, was witness to strategy and reward.

Ironically, there were all the ingredients for deep resentment of the United States in Thailand. In 1966 the US got Thailand to make it an exception across the board to FDI restrictions; from that date only the US could operate, wholly own, and repatriate profits from business in the Kingdom. This was not unlike the 'parity amendment' imposed on the Philippines prior to its independence that occasioned more grief in the affairs of those two partners than any other issue. The Thai saw the concession rather as an opportunity, one which, after all, the Americans had not extended elsewhere. The Japanese simply burrowed behind it and before long had far more significant investments in Thailand in any case. The Americans had the privilege but either didn't care or were smart enough not to exploit it excessively.

Trust In America

The degree to which the Thai trusted their American allies is seen in the Narong affair of 1992, when a prominent northern Thai politician came forward for the premiership with the largest block of seats in the newly elected parliament. Had he been sworn in, General Suchinda, the Supreme Commander, would not have put himself forward, and would never have been put forward by the winning electoral coalition. The great tragedy of the Pramane confrontation, one of the two largest political demonstrations in Thai history, in which the army killed over fifty people in May 1992, would never have occurred, and a canny political leader with a large electoral base would have assumed office. But the Americans introduced an obstacle to Narong's elevation, claiming he had been involved in narcotics. No proof with any legal standing was provided, neither then nor in the commission of inquiry held later. Several Americans who systematically examined the case – including one of the present authors – also failed to find any such evidence. The American motive, by all indications, was irresistibly personal and bureaucratic: ties between its Central Intelligence

Agency station and opposition politicians, combined with the post-Cold War necessity for the organization to show its continuing utility. Yet the American charge was enough to cause the Thai to turn Narong down. At its simplest the Thai were still honouring their benefactor of 1946, the source of much of their aid, thus showing their finest cultural trait – a sense of gratitude that simply cannot be betrayed. Although by the mid-1980s the Japanese had become the larger economic partner of Thailand, in Bangkok the American connection was treated with care and respect. It was thus that Prime Minister Chuan Leekpai could make his celebrated pilgrimage to Washington in early 1998 and return with a billion-dollar list of benefits.

The most serious exponent of Filipino statecraft in the post-war years, Alejandro Melchor, once made the point that Third World states always overestimated the interest great powers took in their affairs; he was highly aware of the inherent patronization prompted by great differences in size.[133] The Thai never made this mistake; the Ghanaians almost always did. In the beginning, Nkrumah seemed to believe not only that the world was mightily concerned about him but that he could solve all of its problems. He could bring peace to the troubled regions of the world; unite Africa under his rule; inspire agricultural development on his country's barren fields. Ultimately, perhaps, he could unify the rest of the world.

As with many of the other issues we have analyzed, Ghana and Thailand represent ideal types. Thailand has been the country that has best been able to get benefits from the outside world and to use its international partners to maintain domestic stability. Ghana, at least during the Nkrumah years, showed the tremendous problems that go along with international hubris.

Aid: Thailand, Ghana and Their Donors

A World Bank study emerged in 1998 that made a startling correlation between aid and economic growth. It seems that in the Third World overall there was at least some positive correlation – but in Africa it was negative. How could this be? In the first place one has to return to our earlier assumptions about the leaderships' real commitment to development – or lack thereof. Aid can be seen, indeed, as a hindrance to élite control, if (for example) it opens avenues, figuratively or literally, to competitive élites or otherwise under-represented provinces. For example at some points late in the Marcos regime more than half of the committed projects of donors were being sidelined by the Philippines government because they were intended at least secondarily to enhance the role of the disadvantaged and dis-enfranchised whom the Marcos dictatorship wished to keep in their place. Marcos's speeches on 'development' were not just specious but constituted disinformation. Thus the first point about aid is that governments in power are more than capable of discerning whether the money is intended to help or hinder their own control and governance. It has been an unusual leader indeed who has been willing to accept aid for the good of the people, when it also represe-nted a threat to his dominance.

Also, as has been shown clearly in states like Nigeria, any form of money given to irresponsible leaders can simply be used to pad their thrones or to stud the boots they use to kick their people. Mobutu rolled his aid into kickbacks for his friends and was able to build his political base thereby. A second point is that the accumulation of aid debts eventually becomes burdensome in itself. In recent years a disproportionate share of the governing élite's time, in the best intentioned Third World countries, has been spent renegotiating terms – their stretching out, forgiveness, or just rolling over until the economy generates enough income to service the interest payments. This is not a small point. The donors have the stability and integrity of their system to preserve; if the whole Paris process is an exercise in illusion ('we will pretend to pay back so that you can pretend that the banking system is intact'), it is an illusion basic to today's international politics. As we shall see, the Thai used the process to their supreme advantage after their 1997 currency catastrophe.

The third point is that aid, being a mixed bag of donors and recipients even in one country, is unlikely to lend itself to wise strategy. Usually aid has been given because the donor wishes to make a point, in the case of the major powers a strategic one: this grants the recipient considerable leverage to use and abuse. The problem was there from the start in Africa. René Dumont, in his famous *L'Afrique Noire est Mal Partie* (*False Start in Africa*), documented the absurdities of French aid to its slavish élite cadres in francophone Africa, including the subvention of greater salaries to the 'parliamentarians' of Gabon than to those of France, and to a larger parliament, though the ratio of population was more than one hundred to one.[134] In the case of Soviet system aid to Ghana, although there was something of a division of labour among the Warsaw Pact allies – the GDR gave intelligence, while the Czechs gave potentially sound industrial turnkey projects. But once Sino-Soviet competition set in, the Ghanaians could play their communist benefactors off against each other without much difficulty. Once the Cold War was over, African leverage only consisted of the last card of the debtor – to bring down, or weaken, the overall international system by failing to sustain its payment of dues.

So where there was no coherence on the part of a governing élite to begin with, there was unlikely to be strategic use of aid at any point. It is difficult to look back over the past half-century and see a refutation of the World Bank's proposition, on the evidence available from Ghana. Aid in Ghana was, it seemed, just another udder, or another point at which the goat could be tethered. But each benefactor developed its own set of dependent groups around its projects, at home as in the recipient country, and the donor became as much dependent as the beneficiary on the continuance of the relationship.

In Thailand we find something quite different, though there too, of course, the temptation of abuse was not resisted in all cases. Bangkok bureaucrats were skilled at turning aid to their own purposes. This is not to say that they were deliberately subverting aid projects and programmes (although of course they sometimes were) but rather that they were using them for high (and sometimes not so high) purposes that donors could not always see. The 'Friendship Highway' by which the Americans opened up the northeast for their own purpose of countering communist subversion, not only opened Issan to greater Thai penetration, bringing the poor northeast into deeper and deeper identification with the kingdom's larger purposes. The highway also opened up the last frontier for Thai agriculture, made feeder roads cheap and thus marketized substantial sections of this largest area of Thailand. The huge sums spent on the border patrol increased regime security but gave the American donors more confidence in the game they were playing in the Southeast Asian theatre.

Where goals were most in conflict was when American agencies, frustrated by the slow pace of Thai bureaucracy – often deliberately so for purposes of sustaining Thai, as opposed to American, goals –

attempted to build up parallel agencies, building up the careers of ambitious and amenable Thai who were blocked in the main channels. The Thai had a genius for permitting partners of their American patrons to develop a power base just long enough to benefit the country maximally in its receipt of American dollars – and then putting the Thai agent in his place. In the meantime, American beneficence was distributed in vehicles with arms joined in the logo – but the programmes, for example Accelerated Rural Development (ARD), were displayed in American initials, and thus irrelevant (because incomprehensible) to the Thai villager. But no Thai was confused as to who was winning the tug-of-war, although the American benefactors, even those seeing through the ruse, reckoned on enough American benefit to sustain the game at their end.[135]

To get the sense of the high level of strategy at which the game was played, we have the testimony of three levels of the Thai bureaucracy: the smartest of the young civil servants involved in fighting the communist insurgency in the late 1970s, the Foreign Minister/ National Security Adviser overseeing and coordinating the work of civil and military agencies as 'infected' villages were targeted for 'reconstruction', and the King himself, the trump of trump cards. 'We had large maps on the walls showing each village in Issan,' the brilliant bureaucrat said. 'We worked hand-in-glove with the military. We shared their tents, their rations; we rushed in irrigation, schools, whatever was needed to bring the village back into the system.'

Thailand was willing to do anything to win; it needed the trust of its American partners.[136] And win the Kingdom did. At the end of the Vietnam War, her eastern neighbours were in ruins and the United States was chafing internally. The Kingdom was truly the only nation to emerge from the imbroglio a winner.

PART II

CHAPTER 5

Development

If the whole world were to develop like Thailand, all the land would be paved and birds would be choking and falling out of the sky. If the whole world were to develop like Ghana, most of us would be starving. To imagine what would happen if the whole world were to develop like the United States, think of one thousand blindfolded drivers barrelling toward a six-way intersection.

With the end of the Cold War, development has become the be-all and end-all of analysts of the Third World from Ouagadougou to Washington[137] but no one can agree on what the word means. If you ask a dozen economists, you will get more than the customary two dozen answers. If you ask most First World politicians, or even most of the people living in rich countries, they will tell you facilely that everyone in the world wants, or should want, to be just like them. As James Fallows has written, 'Americans in particular, tend to view the world as one vast potential expansion of their own culture, containing billions and billions of people who would be Americans if only they could.'[138] If you had asked someone 800 years ago what development was, they may well have talked about wealth; they also would have been more likely to describe a country with opulent churches, temples or mosques. They probably wouldn't have described a land where everyone could get three meals a day or where World Bank officials could ride in their limos from the airport to their hotels without having to worry about potholes.

> Taylor: The people in the Third World don't want anything to do with development.

Tara: They like burying their children?

Taylor: No. But they don't want to live unimaginative lives in some hypothetical developed society beyond their reach. Development is unattainable and undesirable.

Tara: That's what the patronizing rich always say. But every society that has ever been given the choice between trying to develop and modernize versus staying in the Stone Age has chosen the former. Life in a state of nature is nasty, brutish and short.

Taylor: But it's not a fair choice. People with more power always get to stick their arguments down the throats of those with less power. Societies that choose not to develop are plundered. If corporations and fat cats want development, you can be sure that the people are going to get it, good and hard.

Tara: That can't be true. Look at all the 'people power' and student rebellions of the last generation. In each case, it was people protesting for a wider distribution of the goods of democracy and more development. People want to be like the West. Are you saying that corporations foment revolutions by radicals? Are you claiming that the protesters in Tienanmen Square weren't asking for democracy, they were asking for Wal-Mart?

Taylor: Wal-Mart is something that comes along with development and with freedom. People may not want it specifically, but they are willing to take it if it comes along with a society where they are finally giving the freedom to vote – along with the freedom to live a life where every second isn't a struggle searching for crumbs.

Unfortunately, to the extent that the world agrees on 'development', people support the notion that wealth is good and that, with various caveats, money is the soil of the Garden of Eden. Environmental well-being may be a priority, but it's a secondary priority and must come along with wealth, which in practice means after it. The same is true of equitable income distribution and the development of civil society. If you don't have enough food, you won't care if you have the opportunity to vote. Right? If you're poor, you can't afford to protect your forests. Right? Got to get the money, pump up the GDP and run. Right?

Well, no. First of all, it's not as if one day dump trucks full of money arrive in the middle of the night, spill their loot around the countryside and, in the morning, people wake up, look out of their windows and see that, oh neat, development has arrived. This is what Kwame Nkrumah thought and he tried to will development from the top down. Thailand realized that everything has to move slowly from the bottom up and that institutions have to grow as the country slowly moves forward. Think of runners getting ready for a marathon. The one who starts to sprint at the start will pull a hamstring; the one who figures out that she needs to stretch, drink water, study the course and pace herself, is much more likely to do well.

In this chapter we'll lay out our plan for how a country can develop. We don't have a schedule that a political leader can follow – 'develop your country in just 15 minutes a day' – but we do have three steps in a general path. First, countries should try to fulfil basic needs – for both moral and economic reasons. Second, to a considerable extent, countries should keep their essential structures, their identity and the things that make them unique. Third, countries should focus on the freedom of their populations, with freedom based on the notion of people being able to lead the lives that they choose without being restrained by lack of income, health or opportunity. To bring these goals about, the focus of development studies should be moved away from GDP. Money is not the soil of the Garden of Eden and development based on standard models is generally nothing more than a Bacchanalia.

Basic Needs

To move toward development, first fulfil basic needs. People need food to eat, a judicial system that offers them basic protection, and health care to prevent the worst diseases. At the same time, women need to be permitted and able to play a strong role in society. Income needs to be distributed in as fair a way as possible without crippling the rest of economic and political society.

The most important basic need is food; if there isn't any, people can't eat, society can't function and there isn't going to be development to any extent, no matter how many dams the World Bank commissions. No one needs chicken *cordon bleu*, but everyone should have three meals a day and two to three thousand calories. To be sufficiently fed may be a human right (just ask a couple of billion people) but it is more likely to get turned into general policy when recognized as a fundamental economic principle. The conventional economic wisdom asserts that people are hungry because their countries are poor; but it is probably just as correct to say that countries are poor because people are hungry. Food is energy; energy is work. Without food, all we can do is sit on roadsides, looking for shadows and anything to keep the oppressive heat from beating the last bits of vigour out of our bodies.

There is an added multiplier that comes along with an increase in nutrition. Healthy adults are apt to give birth to healthy, unstunted children who are likely to be able to work more productively as adults. While the phenomenon is not well understood epistemologically, it is known that the first few years of life have a profound effect on one's whole future health history: a fact which takes on added significance in a country like Ghana with a bustling and booming population of young people. But this is a heartbreakingly long perspective. Not until 1972, two centuries into the industrial revolution, did a single country experience equality in the growth capacity of children of different social classes.[139] For over a century, each new academic class at Yale averaged out physically larger than its predecessor.

Adequate nutrition also impacts on education. Students who are not well nourished are not able to pay attention in class, do their homework or excel in aptitude tests.[140] In Ghana, young children can be found all over the country, sitting still and apparently doing nothing. But they are doing something very important: conserving energy so that they can continue to live and, God willing, at some point, be able to live actively and healthily. In Ghana it is estimated that, in 1990–1, 39 per cent of all children suffered stunting between the ages of two and five because of inadequate nutrition. In Thailand the numbers were slightly better, 28 per cent. The average for sub-Saharan Africa as a whole was extraordinary and dispiriting, 44 per cent.[141] The latter figure is particularly disheartening when one considers that Africa's best-performing country by that measure was the Sudan, a nation now gripped by terrible famine that has surely reversed most, if not all, of its earlier success.

Caloric increase, however, isn't the whole kit and kaboodle. There must also be nutritional balance. In some cases, more calories can be worse. One of the nastiest things that the developed world has done for the developing world is to export and glamorize taste buds that covet worthless foods or, perhaps more appropriately, companies that peddle worthless foods through massively endowed advertising campaigns. One of the most salient examples is Coca-Cola. Coke has virtually no nutritional positives and its only bodily effect is rotting teeth (not a small problem in Ghana where toothpaste is rare and dentists are rarer). But in Ghana it is widely believed that drinking a Coke is a good way to deal with oppressive heat. In fact, Coke dehydrates the body. Its popularity is not surprising; walk down any alley in Kumasi and you are apt to see a beautiful hand holding a refreshing-looking bottle of Coke. All calories were not created equal and it is important that everyone consumes a certain level of amino acids, proteins, vitamins and other food values to optimize health and efficiency.[142]

Parallel to this increase in basic nutrition needs is a general increase in health needs. Rich countries have doctors, poor countries do not. Studies in Ghana as well as in Ivory Coast and Mauritania suggest that illness detracts about 15 per cent from potential GDP; the figure in the United States is about 1.5 per cent.[143] In Africa, this percentage is only going to get worse. It is estimated that, soon, as many as one in four African adults will be HIV positive; in Botswana and Zimbabwe that haunting figure has already been realized.[144] Moreover, the people in Africa who have AIDS are disproportionately women – in Ghana 70 per cent of the infected are women – and are apt to pass the disease on to their children.[145]

This lack of adequate health care also has dire long-term consequences from a population perspective and because, in a society where people don't expect to live very long, they don't plan for the future as well. There's a final moral point. The capacity to work is the last valuable possession of even the destitute. Failing to cover these basic needs is to strip millions of other human beings of their last true belonging.

Women's Rights

To meet basic needs women must also have their basic rights. As with health, education and nutrition, this is a double winner. A society's development hinges on women, from population to stability to community to basic health of children. But much of the work that women do in the developing world isn't even included in national income accounts and is similarly ignored by all sorts of analysis. Consider this pointed passage from Partha Dasgupta's marvellous work, *An Inquiry into Well Being and Destitution*:

> Educating an additional 1000 girls in Pakistan would have cost $40,000 in 1990. Each year of schooling in that country has been estimated to reduce the under-five mortality rate by about 10 per cent. The total fertility rate in Pakistan is a high 6.6. This translates to a savings of sixty deaths of children under the age of five. The alternative of saving sixty lives with health-care interventions would have cost something like $48,000. But this isn't all. Educated women typically have fewer children. An extra year in schooling in Pakistan reduced female fertility by 10 per cent. Thus, a $40,000 investment in educating 1000 women would avert 660 births. The alternative route of family planning expenditure for achieving the same result would have cost something like $43,000. Nor is *this* all. Increased female education has been found to lead to a reduction in maternal mortality. It has been calculated that in Pakistan an additional year of schooling for 1000 women would prevent the deaths of 4 women during childbirth. Achieving the same reduction through medical services would cost $10,000.[146]

The list could go on and on, and even if there weren't all of these extra benefits to educating women, there is a strong ethical argument that the extension of education is an important and principal good. There are abundant data showing, for example, that women do a vastly disproportionate share of the labour in sub-Saharan Africa – but that the more they have control, the more food is available,[147] and the lower the percentage spent on alcohol and cigarettes.[148] One has only to walk down the streets of Accra – let alone through the countryside – to decide who is working harder. Moreover, educating women is also the single most important means that a country has to limit population growth and the problems caused by overpopulation. There are now six billion people in the world; the number is spiralling upwards, and will continue to do so for at least another generation.

Once women start to have basic rights population growth decreases for two principal reasons. First is the opportunity cost of having children. A woman with no opportunities for meaningful employment, and not much else to do, is going to have lots of children. A woman on a fast track to business success probably isn't. Second, every family wants to have a minimum number of children who live to adulthood. It's cultural, genetic and universal. In poor countries with high infant mortality rates women need to have very large families. In America, if a family wants to have five children live to adulthood, they have five children. In a poor, developing country, if a family wants to be sure of having five children who live to adulthood, they are most likely going to have to have seven.

In 1960, Ghana had a population of 6.7 million. Today the population is about 18 million and is growing at about 3.2 per cent a year, leading to predictions that the population will be 35 million strong, or weak, by the year 2025 – and, of course, multiplication will not then come to a screeching halt.[149] This means that only seventy years after Nkrumah's jubilant declaration in Independence Square, there are going to be six times as many people living in the same land with no corresponding increase in acreage. Having six times as many mouths to feed, given Ghana's limited technological advancement, is going to be quite a struggle. Thailand, by contrast, has so successfully adjusted its population growth downward that it is already closing primary and middle schools in the provinces. A large measure of the difference in the net economic growth differential between Thailand and the Philippines can be attributed to their fertility rates. In 1970 they were both nations of approximately 40 million but 50 per cent more Filipinos have been born since then and this has diluted the gains that could be distributed through what now seems to be a perpetually overcrowded country. The economist – and former Prime Minister – Caesar Virata has argued that this is the most compelling reason why his country will not easily catch up with Thailand or Malaysia, despite their more pronounced decline in the meltdown of 1997–9.[150]

Income Equality

Beyond the moral and economic justifications for meeting people's basic needs, there's also a strong political reason: if people are left out when development comes, the country is apt to go up in flames. At the least, it faces long-run turmoil and discontent. An absence of income extremity has the great value of maintaining social cohesion under the strains and transformations that no one has learned to separate from growth.

Wealth is relative. Life seems much harder when the neighbours are getting rich and you are not – which is why rebellions and revolutions have a way of starting not among the poorest, but those on the way up who see others moving faster than themselves.[151] Part of this is a need for greater expenditure in rich countries in order simply to stay afloat socially – an American family with an income of $5,000 needs to buy a television so that the children aren't left out of school conversations. A Brazilian family with the same income has no such problems. Most of it, though, is just human nature.

Redistribution is thus a necessity in a developing country that wants to move forward because it's not possible to retain social cohesion without it. Sacrifices must be made to ensure equity along the way. It's often better for society overall for the poorest man to be given one dollar than for the richest to be given two. If everyone has a stake, everyone is going to work to bring the nation to the next level of development. If people are left out, anything that has been won is likely soon to be lost. Moreover, if people are left out, the country won't be able to move together, and, at some point, the essential structures that are such important glue politically, economically and culturally are going to be lost. This is why attention is justly being focused in Thailand on the widening gap between rich and poor.

Asia has been known for its relatively equal distribution of wealth, although Thailand has been an unfortunate exception (in Thailand the 10 per cent richest people have 37 per cent of national income. In the United States, it's 28.5 per cent and in Ghana it's a very equal 27 per cent).[152] This may partly explain why Thailand has had a relatively turbulent decade with conflicts often breaking down on class lines, while Ghana has been slightly more stable. Ghana's relatively equal distribution is surely, in a twisted sort of way, what helped to get the economy back on track in the early 1980s. When things go bad, even the ministers feel the heat and, when that happens, policy changes. In neighbouring Nigeria, the fat generals who ruled the land through the 1990s never had to worry about their next Mercedes; they stole everything and were oblivious to any economic pain.

Moreover, as we argue throughout this book, developing countries must strive for equality before the law and in terms of civil and political rights. Basic needs are not confined to food, medicine and gender equality. There are also basic needs for minimal rights and justice. People need to know that homes are not going to be sacked, that they can keep hold of the possessions they are to able to buy and that they have some recourse to a court of law. Without these protections, people do not have any sense of freedom. As many people have argued, one prime reason that Great Britain, a tiny island that looks less imposing on a map than Mali, was for so long the world's greatest power, is that it was the first modern nation with the rule of law: diamond merchants could come from Europe knowing their valuables would not be seized; the China trade could flourish because the Crown didn't seize private property except by due process. People should be allowed to live as they please; and if they aren't, there's not much hope for development.

Essential Structures

For a country to develop, it needs – beyond the basics – to hold onto what makes it what it is. As long as the world remains divided into states,[153] with decision making in the hands of two-hundred-odd governments and their provincial authorities, a subjective and relative dimension must remain in any attempt to define development. One size cannot fit all.

Every society, and the state arising from it, has 'essential structures', salient and defining characteristics which it has no intention of changing. Some of these are obvious and largely determined: geographic and strategic, for example. Historically, few countries have elected to diminish themselves in size[154] or wealth; nor have any in Africa – with the sole exception of Ethiopia's final concession of independence to Eritrea – deliberately altered their boundaries, despite the lunacy of the arbitrary lines drawn at the Berlin Conference.

Those lines are all the states have, *ab initio*, to define themselves internationally.

Religion can also be an essential structure. A fine description of the importance of Buddhism in Thailand is offered by one of our students:

> When foreigners think about Thailand ... they think about Buddhism.... When a Thai thinks about himself ... the answer goes elsewhere.... Does this mean that Buddhism is not important to us? No.... Buddhism penetrates so deeply into the inner self of every Thai that people are no longer aware of its presence.... Most people practise [it] without even realizing it. Thus, it is not Buddhism as a religion but Buddhism as the Way that makes it so crucial.... Saving face, avoiding direct confrontation, passive participation, social hierarchy of class structure, and all other Thai values can be traced back to and explained by Buddhism.... It is this Way that holds us Thai together as a united and homogeneous people....[155]

Necessarily, culture is an essential structure. No country is willing to accept policies or plans that violate cultural norms and behaviours: religion, social patterns, and ethnic survival come in here. But where do we put the cultural traits that have permitted long-lasting dictatorships to survive without popular support? Culture, which is everything and nothing – from establishing the pentameter as the national metre to attitudes toward theft – is an ever-pervasive presence, always altering, always resisting alteration at this point and that. Churchill once defined cultural change as 'Romans turning into Italians'. Tremendous change occurs – non-literate societies may turn their language inside out a couple of times in a century – but the overall stabilizing weight inherited from the ancestors, from weddings to judges' wigs, is very dangerous to compromise all at once. The global drive to the lowest common denominator is doing no long-term good, even to Rupert Murdoch.

Still, despite their importance, 'essential structures' can be self-defeating. White domination in apartheid-ruled South Africa was destined to be defeated. The domination of Israel by religious conservatives opposed to the peace process has come to look similarly self-destructive. The abuse and disempowerment of women is an essential structure in many countries, particularly in the Islamic world – and small wonder that economic historians like David Landes see a strong correlation between the role women are allowed and the economic progress of that region.[156] But typically, essential structures have come to imply general prosperity in a peaceful context. States seek to adapt to internal and international realities, on their own timetable where possible. But essential structures don't count as such, unless they are, in some intuitively satisfactory way, truly *national*. A simple and obvious test is whether the regime in power is willing to put any desired societal trait to the vote: rule by non-elected politburo in China, or by white minority in South Africa, for example. We doubt, in an age of globalism, that any trait which a regime is *not* willing to put to such a test will survive. Our standard is empirical before it is normative.

The realization that regimes – particularly in Africa – were not only *not* truly concerned with 'development' but willing, indeed eager, to sacrifice national growth for regime survival, is a recent one, little digested in development literature. But it was a proposition advanced by some observers as baobab trees began to sprout and entrench themselves. We hardly consider such regimes part of any country's essential structures – although in so saying we are probably dispensing with a majority of the developing world's leaderships at one time or another.

'Development', then, is the process of adapting essential structures in both political and economic directions so that cultural patterns can be maintained while enhancing the wealth, increasing the legitimacy, and securing the boundaries of the state and nation. Second, development depends on adapting these structures as much as possible, at one's own pace, to increasingly dominant international values and standards. These include the obvious and compelling central reporting requirements of national accounts for international organizations – *transparency* of course; but also, increasingly, global standards of human rights. 'Democracy' in the sense of accountability and fair elections is increasingly the international norm against which states must measure themselves, eagerly or otherwise.

Our definition, however, hinges on its insistence that an un-homogenized process of national adaptation be permitted, that cultural patterns may persist so that individuals may continue to develop self-esteem at both personal and national levels. So long as the Chakri dynasty supplies honourable monarchs and so long as

Ghanaian ethnic groups continue to provide identity without destroying national cohesion, Thailand will remain a monarchy and Ghana will have a role for chiefs and a sub-national king like the Asantehene. In fact in 1999 the briefest perusal of the Ghanaian press revealed that the chiefs were receiving rather more attention – and presumably enjoying a much larger role – than we saw thirty years earlier. Yet there remains the persistent and strengthening trend noted by Thomas Sowell, the 'emergence of the elements of a common world culture, shared by at least the educated people of every continent'. This may offer the hope of 'ultimately transcending the many group differences which may seem so colourful and delightful in theory, but which have all too often been bitter and lethal in practice'.[157] And if we do indeed get 'civilization in the singular' (Braudel), then élites in Ghana and Thailand will have the same ultimate sense of where their societies are tending, even if some of the paths toward that common destination meander apart.

The key here is balance between tradition and modernization. As Kwakku Sakkyi Addu, the BBC's Ghana correspondent, puts it: 'McDonalds doesn't have to kick out fufu.'[158]

Environmental Protection

Essential structures are also more than social and political. Another essential structure that countries need to protect is their environment. Environmental devastation has been one of the central problems with growth in the twentieth century: when scholars and anthropologists look back a century from now on our world today, they will be appalled that we knew so much and yet did so little.

Economic, spiritual and ethical reasons have prevented rich and developing countries alike from focusing on the importance of preserving one's environment. This is understandable (a country in which people are starving is not going to be thinking a great deal about the long term) but tragic and short-sighted in every regard. It is impossible to make the ethical claim that one should refrain from destroying a resource when the choice is either to do that or to starve. This is a particularly difficult position to defend if one is from the affluent First World where so many natural resources have already been destroyed and where our consumption levels are the engine that runs the machine of worldwide environmental devastation. A man who has dumped a truckload of sludge in the river doesn't have a lot of moral standing when he tries to stop someone else from doing exactly the same. But still, people are supposed to learn from each other's mistakes, and nations should too. Creating a desert just so a single decade can live well is not something that any society should do or that any society should have to do.

The spiritual element of environmentalism is the hardest to explain. Humans come from the earth and one day will return to it. Protection and love of the land is a core belief in numerous traditional cultures and religions. The smell of a forest after a rainstorm or the feeling that one gets after jumping into a cold clear lake: as our opportunities for such experiences become rarer, as toxic chemicals infect the lakes and rush up the food chain, as species after species dies away and pristine wilderness succumbs to the bulldozer, we are losing a lot of what makes us human.

We are also losing potential. A country that has ruined its water supply, or that has so polluted its land that nothing can be grown, is not a country that is going to develop. China, for example, may well find in the next century that it's impossible for an economy to grow in a land where it's now nearly impossible for a tree to grow or for a child to breathe clean air. Natural resources are an essential structure. Trade-offs must be made, but once the last mango tree is felled, there's no hope of harvesting anything further.

Ghana and Thailand and the Environment

Both Ghana and Thailand are guilty of near-critical assaults on their resource bases. Thailand has plundered its incomparable stands of teak and Ghana has ravaged its rainforests. Now, as further millions of Thais and Ghanaians have to be fitted into the same land, and feel the imperative to get rich that only increases with greater wealth, the environmental noose only gets tighter: as Bangkok smothers up-country Ghana gets rawer, balder and bleaker. Thailand may well be developing a civil society that will prove useful in the long run, but the house may be trashed from the party in the short run.

No matter how you spin it, Thailand has been a disaster environmentally, inflicting grave enough problems for those alive today while staining the world for generations to come. The animals that make up so many of Thailand's myths are all but gone now, much like the buffalo that roamed America's prairies a century ago; the natural resources that helped Thailand's agriculture boom have all but vanished. To quote the grave assessment of the fine Thai economists Pasuk and Baker in their best-seller *Thailand's Boom*:

> Over the past generation, Thailand's environment has taken a beating. Forests have been chopped down. The city has become jammed, ugly, polluted. Industrial wastes have poisoned the air, killed off fish in rivers, made some villages scarcely habitable.... This has not been the result of simple carelessness. Rather it has been a by-product of the way that Thailand has chosen to develop.[159]

An economy growing as fast as Thailand's imposes an intolerable strain on the ecosystem around it. We have more power to destroy this miraculous entity, our biosphere, than we have to understand it.[160] But there is strong evidence of change. An opinion poll showed 85 per cent of Bangkok teenagers (15–19) chose the environment as their key concern – above economic development, the rich–poor gap and the decline of religion. Even in the poorer regions, where both economic development and environmental degradation have been more limited, environmental concern everywhere scored highest: a majority of people in all age groups up to the age of 39 chose it as their most important concern; above that age, strong pluralities still gave it priority.[161]

In business, Thailand was operating at a high enough level to see the virtue of environmental steps far in advance of more developed states. At a time when Russia was begging for delays in the implementation of CFC phase-outs, Thailand – along with Belgium, Germany, Mexico and the Netherlands – 'successfully forged voluntary pacts with both producers and end users' of ozone-depleting substances.[162]

Freedom

The third point, after basic needs and essential structures, is that the goal of development must take in more than money and numbers. Amartya Sen and Martha Nussbaum have developed a very useful model for looking at the ends that development should try to pursue. Their principal assumptions are that looking at society through a hedonistic lens is unhelpful (people don't always choose what's best for them or those around them; think of cigarette smokers who don't want to smoke but who can't bear to starve the beast inside), as is looking at society through the lens of revealed preferences. But instead of stating absolute values which societies should follow, Sen and Nussbaum lay out a list of Aristotelian goals that increase what they call the 'functioning' and 'agency' of society. These goals are, of course, what maximize freedom (as Amartya Sen broadly and carefully defines it).

Nussbaum calls the theory, 'the thick vague conception of the good', defining the good as 'being able to live to the end of a complete life, have good health, avoid pain and enjoy pleasure, use the five senses, to assess and critically revise a conception of one's own good, care for others and nature, play and laugh, live one's own life in one's circumstances'.[163] The list sounds more like something from a motivational poster than from Aristotle, or Sen for that matter, but the point is critical. There are things that are universal goods and, while we probably shouldn't try to legislate them into existence, they should be aims for society: its development should be judged in some measure by how well these needs are fulfilled for its citizens.

We agree with Sen that, following this point, development really boils down to freedom: the freedom to live one's life as far as possible in the way that one chooses – whether this means the ability to choose what one wants to do during the course of a day without having to worry about scraping around for food, or not being coerced by the state for contrary political views.

Choices and Development

A key element of function, agency and freedom is that people are able to have autonomy over what sort of development path they take. There are desperately poor villages in rural Ghana that have very little access to the outside world but which seem to be full of people happier than almost everyone in developed countries like the United States. For example, in the lakes of northern Ghana there lies the village of Mamprusi; the locals call it 'overseas' because it's so hard to get to. At least according to rumour, marijuana is openly sold on the streets of Mamprusi, no government representative has been there in thirty-five years and the residents have never seen a policeman or a foreigner.[164] Of course we can't verify this because, if we could, it wouldn't be true. In villages like Mamprusi, and most other villages, many residents never dream for a second of the headlong bustle of Accra, much less New York City. There are also, of course, cities like Des Moines in Iowa that wouldn't give up what they have to be like New York. Are the people living in these cities being coerced into staying still and having their freedom of mobility taken away? No, they have the freedom to move to the Big Apple; they're just not exercising it.

Taylor: You know, there's probably more that we in the United States can learn about life from Bolatanga than vice versa.

Tara: Like what? Like how to live an impoverished life that conks out, on average, at about age 45?

Taylor: No, like how to live a life where community matters, where people care about one another and where life is sustainable.

Tara: For how long?

Taylor: Think about it this way. How many Americans are satisfied with their lives? Next to none. How many of the people in the village I lived in as a Peace Corps volunteer were satisfied? Almost all.

Tara: Of course they're satisfied; they have low expectations. You would too if you were born with nothing. Sheep are happy. That doesn't mean that people should live like sheep.

Taylor: It also doesn't mean that we should aim to live like wolves, beyond our means. The entire world can't live like America. The entire ecosystem would collapse in minutes. If we let the people in rural Ghana keep on living the way that they want to, we will all be better off.

Tara: Perhaps we should try to mix the best of both worlds. Keep the values of Bolatanga and give them the benefits of advanced American capitalism. Give them medicine. Give them access to

Taylor: the internet. Allow them to learn from our mistakes and encourage them to keep their forests healthy and their air clean.

Taylor: That doesn't work. Look at Accra. Everyone there wants to be like the United States; they all wear Michael Jordan T-shirts and ask for your address, as though you will someday be able to help them get a visa. Life is miserable there. We just can't let the rest of Africa become like that. The people in Bolatanga don't know that they are poor and, thus, they don't care.

Tara: So we should stop exposing them to American culture.

Taylor: Yes.

Tara: Even if they want it?

Taylor: Yes.

Tara: Even if they are willing to die for it, as many are? Are you saying that you know more about what Africa should want than Africans do?

The issue raised by the strangely contented Ghanaian villagers is doubly crucial: a clear repudiation of any one-track logic of development and a yet larger posing of the issue of choice. On a very simplistic analysis, a just society (or the best society) is one in which everyone has her needs, can fulfil all her preferences – and is maximally informed of what choices are and could be. This is a somewhat hedonistic approach, based entirely on the fulfilment of needs and desires.

But what about a society where all the women choose to be circumcised? Only considering the brutal alternative – societal expulsion or worse – is this a choice. People that have been born in difficult situations often have low expectations, and it would be a dubious distinction for a society to consider the fulfilment of low expectations as a success. Doctor Johnson said that we should not be satisfied with what would satisfy an animal, or, as Amartya Sen puts it, ' "He that desires but little has no need of much" may be good advice for contentment and for coming to terms with a harsh reality. But is not a formula for judging well being. Nor is it a recipe for social justice.'[165]

But there is a very difficult line to draw here, since there are undoubtedly societies that would genuinely prefer to hew to the Buddha's way (or indeed the wealth-rejecting way of Jesus of Nazareth) and would certainly be better off if given solitary places to meditate in peace than if all were forced to drive BMWs and eat luxurious meals with golden forks. There are also a few people like Thomas More who genuinely like to wear hair shirts. The line to draw here has to be subjective and has to allow for considerations of choice, information flows and tradition. If someone wants to be poor, just because she knows nothing better, or because she has come to expect that, then she should have other options seriously presented to her. If someone wants to be poor because she can't stand the notion of being rich, then indeed she is richer still.

Gross Domestic Product

The issues of functioning and agency are not, unfortunately, at the core of development studies. That inner sanctum is reserved for GDP.

Bruce Rich of Environmental Defense recounts an old story: a drunken sailor is groping for his wallet under a street light. 'Where do you think you lost it?' asks a friend. 'Oh, about a mile back, but this place has the most light.' GDP is the easiest way to quantify something and call it an economy: it's the first place that any political scientist or economist looks (just as it is the first statistic that we cite in our introduction). But it would do a world of good to start dissociating economics from this seductive skeleton. The technology and the information are there; it's just hard for people to change their ways and start thinking about development in totality, attending to much vaguer (thicker, intuitively richer) notions of functioning and agency.

GDP[166] is the most important indicator in development studies today. In 1992, the World Bank defined a 'low-income economy' as one with a *per capita* income of less than $675 and a 'lower-middle-income economy' as having a *per capita* income between $675 and $2,700. The United Nations even uses the term 'least developed countries' (LDCs) to group certain economies and, for the most part, bases this measure also on *per capita* income.

There are five central problems with GDP. First, it doesn't take into account environmental factors. Every time that a Thai logging company chopped down an ancient forest, Thai GDP increased. Does GDP actually mean, as some facetiously suggest, gross domestic pollution? It's like the Mad Hatter's calculator that can add, but doesn't know how to subtract. Second, GDP does not take into account issues of income distribution. Many of the countries in the Middle East have extraordinarily high levels of GDP, but this money is distributed among very few people.[167] The same is true in Nigeria and is becoming true in Thailand, but not to the same extent in Ghana (where very few people have any money). A rising tide hasn't lifted more boats; it has carried the yachts and flung the dinghies on the mudflats.

Third, GDP ignores factors central to the quality of life: longevity, health, freedom, civil society and many more. The people of a country with a *per capita* income of $1,000, the right to vote and a life expectancy of 75 years, would not trade their position for life in another country with, say, a *per capita* income of $2,000, a life expectancy of 25 years and random arrests by the local police. Fourth, GDP does not distinguish between missiles and food; it is a measure of means, not ends.[168] There's no difference, as far as the accounting goes, between a pair of shoes that you buy for $100 and wear every day for two years and a pair that you buy for $100 but then throw away. Fifth, GDP does not take into account household work, like parenting – demanding, necessary and unpaid. If a mother and a father abandon their children in order to run a brothel, GDP increases. If a husband or mother quits his or her job to take care of their family, GDP decreases. Diligently wash your dishes after dinner and GDP stays constant. Throw them out and buy a new set and GDP increases.

To see a very clear example of reasoning from GDP, or of classifying economies by how much money they have, consider that, according to the numbers, what has happened to South Korea since the 1960s has been almost exactly the same as what has happened to Libya. South Korea, however, has built a balanced economy, decently distributed its national income, offers general opportunity to most of its citizens, and has a vibrant civil society. In 1998 it elected as president a populist dissident whom a previous regime had tried to kill. It put two of his predecessors and the son of the third living president in jail – for corruption. Korea has joined the ranks of the developed world and its musicians play on world stages. Libya, by contrast, has become rich almost solely because of the increase in oil revenues and has nothing much more to show for its wealth than a cluster of mansions – except for poor brotherly regimes and terrorists, and a bloated military.

So What, It's Just a Number

GDP is just a number. But newspapers, international lending organizations, economists, authors and, it seems, most other tuners of public opinion balance their judgements on the whole performance of an economy by this number, and make decisions based on it. In Brazil, as in many countries during the 1980s, the World Bank demanded a certain increase in GDP if it was to continue its lending programme. Brazil met this goal partially by accelerating its rate of deforestation.[169] The same has been claimed by different Ghanaians who argue that the World Bank, during the Economic Recovery Programme of the early 1980s, in effect ordered a vast increase in logging exports.[170] This was partly done to earn foreign exchange, but it also made Ghana look as if it was booming: suddenly, it was able to put on the costume of the Bank's needed success story.

The greater problem is an obsession with wealth, as defined by money, in the world's rich countries. People aren't necessarily happier or better off when they get more money. Think of your friends with the most money; life may be a bit easier, but it's not always better. The same above a certain line is true of countries. Welfare increases depend more on non-economic factors than on economic ones. Moreover, our current obsession has cost us perspective. Protecting the environment has become a tangential goal to development; it's usually what comes next, but never what comes now. Family structures and traditional communities are often broken apart. In Colombia, Occidental Petroleum is trying to build a pipeline across land held sacred by the indigenous U'wa. The U'wa abhor the notion of this development so much that they have threatened to commit mass suicide by walking off a sacred cliff if the pipeline is built. Perverse as it may be, when it's built, Colombia's GDP will increase and the U'wa who don't kill themselves will probably get rich and live in a society much more 'developed' than before.

The easiest resolution of the problem of using GDP as a two-dimensional frame to assess an (at least) three-dimensional world has simply been to create more measures. In 1979, the Overseas Development Council created the Physical Quality of Life Index (PQLI) which ranks countries by their performance in three categories: life expectancy at age one, infant mortality rate, and literacy rate weighted against the difference between the score of the most advanced nation in the world and the least advanced.[171] The United Nations later created a measure known as the Human Development Index (HDI) which operates like the PQLI except that it is framed by educational attainment, literacy and GDP. Both are somewhat confusing, arbitrary and flawed, if only because they implicitly assume that development is a zero-sum game. Were the literacy rate in the least literate country to rise, the HDI or PQLI score in all other countries must fall. Would Ghana be less developed if more people in the Sudan could read?

A reciprocal difficulty comes with slapping values on the environment and the other goods that GDP ignores. Output is tangible and easily measured. But it is much harder to determine how much time a mother spends with her child, let alone assess the quality of the time. In much the same frustrating way, it's not so hard to put a value on a tree's potential use as lumber, but it's quite a challenge to determine how much of a role it plays, and how valuable that role is, in the life cycle of a rare beetle.

The Thai social critic Sulak assures us that

> The only solution for the present human predicament is to challenge the present trend of modernization fundamentally – beyond the material approach to development …. Human development toward truth, goodness and beauty must be the order of the day; one must return from the profane to the sacred.[172]

Sulak often tends toward hyperbole; but he does make a very important point. Sometimes, measuring welfare with numbers can be like measuring a song in kilogrammes.

There is an old saying that war is too serious a business to be left to soldiers: development is too serious to be left to economists. Sociologists and philosophers must have their say, as must biologists, ecologists and, of course, the people. 'We are in the universe's belly,' said Justice Holmes, 'not it in ours.'

CHAPTER 6

Economic Development
in Africa and Asia

The eight tigers – Japan, South Korea, Taiwan, Singapore, Malaysia, Hong Kong, Thailand and Indonesia – followed eight different paths to economic growth. To borrow from Tolstoy, they have certain likenesses in their successes but they were distinct in their defects. Japan and South Korea were relatively protectionist while relying on unreciprocated free trade with their American patrons. Hong Kong opened almost all doors and, while still a colonial territory, became stunningly rich. Indonesia, although it came to be guided by virtuous economic principles and plans, allowed vast unearned wealth to accumulate in the hands of the Suharto family. If Singapore is a young Mozart diligently writing music for 18 hours a day, Thailand is an almost equally accomplished Charlie Parker showing up on the bandstand swaying from left to right with a flask of bourbon in his hand.

The different states south of the Sahara have also slid down varied paths to economic chaos. Nigeria's leaders destroyed their economy despite huge natural resources, while the kleptocrats in Burkina Faso (formerly Upper Volta) had the easier task (although it was less fun) of ruining a naturally poor country. Tanzania tried and failed with socialism; Kenya demolished an ostensibly capitalist system. Ivory Coast started quickly and then stumbled; Zambia hit rock bottom right from the start.

That said, there are still a few fundamental economic lessons – a few things that all these Asian economies did well – from which Africa should learn, and a few other things that Africa has done that should be continued. Mozart and Charlie Parker are different but they're both also clearly miles ahead of Salieri or Kenny G.

The Numbers

First, some statistics to set the tone. Electricity production has increased by 58 per cent in Ghana since 1973 and by 1,148 per cent in Thailand. Inflation in Ghana since 1964 (the first year for which data are available) has multiplied 1,310 times beyond Thailand's. One cedi could buy then what 7,808 cedis can buy today. Ghana's health expenditure *per capita* in 1995 was $4. Of Ghanaians over 15, 35.5 per cent are illiterate, as against 6 per cent of Thais. Ghana's population is growing at such a rate as to double in 19 years, while schools are already being shut down in Thailand thanks to the success of the population programme. Almost half of the population of Ghana is under 15 years old.In Thailand there are 70 telephone lines for every 1,000 people; in Ghana, four.[173] We might be comparing centuries rather than countries.

The comparison that, for better or for worse, gets the most play in international circles is that in 1957 the average Ghanaian was richer than the average Thai. But in 1996 the average Ghanaian earned $420 per year and the average Thai $1,855.[174] The gap (which the Asian collapse has narrowed in the past year) remains of the order of at least four to one. And the sad thing is that many of the reasons for this are hardly opaque. The sources of waste and repeated self-injury are usually all too obvious.

A Baobab and a Mango Tree

There are numerous micro distinctions between the way the two countries managed their economies. But the central macro distinction is between development from the top down, like the baobab tree, and development from the middle outward, like the mango tree. The micro distinctions between Asian tigers and African hyenas can be traced in foreign direct investment, agriculture, trade and education. They can also be seen in the deeper identification with their peoples and the longer time horizons of those who controlled the tigers – a distinction not in terminology but in spirit. The state in Africa remains an essentially artificial construction: a rolled-over colonial *apparat* – rooted not in local experience but in the administrative practices of the metropolitan powers (which had given up a 'divide and rule' policy within living memory, and were more familiar with frontiers agreed around tables in London or Berlin than those located in the soil of Africa). As we argued in Chapter 2, the leaders to whom African nations were entrusted had not won their way to power because of their grasp of economics; placed in control of nations within combustible ethnic situations, they deemed their first priority to be the consolidation of power. Compulsorily unchallenged, certainly un-ashamed, soon enough these leaders were looting their national treasuries and thereby installing a culture of kleptocracy.

We have already touched on the many other reasons that worked toward this contrast – and we will return to them – but our point is the central one: to the Africans, independence and power, 'the political kingdom', were not merely necessary but sufficient. To the Asians, guided by a more revealing historical perspective, political power was only one leg of sovereignty. African leaders willed development by command; Asian leaders sought development by cooperation.

This difference is particularly true of the riders of the tigers, but it is also somewhat true of ordinary citizens. In Thailand, as we have noted before, newspapers inevitably focus on the region's and nation's growth – a self-reinforcing approach that creates a positive feedback loop. When you care about getting rich, you are more likely to get rich, even if, once you are rich, much of your national identity is apt to get caught up in your affluence. Ask someone in Kuala Lumpur or in Bangkok about her city and the odds – at least until mid-1997 – have been very good that she will bring up recent economic growth. In Africa, ask someone about her country's strengths and she will probably mention matters to do with culture, family or community. Show up at a meeting on the dot and you will probably be ridiculed for not setting your watch to 'African time' – a euphemism for being late. There are certainly virtues to the African model, but rapid economic growth is not one of them.

Kwame Pianim, the brilliant and energetic Ghanaian economist banned from running for political office by President Rawlings, makes a similar point. To him, much of Ghana's malaise stems from a plain lack of desire to do work. 'You can get an economic blueprint from the IMF, but the spark has to be homegrown.'[175] In Ghana, the people expect to be robbed by those in power, and have no models to motivate them; no economic theory, however pure, offers the inspiration of effort rewarded, of visible well-being. But one may still hope, remembering the optimism of one-time New Patriotic Party Presidential candidate Nana Akufo-Addo: 'Rawlings set up the markets, our job will be to make them work.'[176]

The Price Is Right

East Asian leaders have gripped Adam Smith's invisible hand, while for forty years African leaders tried to cut it off. The tiger trainers recognized that no man, no business and no government is infallible, capable of predicting precisely what people will want and need. Oceanic Asian governments didn't set prices and endless controls – except Burma which doesn't count.[177] The exception proves the rule: the Philippines remained the region's sick economy until it freed up its system in the 1990s. In Africa, on the contrary, markets were closed off from the world: the government set prices (indeed Jerry Rawlings's thugs went through the marketplaces in Accra, literally flogging market women who were not selling at the ordained rates) and then closed Accra's biggest market altogether[178] – but then, Flt Lt Rawlings was running a police state, not a corporation. From Nkrumah's day on, a small clique of politicians seized upon the commodity institutions set up by the colonialists to meet the objectives of an age of imperialism, world depression and global war, in order to monopolize hard currency.

Why this difference between Africa and Asia? In part it came about simply because Africans trusted the world less. After slavery and colonialism, the belief that international markets were a nemesis to be avoided held a lot more credibility than the view further East that international markets were dangerous, but also a great opportunity to learn from and, eventually, to conquer the world. Even after he had been deposed, Kwame Nkrumah believed that his failure had been a Western plot. In 1968, two years after being forced out of power, he wrote: 'The forcing down of the price of cocoa was part of [the United States and Britain's] policy of preparing the economic ground for political action in the form of a "coup" and a change of government.'[179] This is as likely as the proposition that the continued disk errors sustained by your authors on this project were viral implants by government spies obsessed with subverting our work. No politician believes that his fall was his fault: but Nkrumah's vision from exile of the Anglo-Saxon powers forcing down world commodity prices to fix his wagon may remind us of the projector Captain Gulliver met in Lagado, planning to keep the municipal sundial accurate by adjusting the motions of the sun and the moon.

By 'open to the world' we don't mean that there was always free trade in Asia (although there was certainly more there than in Africa). In Asian economies there often was a great deal of protection – South Korea, for example, had enormous trade restrictions and export subsidies to help its domestic industries to develop before they had to face world competition.[180] But beyond the issue of free trade, there is the more important open-economy issue, in that Asian governments as a rule never set prices or fixed investment. In Asia the market ruled, except where government decided otherwise; in Africa the default position has been the reverse.

A parallel can be drawn with leprosy. Lepers don't lose their limbs spontaneously; they lose them because their nerve connections are cut off. Thus a leper can go to sleep on her arm, cause a blood clot and not even notice. Or, more dramatically, she could put her hand on a stove and lose it because there is no automatic trigger to tell her that something is wrong. Africa, with its price controls, cut off this critical feedback loop; Asia did not. Sen has written that to be against markets is much like being against conversation. Numerous African leaders, astonishingly, have managed to be against both.

Today this dynamic is beginning to change. Africans are beginning to trust the world more, and Asians have learned the danger of considering themselves infallible. Ghana spent the last decade eliminating price controls,[181] opened up to the world, and is completely reversing the economic legacy of Nkrumah. Its people are beginning to develop a market and a culture of competition and this is one of the reasons that there should be much hope for the country. On the other hand, Thailand spent the last few years convinced that it had figured out everything to do with growth – whereupon bankers began to make bad loans, hide information from the world and reinforce the crony capitalism that eventually led to the crash, assuming economic growth would provide cover. As we can learn alike from Nkrumah and from Thailand in the 1990s, the easiest recipe for disaster is the belief that you know everything there is to know.

Foreign Investment

If there has been one major change over the past thirty years in economic relations, it has been the increasing influence of electronically supported international/transnational dealings and the corresponding decrease in power of the vertical state, everywhere apparent in the fast-reversing ratios of foreign aid and corporate investment in the Third World. By 1997 private capital flows were five times the official inputs, reversing the terms of the relationship only five years earlier.[182] The fact that the '150 account' in America – the foreign affairs budget – had declined by half in real terms over a single decade, during which the outside world's population had increased by 15 per cent and its wealth by considerably more, only shows that the action had gone elsewhere – somewhat to Treasury and Commerce, but above all to the real engine of American affluence and influence, the corporate sector.

As a key variable FDI has only recently become significant. Even at its predictive height (1996), FDI accounted for less than about 0.3 per cent of world economic enterprise. As recently as 1990, only 15 per cent of FDI went to developing countries. But FDI sextupled between 1990 and 1996, which indicates how elastic and pioneering it is, that it is coming into its own, and that it is likely to grow rapidly in the future. By 1997, 40 per cent of it was going to the Third World.[183]

One of Thailand's advantages in attracting this FDI has been its status as one of the 'flying geese'.[184] A formation of geese on the wing generally possesses one clear leader, a few following in formation, and a few more in each succeeding flight group. By this analogy, Japan is the lead goose, developing first and arousing others to follow. In the 1960s, for example, it was heavily invested in primary manufacturing – shoes, clothing, cheap watches – but within a decade had graduated to high-grade consumer goods, leaving shoe production to new Asian economies. Soon this second tier – Taiwan, South Korea and Hong Kong – had themselves moved upward, while Indonesia, Thailand and the Philippines had replaced them on the first rung. So the process unfolded, until by 1999 Taiwan was the world's third computer manufacturer – outsourcing to the likes of Subic Bay in the Philippines, lately a US naval base, now a Taiwanese enclave. The countries just followed each other in order, like six brothers and sisters making their way through grade school and college.

Africa did not position itself to take advantage of the change in the importance of FDI – to the very faint degree that it was even aware of it. Rulers throughout the continent were very reluctant to allow foreign investment, even as East Asia courted it. In Accra, the Ghanaian leadership looked askance at Western investment from the start. Perhaps it was inevitable: the commanding heights of the Ghanaian economy – Ashanti Goldfields, Kingsway – were foreign-owned. These companies, which, with the small-scale but successful traders from the Middle East, were all the serious capitalism visible prior to independence, were thus symbols of external influence, even control. Ghanaians thought independence meant that they could seize anything in their territory. They wanted the whole thing. Even in the early 1970s, after the seemingly obvious lessons of the Nkrumah period, the Ghanaian intelligentsia went on witchhunts against potential foreign investors like the British pharmaceutical firm Abbott Laboratories, which proposed a substantial undertaking. It was the intellectuals – more precisely the organ of academe, *The Legon Observer* – which did the dirty work.

Even from the days when America seemed bogged down in Vietnam, it conferred prestige in Thailand to work for Citibank, American Express, or Philip Morris – not to mention the income, although only recently has the differential between private-sector and civil-service salaries more than compensated for the historically far greater standing accorded to those serving king and country. And this is only one of the secondary reasons why the flow of FDI to these two countries, even after adjusting for population size, was several orders of magnitude greater for Thailand over the past forty years. After the Plaza Accords of 1985, when Tokyo under extreme pressure agreed to revalue the yen, and the subsequent export of vast capital abroad, a billion and a half dollars flowed into Thailand alone in just five years, more than the total foreign investment in all of black Africa in that entire period.[185]

More importantly, attitudes towards FDI are changing, and thus accelerating the process. Ten years ago, in most Third World countries, the perception was that rapacious Western firms were hungering to come in, and that only the protective veneer of national laws kept them from taking over.[186] Far from drooling at the gates of Third World labour markets, the multinationals were gripped by a grand diffidence bred of too much pain and difficulty. It was the all too clear memory of a din in their ears, of the Pérons of this world denouncing and nationalizing them, buying them out on unfavourable terms, and then running their countries into bankruptcy;[187] of all their oil investments in the Middle East being seized; and of endless controversy over even rather modest proposed investments. Small wonder that, as we have seen, as of 1990, 85 per cent of FDI stayed within OECD countries – *only then shifting as Third World countries reformed.*

The resistance to investment was itself largely a function of the defensive self-importance of the unfulfilled élites of the marginal world – these men who, a full generation after the metropolitan powers had thankfully cut the painter to their unfruitful empires, twenty years after even well-meaning America had seen their insignificance, were still bolstering their badly damaged sense of consequence with the fantasy that they had assets for which the great powers longed. Commodore Perry saw Japan's industrial potential in 1854; we are still awaiting the visionary who sees that of Honduras or Mali. Cultures which are snobbish and mandarin toward crass trade should not be surprised that crass traders find better things to do than enrich them.

In 1963 Ghana passed a new investment act, intended to make foreign investment a more attractive proposition: droves of potential British investors came to visit. In their five-year plans Ghanaian economists laid out a role for foreign investment – a highly constrained one, but nonetheless a role. One of us wrote thirty-five years ago that it looked as if a genuine and profitable partnership between British capital and Ghanaian socialism could exist within the framework of the seven-year plan. But Nkrumah assigned every attractive slot in the plan to the state sector, and bought out (on very dishonest appraisals) private investors whose success was politically threatening. Graft, hoarding, corruption, and maladministration became endemic. The fear that remained was not that British concerns might be nationalized, but that Ghana's economy would deteriorate enough to render British investments worthless.[188]

FDI also conjures up complex emotions and erroneous economic models. Do Americans recall their anxiety at the Japanese purchase of a motion picture studio, Rockefeller Center, and a famous California golf course? That was a decade ago, before the Japanese 'miracle' dried up: today, the British, the island empire people forgot, own more property in the United States than the Japanese. Industrial leaders who needed to invest in the Third World – for reasons of resources or cheap labour – accustomed themselves to long lectures from the local leadership on the perfidies of neo-colonialism.

Nowhere was such a reception more certain than in Ghana. Edgar Kaiser, the country's largest investor, spoke for many others when he told Nkrumah that Ghana couldn't really expect investors to bring money into a country whose newspapers daily reviled, insulted, and offended them.[189] It took courage and farsightedness to invest in such countries, so very few did. On a much larger scale, India performed the same feat, attracting only a trickle of token FDI until the Chinese miracle, sped by the greatest flood of FDI in history, woke the government up. The financiers of Mumbai finally had their day: in the 1990s investment began to pour into India, and the percentage of Indians in poverty began finally to drop.

While Ghanaians were learning how to drive away investment, Marshal Sarit came to power in Bangkok. Just as Ghana was building up its state enterprises, with such disastrous consequences, Thailand was receiving a justly famous World Bank mission that would call for the dismemberment of the same. Of course the timing was fortunate. The SOEs (state-owned enterprises) were largely associated with the Ratchakru group, whom Sarit had thrown out of power, so he could do well while doing good in following this virtuous economic advice. 'The state enterprises in distribution were dismantled. Some of the state factories were sold off to private owners. No new enterprises were begun except for public utilities. Sarit espoused the US language of development....'[190] And small wonder: as Pasuk and Baker also point out, the Sarit coup 'brought into line the strategic interests of the US, the dictatorial aims of the Thai military, and the commercial ambitions of domestic capital.'[191]

Nonetheless, Thailand, although not at any point hostile to foreign investment, was a bureaucratic state *par excellence*, burdening investors with regulations that discouraged the inflow of serious money. Even immigration was resisted: the routine complaint among the *farang* community was the degrading long days in line renewing visas every three months.

Something happened in the late 1970s, about the time that Walter

Wriston's message from Citibank was coming on powerfully. Markets worked, socialism failed, but serious countries like Thailand still had to undertake reform, streamlining bureaucracy, if they wished investment on a serious scale. When General Kriangsak was Prime Minister (1977–80), very competent ministers and permanent secretaries began taking the advice. The Japanese had already patiently established an investment beachhead in Thailand, where they felt comfortable: a fellow monarchy, a Second World War ally (that belief alone was a triumph of Thai tact and cunning), and a country sharing many values. Soon they were allocating a tenth of all their aid to Thailand. By 1985, when the Plaza Accords were signed, Thailand was in an enormously favourable position to welcome the billions of new FDI available; by 1990, as we have seen, the country was getting more than a billion dollars of Japanese investment alone.

Domestic Investment

It almost goes without saying that domestic investment is as important as FDI (in Korea, it has always outmatched FDI to an astonishing degree). Not surprisingly, there have been similar problems for African states in attracting this sort of investment, partly because the baobab tree hates competitors. According to numerous economists in Ghana, every president of the nation has seen private business as competition, not as potential support. Today the biggest factor impeding investment is probably the fear that President Rawlings is simply going to hold on to power like a typical African despot. Ghanaian businessmen don't trust Rawlings and, just as a farmer won't want to raise chickens if he knows that a tax collector is coming to carry off all the eggs, they don't want to start enterprises that will be nationalized by the government as soon as they are profitable.

Africa has two troubling historical tendencies. The first is toward violent changes of government and chaos. Ghana, for example, has never had a peaceful, full-term, government transition. This isn't the United States, where you are reasonably sure that power is going to be passed on constitutionally in four years and, if justified in its exercise, to someone of similar views. It's more likely that there will be an accident in an airport, and suddenly an until-then-obsequiously loyal cabinet member or ethnic agitator will take charge. True, Thailand has had its litany of coups, the last in 1991. But coups in Thailand have had a surreal quality; as described in Chapter 3, little blood is ever shed and the coups scarcely ever even block the traffic. Sometimes they have actually furthered the orderly conduct of business. As late as 1991, the business community, local and *farang*, cheered the coup makers on. Until recently coups were virtually the agreed-upon mode of rotation within the élites and an occasion for smart civil servants to enact reforms.

The second trend is that Africa has a history of seizing business profits. As noted earlier, some countries simply created a 100 per cent tax bracket on any income over $35,000. Others, like Zaïre under Mobutu, confiscated the assets of the middle class down to the most basic level to avoid a (very hypothetical) political threat.[192] In Ghana there is a law making it illegal to carry out 'any act with an intent to sabotage the economy'.[193] This formula is evocative of the memorable line of that patron saint of African dictators, Humpty Dumpty – 'words can mean what I want them to mean, neither more nor less'. In the past it has been applied simply to take money away from people who are making profits or to shut down businesses that the government didn't like. Businessmen who weren't scared off by the erratic government of Nkrumah, or the nonsensical ones of his followers, were surely scattered to the winds by this statute.

Even today there are tremendous disincentives to investing in Ghana, the prime one being that a business can never really be sure how the government is going to treat it. The days of instant nationalization may be gone, but even that lover of free markets Jerry Rawlings has on occasion astronomically raised the prices of essentials like electricity. Even today, there is a huge infrastructure problem – there simply is not enough electricity generated in Ghana. Over the last two years, surprisingly low rainfall has dropped the Volta Lake way below the dam's capacity. For nine months there was power rationing throughout the country, the lights on one night and off the next: a bore if you are a journalist; crippling if you are a factory worker. Admittedly these are problems exacerbated by nature, but prudent countries provide against such contingencies. The whole atmosphere in Ghana is uncongenial to business: it takes, for example, half an hour to cash a traveller's cheque – if you can in fact persuade even the Standard Chartered Bank to *cash* the damn thing.

Foreign direct investment generally makes a country richer, but there are certainly cases where it brings much more harm than good. For some countries, getting richer in the short term only entrenches a rotten government and thus brings more poverty in the long term. If a country has an unrepresentative or indeed hostile government, FDI is not going to be a force for good. Like foreign aid, FDI is a means to an end, and if the government's ends are bad . . . .

Burma is the classic example. For the past decade, the repressive Burmese junta has been propped up by foreign investment, most saliently by UNOCAL, the American gas giant, and has used this money to maintain some sort of financial stability while continuing to oppress its citizens. If investment were to go, the junta would be more likely to go bankrupt and collapse – and pretty clearly this would be a good thing for Burma.

There are two main ways to deal with such a situation. The first, the option that businessmen universally favour, is called constructive engagement, dancing with the devil. The second is sanctions, which sometimes work (see South Africa) and sometimes fail miserably (see Cuba).

Currency Markets

Unfettered capitalism and FDI are both very mixed bags, and both Ghana and Thailand have suffered because of currency markets. Ghana suffered because the government set rates the way that Butch Cassidy would have set bank security codes. Thailand suffered because unregulated global currency markets deal with markets the way that Butch Cassidy dealt with safes.

In Thailand, up until July 1997, the government stabilized the currency near 26 baht to the dollar. If there were more sellers than buyers at that price, the government would either raise interest rates (slowing economic growth but making the baht more attractive), or use some of its dollars to buy baht in the open market until the price returned to 26. If there were more buyers than sellers, the policy would be just the reverse.

The trouble with such a policy comes when currency traders

perceive that the government will no longer be able to defend the currency either because of economic weakness or because the government is running out of reserves. From this moment on, there are far more sellers of the currency than there are buyers, and it takes either exorbitant interest rates or more and more dollar reserves from the central bank to maintain the price.

Two main problems, personal and impersonal, had worked offstage to bring the sudden collapse of 1997: the Prime Minister, Chavalit Yongchaiyud, had been carried away by Thailand's growth over the past generation. Whatever he did, the economy boomed. Chavalit developed unlimited faith in his own abilities and, because money means more in Thai politics than even in America, he became more and more indebted to Thai businessmen (all of whom were bound to take a bath with devaluation). As the currency weakened and sporadic attacks revealed his policy's weakness, Chavalit held on and believed that he could will the currency to stay strong, as Canute attempted to hold back the waves. Currency traders kept pounding, however, until, like a high pressure hose firing on soft clay, they gradually wore everything away and the baht collapsed.

Chavalit's obstinate position did not encounter adequate opposition because of the impersonal factor: the underlying economic problems in Thailand were almost precisely the opposite of the ones that had caused the collapse in Mexico a few years before, and analysts had not immediately grasped the weaknesses. In Mexico, the problem was over-consumption. Billions of dollars had flowed in and been spent on expensive cars and luxury goods. In Thailand, billions of dollars had come in and been invested, and then more had been invested, and then even more had been invested and lent out. This was hardly a problem in standard macro-economic terms and it wasn't until increased prices and indebtedness had reached crisis proportions that people took notice. Only in July 1996, one year before the devaluation and well into the cycle, did the IMF first argue that Thailand needed to devalue.

Currency Machismo

Ghana's currency problem, although similar, was caused by governmental greed, not international speculation. The clique in power simply set an artificial exchange rate, arrogantly higher than it had any hope of commanding on an open market, penalizing such potential exporters as farmers and benefiting the unfailingly well-connected importers. Government policy is more concerned with state dinner parties than the needs of average farmers.

Governments also have a bias toward high exchange rates as an index of national grandeur. During the late 1980s, the television news ran nightly reports on the fall of the American dollar against the yen as it might follow the record of a team heading toward relegation from its league. Jeffrey Herbst describes the pressures brought upon the government of Ghana against devaluing the currency, as was so clearly necessary, in the early 1980s: 'In part, the need to have a strong cedi was tied to the desire of many Ghanaians, who had seen their once proud country decline into bankruptcy, to recapture some of the nationalistic spirit of the past by confronting international financial institutions.'[194] At this time, the *Accra Daily Graphic* ran an article arguing that

> It is as if the IMF is some sadistic monster which becomes angry at seeing people happy.... One also recalls with pride how Ghana's own Osagyefo rejected the Fund's pressures to devalue the cedi in the early 1960s.... Unfortunately many of the leaders Ghana has had after Nkrumah did not have the courage of the Osagyefo.[195]

This reflexive opposition to devaluation weaves a negative feedback loop. The economy gets worse, so the need to devalue increases, but the opposition to devaluation becomes even stronger, which makes the economy sink still further.

Floating the exchange rate takes guts and a real desire to do something good for your economy. The benefits only accumulate over the long run: increased production, more efficient markets, more honest trade, bought in the early days by rising prices, dislocation, bankruptcies. Kofi Busia devalued the cedi in 1971 and was overthrown within weeks as Colonel Acheampong led the military to capitalize on popular outrage.

Not only did the clever fellows in African capitals discriminate against farmers with their exchange-rate fantasies, they also embarked on what, had it been guided by rational motives, could only have been a systematic campaign to bankrupt their agricultural sector. Thailand did the exact opposite, and was one of the few Asian tigers to be able to develop its agricultural export industry. The statistics are surprising, if a bit horrifying. In 1961, Ghana had more agricultural land available than Thailand. By 1994, Thailand's exceeded Ghana's by 65 per cent.[196] Ghana's overall crop production was higher in 1971 than in 1990 while in Thailand crop production almost doubled during the same period.[197] Obviously the differences have extended beyond just simple industrial development. In fact, one might be inclined to think that, over the past generation, Thailand's agricultural output would have declined relative to Ghana's owing to the large number of people who entered the industrial sector. But that's obviously not the case. Right from the start Thailand's governments understood the essential priority of agriculture, if only, to borrow from Willy Sutton, because that was where the money – and the people – always were. And with the money, the chance to make real changes. 'The main impetus behind Thailand's economic growth in the 1960s and 1970s was the growth of agriculture,' as the World Bank study *Thailand's Macro-economic Miracle* observes.[198]

Marketing Boards

Marketing boards caused a great deal of this difference between Ghana and Thailand. Marketing boards, like smallpox, were introduced into Africa by the colonialists. They exist, ostensibly, to guarantee prices to farmers, but what they eventually end up doing is guaranteeing that the government can always buy crops at below market rates. The first problem that Ghana's cocoa industry faced was massive corruption and inefficiency. While quite possibly well intentioned, the cocoa marketing board ended up as a major hindrance to farmers. Moreover, with a few exceptions, marketing boards have failed. The board essentially cuts the farmers off from the laws of supply and demand and, taking into account the board's incentive to pay as little as possible, farmers are given consistently low rates, even when the market price is high. Even today, as Rawlings tries to reform the marketing board, his goal is merely to enable producers to earn back 50–60 per cent of the international export price. In other words, if cocoa is sold for a dollar, Rawlings wants corruption to be eliminated to the extent that the farmer who produced the cocoa gets at least fifty cents. In the past, the farmers have earned as little as 15 per cent of the world price.[199]

Moreover, even by the standards of marketing boards, Ghana's cocoa board has been remarkably inefficient. By 1992, when President Rawlings finally lost his temper with the board, the staff had doubled since the early years of independence, while crop production had been cut in half. Today, Rawlings is trying to cut the size of the board down to about 10,000.

Cocoa production in Ghana also runs up against the simple problem of poverty. Poor countries just don't have the infrastructure to run industries such as cocoa and a very large percentage of the annual crop is lost because of poor transport on Ghana's miserable roads, and inadequate storage. In 1965 Kwame Nkrumah spent millions of dollars constructing silos to house the excess cocoa crop. Not having the advantage of savvy scientists on his side, he didn't realize that, in Ghana's tropical climate, the crops would turn to worthless silage.

Similarly, there is the crucial problem of time perspectives. As one travels around Ghana, one notices immense areas of land that are simply covered with bush – potential crop land that isn't producing a single thing. Why aren't there cocoa trees there? Well, the main reason is that it takes about three years from the time that a cocoa tree is planted until it bears fruit, and no one can afford to wait that long. There simply isn't enough capital to be able to plant trees and sit around. If you talk to cocoa farmers in Ashanti region, they all want to buy land, plant trees and harvest. The trouble is, they can't. Ghana also refused (or was unable because of its other priorities) to develop the infrastructure – and in particular the roads – to run an agricultural economy. Thailand, on the other hand, had a vast network of roads built by the United States in the 1960s. Today, only 24.1 per cent of roads in Ghana are paved.[200] One recent study estimated that 25 per cent of Africa's potential agricultural production was destroyed or simply made unworthwhile by appalling transportation or yet more appalling roads, and by other problems with the national communications infrastructure.

A further problem facing Ghana's cocoa production and all African farming is that – despite the Western rhetoric in support of free markets – the United States and European countries are notoriously protectionist when it comes to agriculture. Not only are tariffs imposed on imports, and farmers given state subsidies, but there is a myriad of health regulations, partly designed to protect American consumers, partly to protect narrow farming interests. This is not surprising. There are few multinational agricultural industries to lobby for open agricultural markets and the domestic farming lobby, of course, wants to be protected. The unfortunate end result is that African nations have a much more difficult time exporting their agricultural products, one of the few export items in which they have a comparative advantage in production and that they should be able to exchange.

Education

The tigers' economic success can also be attributed in no small part to their energetic promotion of education. Africa neglected – sabotaged – educational spending and paid a great price. In Ghana, for example, according to 1993 data, 40 per cent of the population was illiterate, and unsurprisingly so: the state was spending the equivalent of $25 a person on primary education and $68 a person on secondary education.[201] In Thailand the numbers are very different. If you look at the most recent educational performance test results, seven of the top eleven countries are in East Asia. Japan has the longest tradition of educating its people. During the Meiji Restoration, primary school enrolment rates were raised from about one quarter to nearly 100 per cent.[202] People were still surprised that the Japanese started bringing off things previously confined to Caucasians, but there was no arcane secret.

Education matters not just as a good in and of itself – it allows people to read, to have more work options, in short to lead more fulfilling lives – but also because it increases industrial productivity. If someone is educated, and if she can read, she is much more likely to be able to learn new tasks and complex skills. One can also argue that education is an important factor working for democracy – after all, an electorate needs to be able to understand the policies of the people to whom they award their votes.

Tara: Ghana is doing much better than it was fifteen years ago.

Taylor: You must be joking. People can't get one square meal a day here. Fufu is a food of the upper class.

Tara: No, they can't get three squares a day, but three is more than one so they're doing better than fifteen years ago.

Taylor: I can concede a little bit here. GDP *has* gone up in the past fifteen years, but it's been hollow growth, built on loans. We haven't improved; we have just taken money and we are going to pay for this down the road. Plus, borrowers have no dignity.

Tara: No, everyone has to take loans at some point in their life. Think of it as trying to get from point A to point B. You can walk with dignity, or you can pay a little bit and take the bus.

Taylor: That I agree with. The only problem is that Ghana's bus is being driven by corrupt drunkards, the wheels are coming off, we're spewing exhaust and the roads are so bad that it would probably be better just to walk anyway.

Tara: The problem with people like you is that the glass is always half empty....

Taylor: Or completely empty – like the glasses of almost everyone who lives in any village in this country.

Does Africa Have a Chance?

The answer will come from the political sphere before we can pass on to the hope of more substantial achievements. Ivory Coast, a country that was beating Ghana hands down throughout the 1960s and 1970s, winning its historic bet against Nkrumah, experienced from the late 1980s a decline almost as precipitous as Ghana's had been a decade earlier. A senior adviser to the French Minister of Economic Development observed that we could have the 'hour long explanation ... or the two-word explanation.' We asked if the two-word answer was hyphenated. Houphouet-Boigny, the sage of Yamoussoukro, had brought foreign investment from Paris and Wall Street, and was the first African to bring his country to the Eurodollar market. But in his dotage he so canted the government budget – maybe half a billion on the appalling cement replica of St Peter's in his home village – that it verged on bankruptcy. The same is true in country after country. Idiot leaders have led to idiot economics. Houphouet started as a modernizer who had to display some Big Man traits to be effective; he ended as a Big Man hollowing out the hard-won treasures of his modernization. They all stay too long. That in itself is sufficient justification for democracy.

Africa's main problem, however, is that ultimately it has wanted development from the top down, rather than, as in Thailand, from the middle out. Nkrumah destroyed the Ghanaian economy by building showy projects – a foolish motorway to nowhere, nevertheless 'built to the highest standards of the world'. Political conditions made full development of the showpiece Volta River Project almost a non-starter. The useless conference centre he built for the OAU's 1965 heads of state meeting in Accra swallowed the last of the treasury's riches. The monument for the last forty years of the African ordeal should be a statue of the Unknown Tyrant, pouring fortunes into a bottomless pit.

Africa has a chance, but only as the old leaders – and, let us hope, their legacies – die off; only as the nations begin to recognize that open societies are the vital ones, that agriculture does not detract from a nation's dignity, and that human development may make people worse subjects, but wonderfully better citizens.

CHAPTER 7

Corruption, from Nibble to Gulp

Between the start of our research and the completion of the manuscript, Sani Abacha died and Nigeria nearly died with him. President Suharto lost his job, though not his piggy bank, and the Asian economies began to sputter back to health after the contagious illness that spread from Thailand. Boris Yeltsin flailed helplessly as the country that defined the Second World continued its slide into the chaos of the Third. All of these monumental events were due in no small part to corruption.

Corruption has prevented Nigeria becoming a nation, has derailed Indonesia's standing as one of the Third World's most adaptive countries, and rotted Russia's democracy before it could take hold. More generally, it has been the gangrene which has made the Third World's other ills incurable. Corruption isn't the be-all and end-all of economic pathology but, as any experienced student of the Third World knows, it is central to understanding government, corporate matters and administration therein. 'It would not be wrong to say that corruption is the single most important reason for our economic meltdown,'[203] said the Chulalongkorn University economist Pasuk Phongpaichit of the collapse in Thailand, itself the single most important reason for the collapse in Asia. The same could be said of country after country, from Congo to Korea.

Corruption, though, is far more easily denounced than defined. Even in the most exemplary democracies today, to promise a tariff or an import quota at election time – bringing the government in as guarantor of a cartel against foreign competition – is just healthy democratic peacemaking. But that's almost as bad as the kind of corruption that the same countries rail against. Corruption has always been with us, but in the developing world it has such lurid significance because it is not occasionally aberrant but completely atmospheric, the standard return upon cultures in which rights are defined in terms of those who have the weight, not of a common citizenry.

Thus corruption ranges from primitive taxation to the sale or trading of public office (there was an open legal market in military commissions up to colonel until halfway through Queen Victoria's reign in England); it includes the sale at grotesque prices or simply purchased neglect of the public domain, from the Yazoo frauds of the early Republic to the amazing casualness of Brazilian authority to its rainforests today; it takes in simple judicial manipulation or (crucial in an information age) regulatory malfeasance: how did Japan let its banks and insurance companies march so far into the swamp? The continuities of corruption run around the world. The breakpoint comes between cultures which can discern the non-zero-sum returns on overall honesty, and those where revolutions take place to put fresh hay into the trough.

Sometimes the institutionalization of corruption reaches comic proportions. In the nineteenth century, each Thai king appointed officials to 'harvest' taxes, for doing which they were to withhold a proportion for themselves, literally called 'eating the economy' – although 'economy' is too modern a word here. (Similarly, in *ancien régime* France, the Crown directly leased its revenue authority to tax farmers.) The historic *sakdina* system simply entailed the King's bestowing authority and his beneficiaries drawing their livelihoods from those upon whom the delegated authority was visited. Even today, these old habits linger. Politicians in Thailand speak openly and naturally of their well-grounded expectations of 'making up' the cost of their election to parliament – generally around a million dollars – over the first year in office. Throughout the Third World (and in not so ancient times, in all the countries that constitute the First) office has been seen as a way of getting rich or of sustaining riches. *Iustitia est magnum emolumentum*, says a medieval text: justice is a great source of income.

There is a good argument that 'corruption,' which here can include superbowl tickets for cabinet officers and yellow squash import quotas, may well be too weak a word for many societies in which river basins are for sale. In such worst cases as Nigeria, we are talking about the near enslavement of society by a government that rolled tank-like over even the vaguest and easiest aspirations to honesty. Power is so centralized, so primitively focused and so intense that it burns up the very circuits it runs on, even as it consumes the country. Under General Abacha, no decisions were made outside his bungalow; no decisions were made that didn't enrich him; in the end he died, by all accounts, from his own self-indulgence. Abacha created what became almost a mirror image of the classic tragedy of the commons – in the latter tragedy, what no one owns no one maintains. Using the word 'corruption' is surely too weak to describe what happened in Nigeria, but it's a word we have to start with and build on.

Dash

Corruption creeps along four main deliquescences, which we will define as dash, money politics, mango corruption and baobab corruption. Dash, as it is called in West Africa, is the first and most innocuous type of corruption; it pervades all developing societies. Dash can take the form of small bribes, 'presents', Asian tea money, and favours of the sort that just serve to overcome the passive aggression of a swift-moving society that is losing its village personalism and transparency while not yet developing the self-respect we call professionalism. It is particularly prevalent when a low level of bureaucratic identity or corporate spirit, unregarded and unpoliced, makes such lubrication necessary, rational, and unshameful to either side.

> 'Nurse, I would really like to use the bedpan.'
> 'Oh. Unfortunately they are all in use.'
> 'Here's a dollar.'
> 'Here's your bedpan. Have a nice day.'

Dash may or may not act as facilitator of the economies which stand behind these societies. It is an open question whether its cost as an overhead – and the greater costs of delay and obstruction which exact it – offset its facilitating power. Certainly, it helps people at low levels of the bureaucracy in the Third World who may not be paid at all; just as certainly, it throws a monkey wrench into any planning and prudent decision making by adding an arbitrary and often unpredictable level of fiddling and cost to every transaction. More gravely, it helps to sustain an environment of corruption at higher levels. But weighing the benefits against the cost, and taking into account the very small scale, the overall system-wide import of dash is somewhat self-cancelling in the ordering of societies and their priorities. It is more an index of a society's being unprepared for modernity than a cause of it.

Money Politics

A second, far deeper and more malodorous channel of corruption is money politics: the flow of money outside official channels to influence the selection of leaders and their policies. This is the kind of corruption where the people in control of a country's economy try to take over the political system; quite obviously, it is the most important kind of corruption in the First World, most notably in the United States.

This type of corruption may very well debilitate the development of civil society, but it does not necessarily distort economic development or deplete treasuries, although the likelihood of such concealed mechanisms working to the general good seems small. It is just one further step away from perfect competition and thus a drag on development that is hard to quantify. Thailand may be seen as an ideal type of this kind of sleepwalking malfeasance. In 1995, at least one billion dollars – about 0.5 per cent of GNP – was widely estimated to have been spent in the Thai elections, mostly in bribing individuals to vote for one candidate or another. (This would have been matched by an expenditure of something like $36 billion in the US in 1996.) There were some positives to this bingeing; it can even be seen as exercising a positive redistributory effect. Some *kamnans* – village elders or leaders – reached the point where, instead of presiding over the handing out of roughly 300 baht per voter, they bargained for improvement schemes roughly proportionate to the headcount. Thus, a village of a thousand voters could get 300,000 baht (about $11,000 then) – enough for a new irrigation channel.

In the United States, this kind of corruption is executed behind a legal veneer that helps to keep it in line. Money obviously helps aspiring politicians and, in many races, it is necessary – but it's never sufficient as it is in Thailand. In 1994 and 1998 in California, Michael Huffington and Al Checci poured enormous sums of money into their quixotic quests for power but they were forced to spend it on persuasion, mostly through television advertising, instead of on purchase of voters; in the end, even they fell short. In Ghana or Thailand, either surely could have been elected. If Ross Perot were Thai, he could be at least Deputy Prime Minister. But this is still not quite an equivalence. The exertion of the hard sinews of power in a Thai or Ghanaian election confers a certain Balzacian intensity of reality upon a successful politician; but one is being that little bit too sophisticated to equate it with the democratic authority coming from a relatively honest election.

AT A HOSTEL IN DELHI

Taylor: I really want to go to Burma, but I don't have a visa and we have to leave in two days.

Tara: That's not a problem. I got my visa to Burma in a matter of minutes; I just stuck an extra twenty-dollar bill in my passport and asked if I could pay an 'accelerated processing fee'.

Taylor: You just bribed them? That's immoral.

Tara: Why? I get to go to Burma and they get money that they need more than I do.

Taylor: It's what has destroyed Africa and Asia. Political figures accept cash for favours and give cash for favours and eventually the whole state implodes because the only things around are cash and favours and, in due course, neither of either.

Tara: How is that different from America where political leaders push protective tariffs, or tax cuts, that will benefit a very small number of individuals at the expense of the rest of the American public? How is handing cash to voters any different from what we do here?

Taylor: It's no different economically, but it's different morally. It is the first building block in the creation of predatory states. Name one country where petty dash is prevalent and that has an uncorrupted higher government.

Tara: But the people who are deceitful buy things with that money, don't they? The woman who took my bribe is going to go to market and buy some food from someone who will then take the money that they earn from selling food and will use it to buy shoes for her children etc....

Gulp

The third and fourth kinds of corruption, which we shall call 'mango corruption' and 'baobab corruption', are the kinds that command the most startled attention from outsiders and have the deepest effects. These two are the kinds of corruption where state policies are chosen for the monetary benefit they will bestow upon officials and their patrons, at a level of aberration and magnitude so great that the country has to lose. An example would be granting, say, a road construction contract to the brother of a senator (or to a businessman who has 'materially persuaded' the Prime Minister), instead of putting it up to competitive bidding. As we shall discuss below, in many developing countries the whole spectrum of government's business needs are rated by their political 'rakeability', not their social value. If 'money politics' corruption consists of using money to buy or rent politics, usually in order to tunnel through politics to gain much more money, this kind of corruption consists of using a range of means from truly intense corruption to raw military power to seize the economy directly. It was a relatively mealy-mouthed form of this, Professor Pasuk has argued, that brought on the meltdown in Thailand.

While this Herculean abolition of the distinction between public and private is something clearly other than its two weaker brethren, dash and money politics, there is a further distinction that needs to be made. The economy can be eaten according to two different diets and mango corruption is very different from baobab corruption. Under mango corruption, the economic system still operates basically upon what economists style a virtuous model while corrupt ministers, prime ministers and middlemen steal what they can, with only secondary distortionary effects. More money is made, and so there is more to steal. 'A rising tide,' John Kennedy liked to say, 'raises all boats' – including, one might add, those flying the skull and crossbones.

But according to the second diet, the state itself becomes the kitchen; it is set up precisely with the objective of corruption. The aim is not even that of maintenance, as was General Abacha's system in Nigeria. It is driven solely by unreflecting greed; a natural sequel, indigestion, has a way of proving fatal.

With mango corruption, an economy can still greatly prosper; with baobab corruption, an economy is doomed. To illustrate this obviously crucial distinction a superb and recent example is Indonesia, where a family appetite raised on the mango approach grew in the eating into a baobab corruption pathology that ate through the dish with catastrophic results.

Suharto Family Values

Throughout their rule, the Suharto family extracted enormous rents from Indonesia's rapidly growing economy; but up to a surprisingly late point, they maintained an economic system constructed on sound principles under the guidance of smart economists and bankers. They let the economy grow and thus were able to steal more in absolute terms, even if less in relative ones, as their country boomed. Indonesia under their rule expanded: in constant 1987 dollars, *per capita* income increased from $185 to $727 between 1966 and 1996. But eventually the mango corruption of Indonesia's golden years metastasized to consume the virtuous policy. Suddenly, Indonesia was a prey to baobab corruption; next thing, it had collapsed.

In April 1996 Madame Tien Suharto, 'Madame Ten Per Cent', died. But it was she who had held back her six children from going public with their power and wealth. Once she was dead, one son was blackmailing all rival businesses through government purchasing, expanding the sales of his 'Timor' car and trashing every principle of fair trade. A daughter was straddling the expanding road system with her monopoly and blackening the Jakarta skyline with clusters of skyscrapers. Friends were getting their hands on the cash too, and sound economic policies were discarded left and right. The difference between the more or less acceptable republican boodling up to 1996 and the predatory monarchical arrogance thereafter was enough to make the difference between continued success and catastrophe.[204]

One of the greatest ironies of the Suharto family story – one which makes a generic point – is the sheer inefficiency of their corruption as the story unfolded. While in all they may have absconded with $40 billion, by the millennium the take may have diminished to a tenth of that. The devaluation of the rupiah, of which their own greed was the major cause, accounts for much of that diminution. But bad business practices, brazen chutzpah, the use of debt, and the cost of cut-outs all took their toll. Very little 'value added' accrued to the economy by their depredation.[205]

Next door, in the Philippines, a similar story unfolded, only with fewer years of mango corruption. Marcos came to power in 1965 and, in his early years, built the economy, stealing from it along the way but on the whole leaving it in the hands of competent economists. He elicited international support – even for his draconian martial law regime from late 1972 onwards – because of the dramatic economic growth that came with the systematic reforms that were undertaken.

But from 1976, previewing the Suharto family's post-1996 consolidation, Marcos reconstructed the economic system and turned the nation into his own private fiefdom. First he fired Alejandro Melchor, the brilliant chief architect of the growth policies which had brought a resounding increase in trade and industrial sectors.[206] Then he turned the government-run banks into milch cows for his closest friends, already major industrialists and now aspirant billionairess. They got no-risk, uncollateralized loans, with predictable results. His closest friends were given rents from the vast pineapple and sugar industries and allowed to ransack major corporations. As a small example, he used martial law powers to put an excise tax on foreign cigarette filters so that a distant cousin could almost monopolize that industry, accumulate many million dollars, emigrate to Austria and buy a *schloss*. The booming reformist economy of early martial law seized up totally under the crony system; *per capita* income, which had shot up from $514 in 1972 to a high of $688 in 1982, retreated year by year. By 1986 it was back down to $554, barely above its level at the time of martial law's proclamation fourteen years earlier. Marcos had stripped his people naked and put on every single one of his country's expensive robes.

Everything I Wanted to Learn about Corruption I Learned in Nigeria

Nigeria is perhaps the greatest and the saddest example of what can happen to a country when baobab corruption becomes pervasive and of how, once deep corruption becomes a way of life, transition out of it is almost impossible until it has eaten its way to the bottom. Corruption set in at independence, soon became institutionalized, became a way of life when oil began to flow and, in the end, has left the country worse off than if the character-rotting oil had never been found. Between 1966 and 1996 constant *per capita* income increased trivially from $254 to $301, despite the vast inflow of oil revenue – over $25 billion annually at its peak – and notwithstanding the fact that between 1968 and 1977 oil-derived government revenues increased 34 times.[207] Today Nigeria's situation, if dramatically improving under President Obasanjo,[208] is disastrous: not enough food, much disease and, even in the buzzing commercial capital of Lagos, often no electricity. None of this is because Nigeria wasn't dealt a good hand at the outset. The country was probably blessed with more natural resources than any other nation in Africa, with its vast reserves of oil and minerals and its ports.

The ultimate effect of corruption can be seen when it is organized by leaders with absolute power and no scruples whatsoever. In the wake of Sani Abacha's death, it became evident that 'in Nigeria, corruption isn't part of government, it's the object of government,' as one local political scientist said wearily.[209] Gladstone had called the Neapolitan Bourbon state 'the negation of God erected into a system of government'. Not so ambitious but more efficient in their own way, the Nigerian brass pursued more with amazing effect.

Nigeria is one of the world's largest exporters of oil, but it has to import gasoline because Abacha as an act of state let all of the national refineries waste away. Abacha understood that if he shut the refineries down, he would be obliged to ship his crude oil out of the country (stealing a little bit as it left) and then have it shipped back in (stealing almost all of it and giving it to friends and cronies). 'Abacha has increasingly monopolized the trade himself,' John Barman, a London-based oil industry analyst, said. 'There is no deal that does not go through the presidential villa.'[210]

A potentially great nation had been reduced to a racket. About this time, Nigeria became the world capital of the 'Spanish prisoner' scam, filling American letterboxes with bogus offers. Abacha's barbarity can only be matched in impact by Mobutu's decision to allow the roads in Zaïre to go back to jungle to preempt any organized resistance. It can only be matched in brashness, if hardly in scale, by Siaka Stevens of Sierra Leone, who, when told that he needed to privatize government companies, simply founded a private company with one Siaka Stevens as its president and sold everything from himself to himself. Stevens, like Abacha, presumably also made sure he kept his millions outside the country, probably slipping like goldfish through Swiss bank accounts, thereby ensuring his own future and damning his country's.[211]

Corruption in Nigeria is an old story: if Abacha was 'War and Peace', his predecessors scripted 'Gone with the Wind'. In the first republic it was said that Festus Okotie-Eboh, Minister of Finance, charged foreign callers to his office by the minute. In the summer of 1976, after the oil money came sloshing in, Lagos harbour was filled with a mile-long line of ships bearing cement, paying huge demurrage charges, allegedly because a minister found these easiest to tap. The whole baroque monstrosity of theft, not so much an outrage, more a way of life, just kept on rolling, gaining momentum as it pushed the country through the last fifteen years of a perpetually unattainable transition to democracy and transparency. Indeed one Nigerian diplomat has argued – privately – that to blame Abacha for what has happened is to miss the point: President Babangida siphoned off far more money – if over a longer period of time. And he at least has lived to tell of it, indeed by many accounts to buy the 1999 elections that chose a fellow general (and fellow ex-President) to succeed Abacha.

Goats Will Always Eat Where They Are Tethered[212]

Besides the obvious problems that come from having an economy perverted to enrich the powerful, once things start moving in the wrong direction, it's very hard to get them back on track again. Virtuous transitions are much more difficult than the reverse. Corrupt bureaucrats are like headless nails: once you get them in, it is very hard to get them out. As Indonesia is learning – although we are not yet sure whether the energies unleashed by the crisis of 1998 are ready to run down constitutional channels – even near-revolution does not necessarily burn out habits of corruption so deeply engrained. Once corruption becomes everyone's business, it is honesty that looks odd and risky. People who stay in power are people who know how to work the system; in other words, people who know how to be appropriately corrupt (not that they necessarily think of it as corruption). And these people are not going to want to change the ways that have served them so well.

Just look at how resistant even a country like the United States is to campaign finance reform. As we write this, Senator Mitch McConnell has promised a perpetual filibuster to scuttle the legislation, and nearly every Senator seems to be privately hoping that he will succeed. Politicians who are good at dancing around the law, raising vast campaign treasuries, are in power. Similarly, businessmen who have succeeded are used to having financial relationships with the government and know how to operate in that sort of system – largely through lawyers whose day-to-day conduct belies an interest in policy as such. And why would either side want to bite the hand that feeds it?

Thailand and Ghana

Thailand and Ghana also represent corruption in this form, but in significantly different ways. Few countries are thought to be as corrupt as Thailand, yet its economy expanded mightily in spite of it, especially during periods of relative restraint, as was the case when General Kriangsak was Prime Minister and during the long stewardship of General Prem for the King during the 1980s. There is an equilibrium trade-off between growth and shakedown: diminishing the latter surely increases the former.

In absolute terms, the greatest corruption was that of Marshal Sarit: the assets seized on his death amounted to $140 million,[213] a phenomenal sum to squeeze from a peasant society. So far as is known, he kept virtually all his holdings in-country, thus having no impact, save an indirect moral one, on the country's productivity. Moneys siphoned off through lotteries and the like surely fall into the mango corruption category; indeed, Sarit reputedly poured his 'winnings' into numerous productive enterprises around the country which the government promptly whisked away from his stiffening sticky fingers. Surely no single person is directly more responsible – the King at all times getting the larger credit for the stability the Kingdom provided – than Sarit for the Thai economic boom. It is difficult to believe that Marshal Sarit's place in history will be much affected by his corruption, since it is balanced by his enormous role in consolidating the state, launching the modern economy, reconstructing the monarchy, and setting a standard and style of crisp and effective governance (for which he also compensated himself). The important point is that Sarit never took more than the country could easily afford.

Indeed, the top leadership in Thailand was notable, until the mid-1990s, for holding back at least from monumental corruption, even though a few second-echelon military set world-class standards of brigandage – Generals Krit and Arthit, and Field Marshal Dawee. If no national leader, the King aside, quite rivalled Harry Lee for a Spartan and exemplary life,[214] none, apart from Sarit, amassed a world class fortune. General Chatichai started rich and got richer, but his government added more to the wealth of the nation than did any other, and Chatichai's own personal wealth was only .01 per cent of Thai GDP, the relative order of Ross Perot's share of the US economy.[215] It is the Thai style to have farms and a substantial old-fashioned compound in Bangkok, but little ostentation. The new populist government in 1973 stripped Marshal Thanom – Sarit's protégé – and his family of most of their assets, but it is notable that, if they had had large assets in Thailand (and this was not self-evident), they certainly didn't abroad – or didn't spend as if they did. After Sarit, the fear of expropriation and prosecution hung over their heads.

Compare this with the enormous export of Philippine wealth into Marcos's foreign accounts, or the direct augmentation of this hoard by flows from foreign coffers as the price of entry into the Philippine market. Even the other great Thai fortunes, made corruptly by most definitions, did not substantially alter efficient allocation of economic benefits. Field Marshal Dawee Chulasapya was a veteran of the Free Thai, had worked with the OSS to overthrow the Japanese-controlled Second World War government, and was ever after on good terms with the American military, displaying near-genius at promoting projects for Thailand's own infrastructural needs. And he was equally smart at setting up companies to provide the proposed services – 'R and R' for American troops looking for relaxation in Indochina, supplies for the bases, and so forth. The billion or so dollars he made seems nearly all to have stayed very discreetly at home. Like many of his generation, he used his contacts with foreigners, especially Americans, to get in on the ground floor of the structures they were beginning to raise around the world; but this was not as such a misallocation of Thai resources, since the Americans were going to foot whatever bill was required to get the particular job done and to audit it very closely. Only in logging – that environmentally catastrophic activity, which felled Thailand's forests in one generation – can we see Dawee as economically pernicious; and even there, he had no real idea of what the consequences would be.

Thailand also went through several periods of clean government at the top, providing a benchmark for others, to the great detriment of many. It was said jokingly but truly that there were no disincentives to visiting Government House when Anand Panyarachun was Prime Minister: there was parking. Everybody knew what that meant; the lobbyists bearing briefcases of cash knew they were not welcome and didn't even show up. But the brief periods when the brothers MR Seni and MR Kukrit Pramoj were Prime Ministers also provided a benchmark.[216] And although Chuan's first government was brought down in 1995 by a land scam, few would have argued that he was personally corrupt, either, or that his government was as seriously corruptible as the then alternative. The temptations were just too great and his government paid the price. The economy bristled with positive indicators when he returned in 1997, after the meltdown, amid an atmosphere in which clean government was in demand: it was the ultimate proof of his own high standards and of the high regard in which he was held.

But alas: back in 1995 the kind of corruption that destroys growth –

and in this case set off the second greatest economic crisis in world history – was creeping into Thailand: despite those who knew how to steal without debilitating the economy, the foundation was being consumed, as if by termites. By 1996 attitudes had changed and people were becoming enraged by the continual display of wealth and power that had finally emerged at the top in the 'buffet' government of the mid-1990s. Banharn's government had been in power less than a year when the opposition scheduled a very well-researched censure motion against ten ministers. They started with the Prime Minister who, apart from the charges of plagiarism and lies about his ancestry,[217] had 'failed to clarify' allegations of kickbacks offered to government officials by Sweden's Kockums submarine building company. Finance Minister Surakiart Sathirathai was hit by the heaviest charges, starting with his slashing (to a token million) of back taxes amounting to 51 million baht owed by Deputy Prime Minister Montri Pongpanich. The Deputy Interior Minister, Suchart Tancharoen, scion of a fabulously rich Chinese-Thai family, appeared to have cleaned up the most: under his ministerial privileges, land transfers were made to his family worth many fortunes, and his connection with a mysterious Burmese woman involved in illegal logging looked worst of all. Trouble was, no one in knowledgeable circles had any doubt that what was showing was the tip of the iceberg. And within the circles dominated by these ten, no one even tried to deny the charges. It may have been 'government as usual' but it was no longer good enough. Thailand had moved up the ladder. It was now firmly caught up in baobab corruption.

Ghana

Corruption in Ghana started out on a very small scale compared with what came to be seen as *comme il faut* in Africa (and tiny in absolute terms compared with Thailand). But it was in contrast to the high moral tone and aspirations the first Prime Minister and President, Kwame Nkrumah, had set. And the commissions of inquiry set up after his expulsion established beyond any doubt that corruption at very high levels – including the radical socialist Nkrumah himself – was, by the standards of the day, substantial. Krobo Edusei got knowing laughs when he confirmed to the commission that he truly knew what gold bars looked like. Nkrumah had a gold bed and dozens of houses. He also had a new definition of socialism. 'Socialism', he explained, didn't mean that you had to throw your money into the sea. Indeed not, although the Nkrumah government had all but done so. But there was no economic growth in the Nkrumah period, just a lot of show buildings and one great public work financed by the World Bank and a host of other donors: the Volta River Project, the largest enterprise ever undertaken in Africa, whose benefits were nevertheless dependent on a level of ancillary activities which the country was a long way from generating.[218] The soldiers who made the coup against Nkrumah denounced the old order's ripe rottenness with gusto for weeks, or even months. But soon enough army colonels had seized the former cabinet ministers' Mercedes Benzes – or at least their Chevrolets. When Flight Lieutenant Jerry Rawlings executed ex-Presidents-cum-military officers for corruption in 1979, the question was not whether there was evidence thereof, but what were the real reasons for the executions, since everybody at that level was corrupt.

During the 1970s, in particular, Ghana also consistently got its economic decisions wrong in the government's zeal to steal from the state. The most obvious way that this was done was through the manipulation of exchange rates and, in particular, the setting of an artificially high rate. The first problem with an overvalued exchange rate is that it creates a bias against exports in favor of imports. But what an overvalued exchange rate really does is create opportunities for corruption that are apt to keep the regime in power and to self-perpetuate. People who were allowed to purchase goods at the state-fixed phony exchange rate were able to make huge profits. Thus, an import licence was something to be sought with cash – substantial cash – in hand. An overvalued exchange rate also offers tremendous incentives for the creation of a parallel or black market which the government and the police can control as they wish (and which they know they will be paid off for protecting); last of all, it forces people to try to smuggle their goods abroad, again opening the door for corruption on the part of whoever controls the border police. In the case of Ghana, because of the artificial exchange rate, a great number of cocoa farmers had to smuggle their goods across the border; presumably some money was changing hands as that happened.

But Ghana is an important example because there wasn't a pernicious culture of corruption in the country until the late 1990s, for an assortment of reasons – in part because of Ghanaian national pride and desire to escape from the problems engulfing Africa and in part because, while the current government is corrupt, President Rawlings was generally thought, until recently, to be honest. People just don't steal in Ghana the way that they do in Nigeria, and politicians are more honest than in most other countries in Africa. Certainly, the whole country isn't built around the personal enrichment of a ruling élite (with the rest of the country trying to get a share of the tiny bit left over). One of us once got off a bus at the Ghana/Togo border and walked for ten minutes before realizing that he had left his guitar on the bus. Running back he found the guitar on the bus, but the bus driver saw a chance to make a quick dollar.

> 'Did you leave that guitar on the bus?'
> 'Yes.'
> 'Well, I have been watching it; you'll have to pay me twenty dollars.'
> 'The guitar was crammed in between seats, you had no idea it was there.'
> 'Come on, give me ten dollars for taking care of it.'
> 'My friend, this is Ghana, not Nigeria. You aren't supposed to be corrupt here. You're supposed to be nice to Americans and you're not supposed to cheat.'
> 'You're right. We are honest. Go ahead. Bless America and bless Ghana.'

If Rawlings is ever caught stealing blatantly from the state, the bus driver, and thousands of other people in Ghana who have walked away from opportunities to a make a corrupt dollar, are going to be angry. And for good reason, too. Ghana is definitely moving in the right direction, hard as that may be.

All Good Things Go Together

Are global attitudes toward reform in business transactions going to penetrate Thailand and Ghana? It was easy enough to dismiss American legislation against corruption as sanctimony that will only lead to an additional layer of hypocrisy atop the cuts that would simply take a different form. 'The cost of doing business' would continue to be paid by the consumer-customer with the additional cost of hiding it escalating. By the millennium there were signs that this was changing, at least in Thailand. As Amaret Sila-on, a powerful Thai leader at the intersection of business and governance, puts it, 'when Boeing can't offer cuts, it begins to affect everything else'. [219]

Can the hydra-headed monster be tamed? A country like Singapore is simply in circumstances too unusual to provide an operational model. Dash-type corruption will be present in the Third World throughout our lifetimes, persisting as it does at the New York docks and police department. Ironically, corruption of the money politics type may actually be accentuated by the growth of democracy. As a senior government spokesman in Thailand put it, 'It's getting worse. Now there are just so many more mouths to feed, so many more hands out waiting for their share.'

Serious efforts to root out corruption have come – again, like demographic change – at relatively high levels of economic achievement. New York and California taipans bought legislatures in the nineteenth century; periodically, it was said that Delaware had no US senators because the DuPonts were quarrelling. But the progressive movements started soon thereafter and demanded cleaner government. In the new constitution which Thailand made law in 1997, the opportunities for corruption were diminished, it was hoped, by the transparency required of ministers and other high-level government officials with respect to their personal assets so long as they are in office.

It is also possible to root out corruption through the logic of the market. Once corruption is out of the hands of the state, there are often different actors, all trying to make a buck, who will be fighting against one another. If one businessman will only skim 5 per cent off the top, then the businessman who wants to skim 10 per cent off is going to have to lower his price or go out of business. Not exactly what Adam Smith had in mind, but there's a case to be made that it could work. [220]

But corruption may have been made less fashionable by the example and enterprise, and perhaps the threat, of a police general who, having crusaded against it, was made Commissioner of Police in

Thailand's post-meltdown government. General Seri claims never to have taken a bribe – implausible to the point of unnatural, but for the several attempts on his life. In Thailand, the drive against corruption was the first cause to be both serious and popular after the meltdown started, possibly a function of a natural, nation-wide desire to see that no class continued to cut corners at the general expense when everyone else was feeling the pinch so bitterly.

A conversation in 1998 between a senior official much esteemed for integrity, and his graduate-student son, went like this:

'Surely, father, with all of my generation returning to Thailand imbued with ideas of good governance, corruption has to end. We don't want it and can't tolerate it.'

'But it is deeply ingrained in the national consciousness ... ideas change slowly. The wheels within wheels, wherein benefits are passed from one level to another, protect the system. Everybody has, alas, some stake in the existing system.'

'But look at our new government. The Prime Minister is a world apart from his predecessor.'

'True enough. Chuan is clean. Not all the people around him are. Some of the highest have benefited even from the transactions they are supposed to be regulating, those on which the restoration of the financial health of the system are based.'

'Father, we will change all this.'

'I wish you the best of luck.'

Provisions against corruption, as we have seen, were at least a very visible part. A General Seri fan club developed; comic strips, cartoons, and a biography furthered his popularity. Prime Minister Chuan elevated him to the head of the Central Investigation Division and he became a prime feature on national television, hauling bails of pay-off cash into police headquarters and forcing the prosecution of numerous formerly sacrosanct officials. He has gone after governors of the Bank of Thailand and senior bureaucrats involved in land deals on the

Burmese border. Given that Thai people today would agree that their troubles have less to do with their ability to create great wealth than their leaders' determination to skim it, and that General Seri's investigations are manifestly leading toward greater transparency in government, he has become doubly important.

But it *is* changing, as we have seen. Change must be possible in any enduring polity: the notion of bribing an English parliamentarian, heir to rotten boroughs and bought seats though she may be, is surely anathema.

Another example of 'good things going together' lies in the very manner in which even those accused of high corruption do business today. Two Thai social scientists used Narong Wongwan, Prime Minister-designate in 1992, as one of their nine *jao por*, or corrupt godfathers.[221] But there is a logic to high capitalism according to which traditional types of privilege drop along the wayside. One of us travelled throughout Khun Narong's fiefdom of the North for almost a week and found nothing untoward in his investments or business attitudes – even if he drove hard bargains.

Let the Battle Begin

Until rapid economic growth comes to the developing world and brings a higher national consciousness and a rich world of NGOs, there isn't any hope of combating corruption in the form of dash and money politics; rich people will win elections and employees at passport agencies will still demand bribes. But baobab corruption can be combated – and this is what should engage the outside world and patriots inside any developing country. As Kishore Mahbubani, the ranking professional diplomat in Singapore (one of the least corrupt countries in the world and, not surprisingly, also one of the fastest-developing) put it in a list of 'ten commandments' for development, 'Thou shalt acknowledge that corruption is the single most important cause for failure in development'.[222]

What is to be done? Clearly the issue transcends national borders – the Thai crisis spilled over Asian boundaries and set off reverberations in Latin America and Russia – and an interstate organization established to monitor all corruption threatening global stability would be a good idea. Of course, the biggest offenders would be the least likely to ratify such an agreement; for that reason, such a deal is surely a long way off. People should begin laying the groundwork for an agreement, but no one should hold their breath.

But there are short-term steps that can be and are being taken. Already indices have surfaced – like those of the European NGO, Transparency International – ranking countries' corruption. The recurrent and regular ratings of human rights put out by Freedom House have done much to publicize many abuses in that arena, and the US government's ratings have given further emphasis. Ratings count: for investors, bankers, risk analysts, bond-raters. The US government, for example, does not permit itself, without a presidential exception, to extend financial assistance to countries judged at the highest level to spend excessively on their military. The same sort of guidelines could surely be devised for corruption that endangers global stability.

Corruption is a serious problem, but only when politicians are restructuring the state for their own ends, as happened in Thailand, seems to have always happened in Nigeria and is now happening in Burma. This distinction needs to be made and understood so that this kind of pernicious corruption can be stopped. The other forms of corruption, the kinds that float in and out of life in the developing world and will continue to do so until the developing world is developed to something like a Western or Japanese level, should just be left as they are. There are bigger dragons to be slain now.

PART III

CHAPTER 8

Civil Society:
the Main Event

If you had tried to found a Ghanaian chapter of the Sierra Club in 1965, you would have spent more time the next decade studying cinder block walls than unpolluted waterways. Kwame Nkrumah was the only person on the scene allowed any power. Private influence was subversive. Today things are improving. Jerry Rawlings only threatens the people and organizations that he's truly scared of: force is always present, but smart – and courageous – journalists and politicians, playing their cards carefully, survive and build the society.

Thailand is far better. Since 1992, people have been able to form pretty much any kind of organization – and, Lord, have they done so. Organizations aren't yet as strong as in the United States, where they have had generations to develop, but they're growing and, at last look, there were already numerous bodies devoted to protecting obscure animals, distant human rights, and small farmers growing odd crops.

These organizations don't represent all of civil society but they are a key indicator. Civil society is the encouraging human ocean in which swim citizen organizations that encourage people to live as adults, not as stunted children – saying what they want to say and doing what they want to do within ample limits. It should be seen as a dimension of political and economic society. Civil society is not the state or any part of the state's *apparat*. Indeed most of what we now consider as the basics of civil society began as protection *against* the state or any other monopoly of power. As Cohen and Arato argue:

> The political role of civil society ... is not directly related to the control or conquest of power but to the generation of influence through the life of democratic associations and unconstrained discussion in the cultural public sphere.[223]

Or, as Vaclav Havel puts it with his customary eloquence:

> Between the aims of the post-totalitarian system and the aims of life there is a yawning abyss: while life, in its essence, moves toward plurality, diversity, independent self-constitution and self-organization, in short, towards the fulfillment of its own freedom, the post-totalitarian system demands conformity, uniformity and discipline.[224]

The functions which add up to civil society may always have been around – in a less variegated form perhaps. Tocqueville, writing in the 1830s, noted the tendency toward association as one of the central manifestations of American life. We also find that in Britain, as early as George III, the Crown, conscious of a certain unliked Germanity, was subsidizing what we today would call civil society in ways very reminiscent of the present Ninth Reign in Bangkok.[225] Despite these roots, the reality of civil society and its systematic study have arisen in parallel with NGOs and have been accelerated extraordinarily by the internet – proving Thorsten Veblen's point that more recently developed societies move faster in embracing the new because they have less old-modernity to unlearn.[226] Civil society, after all, assumes a certain level of interaction: meeting places, membership lists, something more than the ascriptive society offers. Herodotus, child of the arguing Greek world, pointed to the absence of market places in Oriental metropolises.

But an understanding of civil society must also go beyond the established distinction between *gemeinschaft* and *gesellschaft* to add the subtle bonds within a community: the cultural traditions, religious litanies, rules of lineage – whatever goes to create a self-perceived 'we group'. Lee Kuan Yew can well say that the United States has no civil society and mean it, in at least one sense. After all, civil society is more than just the number of organizations that operate within a country's borders; it is also found in the day-to-day interactions of people and in the bonds they feel towards each other, towards their communities and towards their nation.

A classic example of the process at an early stage manifested splendidly in the Philippines. In 1983, when the opposition leader Benigno Aquino was assassinated, international organizations converged on Manila. With the Filipino Catholic Church in the front line as Manila's bishop, Cardinal Sin, summoned the faithful to the streets, and with the mainstream Filipino army and its nominal chief General Ramos not far behind, it is small wonder that change came wondrously. Having overthrown Marcos, the serious NGOs looked for further vocation, after the media had packed up and passed on. The drought in the Visayas and the subsequent near-destruction of the economy of these once-prosperous islands gave these organizations a deeper role. Before long NGOs were part of the process throughout the archipelago, but now they were in a position to reinforce traditional community beliefs and values.

The Ilocano élite from Pangasanan, governing the Philippines from 1992 to 1998, sought to bring a vast industrial investment to Iligan Bay in their home territory. The fishermen resisted, gathering almost overnight into environmental NGOs. 'These people haven't had an increase in their standard of living in several generations ... what is their problem?' asked President Ramos's close associate, the formidable General Magno. Their 'problem' was that they were already suffering too much pollution from rapid industrialization, and did not wish to see their deep-rooted way of life evaporate completely, no matter how great the economic benefit, even possibly to them. A similar process is under way in South Africa as the thousands of organizations that sprang up to defeat apartheid look for new meaning and useful work.

Civil Society in Thailand

It is an index of Thai dynamism that there was so *little*, not only of civil society but even of state organization, until so very recently. Only towards the end of the nineteenth century did the sleepy monarchy in Bangkok awake to the need to consolidate the country or lose it to colonialism; and then – reawakened in the 1960s, with US prodding – to assert its authority against a threat centred on Vietnam, this time the communists instead of the French. Before this, there was no civil society – no institutional connection beyond an irregular tax collector – beyond the confines of the village. Not only was the structure of governance, asserted from the centre, plainly lacking, but there had always been enough land to prevent the development of feudalism and to preempt the organizations that would rally against it. No dukes, no mafia.

Even when central organization did start to take on substance, it grew very slowly compared with the other changes that made up the astonishing overall acceleration of Thai society. William Klausner, the distinguished *farang* student of Thai culture, has evoked his own culture shock at returning in the booming 1990s to the village he had lived in as a young Yale graduate during the mid-1950s – in the poorest area of the poor Northeast, when there was no running water or electricity – to find villages paved over as Mercedes parking lots. Very great changes, very few years: no wonder that parallel and intermediate institutions were crowded out of the light by activities which could duplicate established developed-world activity. To steal from Tolstoy again, all core industrial activities of a certain type are alike, but social reactions to them are intensely individual.

In other words, it all happened in a very few short years and it's no wonder that civil society was so slow to develop that attitudes at the centre toward intermediate organizations were sceptical at best. Even the organization of labour in the cities did not keep pace. As Pasuk and Baker explain, there were forces countering any movement that labour made towards organization. The first was that vast amounts of labour – mostly Chinese – continued to arrive in Thailand throughout the country's early stages of growth. These new workers reduced the leverage of organized labour. If a thousand new people are going to move in to replace you the minute you go on strike, you had better be a flexible negotiatior. The second reason was the élite's belief that labour was a central threat to their authority and to the economic growth that had become the chief goal of the new economy – and the trump card that kept them in power.[227] In the end, the élite was proved right – the pie did expand so incredibly rapidly that there was more for labour later than there could conceivably have been had workers had a fair return on their contributions in the 1960s and 1970s – and so we may have to temper our sense of the equity involved. When the Labour Relations Act of 1975 legalized unions, the new workers took their dividends in undammed prosperity, not class consciousness. Only in government institutions, with a special interest in visible harmony, did unionization flourish.

Thailand during the Boom Years

What peasants driven into slums dream of can make life difficult for the dominant class. The boom that gave people three meals a day, saved their babies from dysentery and brought electricity flickering into their shacks was like a whale beneath a rowboat, upheaving the high pretences of the old world. Historically, 'King, country, *Sanggha*' had filled the horizon. But as the economy boomed the country into the 1990s, the *Sanggha* (or Buddhist brotherhood) was counting less and less, the King no longer directly governed, and the army had to work at being respectable – all the factors that traditionally had ordered Thailand were losing substance in the new light. There was general loyalty to Thailand as a concept and as a reality. The problem was what was in between. Within the Sino-Thai community, Confucian principles still had enough clout to provide intermediary institutional linkage, but as traditional society broke down at dizzying speed in the country, as a whole, it was less clear what could replace *Kamnan*, village headmen, and *Sanggha*. The country had, in Chai-anan's memorable perception, become 'ungovernable': perhaps orderly government would work for those who reasoned processes through – only human societies do not so operate. 'A rational army would desert,' said Frederick the Great. Or, as Hilaire Belloc said of the water spider, 'But if it ever stopped to think … how he can do it, he would sink.' Conflict is unavoidable, Chai-Anan went on, because there is a clear state-versus-the-people relationship – there are few remaining restraints effective enough to keep the disenfranchised or non-allied members of Thai society under control.[228]

Sulak Sivaraksa, one of the most vocal opponents of present Thai development, quoted an old Thai saying:

> 'There is rice in the fields, there are fish in the water.' This saying does not simply describe the abundance of food resources available to the populations of the region in the past, it also aptly describes the simple life of self-sufficiency that existed among village communities in Southeast Asia before the advent of colonialism and neo-colonialism…. [Communities] were governed and protected by their own institutions: the family, the community and the seniority system.[229]

Sulak goes on to argue that modernization threw everything into upheaval, creating a temporary vacuum and lack of structure. But this was a particularly modern gap, to be filled at least partially by a particularly modern response: the rapid growth of NGOs. From the beginning, these NGOs have greatly influenced short-term issues (Sulak coordinates an environmental NGO which has protected forest resources successfully) but they have also woven new societal bonds. For a time the parallel development of corporate power was so rapid that the titans could sneer; but as the meltdown made many people dependent on NGOs for a livelihood and washed a more humane government into power, the titans were somewhat humbled. No longer were NGOs the butt of a rather tiresome family of jokes all starting from fact that 'ngo' was the Thai word for 'stupid'.

Civil Society in Ghana

Ghana was born of civil society. J. B. Danquah, founding leader of the nationalist movement, used structures implanted during colonialism to enlarge the area of autonomy. His party received substantial assistance from British anti-colonial organizations but Danquah's fatal decision, all too literally, was to invite an original, impassioned but not too thoughtful Gold Coast expatriate to return from the United States and take over organizing the party. Kwame Nkrumah, organizationally astute, wasted no time in pulling Danquah's party right out from under him and then, independence won, treated every alternative nucleus as a centre of resistance to his rule. Only nine years after independence, if you rubbed Kwame Nkrumah (or anyone whom the Osagyefo supported) the wrong way you could, and probably would, be detained in prison without trial.[230] Nkrumah jailed Danquah, one of the most intellectually respected men in Africa, not for violating the law, but for crossing him politically. In 1965 Danquah died in chains.

Nkrumah saw political development as a threat, not because he was a tyrant at heart like Mobutu or Stalin, but because he genuinely believed that he was at a higher level of consciousness than the rest of society. He believed that he knew what people would really want could they but obtain optimal awareness as certified by one who knew. And so, if people disagreed with him it was not because they might be wrong but because they had failed to understand themselves correctly (Thoreau said that if someone came to his house to do him good, he would run for his life). It is this argument that Lenin deployed so effectively to justify his destruction of all serious opposition. He 'knew' that he was working to fulfil the true wishes of the Russian proletariat, even as he knew that most of the Russian proletariat was opposed to him. Undoubtedly, Nkrumah wanted what was best for Ghana and for Africa and hence, by all too easy a transition, what was best for Africa was what he wanted. Such blind and egotistical creatures as stood in his way – by disputing his arithmetic, for example – had to be silenced. This was not a formula for lively civic debate.[231]

After Nkrumah was thrown out, the next great failure of civil society in Ghana came during the rule of Colonel Acheampong, who saved the state from his predecessors to deliver it to himself and to his cronies. Civil society wasn't going to do him any good. Kleptocracies only thrive when there is no one to call them by that name: the corollary of this has been the central African problem for the past 40 years. Men come into power because it is a way to access wealth and they don't want anyone to interrupt them while their fat hands are in the cookie jar. Theft makes enemies, especially of rival robbers; regimes fall, but the river of corruption takes the same turns.

Until the late 1970s, Ghana could not even develop a 'we group' – the bare minimum of civil society. Finally, it did show precisely that. After six years in power President Acheampong had stumbled over one threshold after another, whether in politics, economics, or foreign policy. It was still possible to make things worse, and he succeeded. The most accomplished Ghanaians indeed endeavoured, at great personal risk, to resist the greasy slide. A 'People's Movement for Freedom and Justice' was formed by William Ofori-Atta, a royal Akan and independence leader; Komla Gbedemah, the most competent of Nkrumah's ministers (dismissed early on, of course); and the popular and dashing young General Afrifa, who had spearheaded the 1966 coup. They were actually able to force a referendum to establish a new republic – immediately rendered meaningless, however, when Acheampong decided that ballots would be counted in military and police centres.

With the new rules for counting, of course, his proposed 'government of unity' won, and immediately began arresting opponents of his

Supreme Military Council.[232] But Acheampong had miscalculated. Students boycotted schools, the Association of Recognized Professional Organizations called its members out on strike, banks and hospitals closed, and finally, on 5 July 1978, an almost anticlimactic coup arrested Acheampong in favor of General Fred Akuffo. Akuffo was not a tyrant; he was too busy stealing, with more energy and less shame even than his predecessors. The disillusionment and cynicism of this sequel to heroic goodwill did much to sterilize the energies of hope and enterprise necessary to awaken a civil society; and then, as the fabric of the state caved in under Akuffo's rottenness, there emerged the purposeful positive tyranny of Jerry Rawlings.

Rawlings handed over to the civilians; found them corrupt; brutally returned; and finally, if tentatively, began to concede a compromise and ambivalent liberty – in part because he does seem to possess a strand of cranky idealism. More importantly, he knew in the early 1980s, as he knows now, that to stay in power, he had to concede something – 'less power but more lasting' is the motto of the tyrant in Aristotle. If his power did not last, he was likely to end up before the same firing squad to which he had dispatched his three surviving predecessors.

In Thailand, a thousand flowers bloomed in the aftermath of the uprising of 1973. The country had leaders in the wings, from the old élite, who could at least cope while the forces bottled up under the economically progressive but politically oppressive former regime moved into the political arena. Students wrote passages from St Augustine on public monuments ('What is a state, but a band of robbers, organized to pillage the people....') and moved into the bureaucracy to sharpen its cut. Organizations, from labour unions to political parties, sprang up everywhere. The old clock of the epoch of Western power and protection was running down; American forces were moving out; South Vietnam was foundering; no wonder the military feared that the students had gone too far. By 1976 a coup had installed the narrow and repressive civilian functionary, Thanin Kraivixian, a disaster from the start. A student effigy thought to be a likeness of the Crown Prince at Thammasat University gave the military the excuse for another bloodbath, which prompted over a thousand students to take to the hills and join the flickering Communist guerrilla movement.

Over and over Thailand has shown a genius for renewal, change and growth. The reforms enacted in 1973–6 empowered many new elements and gave them a sense that they could meet the new world with a confidence that came from within. Even so the radicals had gone too far, given the regional environment. The military leaders of the mid-1970s saw that their coup was self-defeating. Into this vacuum of solutions there rode a remarkable 'man on a white horse' who articulated the problems both literally and symbolically. General Kriangsak was popular and had followers throughout the nation, including in the press and academe. Accepting that political reform, which he had long advocated, would have to go forward,[233] he also understood that it was not realistic for civilians to govern – yet. And so, the choice was between him, on the one hand, and ideological zealots like Thanin or the very visible hard-line generals on the other. His coup was popular, but crucially he did not stop at throwing the rascals out; he moved straight on to reinforce the still largely inchoate alternatives to oligarchy and barrack-room bullying. The students in the hills started drifting back under amnesty; less than three years later, when Kriangsak could not command a majority in the parliament he had revivified, he showed how seriously he took it by conclusively and undramatically resigning.[234]

Thailand's lack of civil society pointed to the military as both problem and solution. It must be understood that in the Thai subconscious the military has a special place and meaning. Historically generals have had interchangeable civilian and military roles, and well before today the 'we vs them' mentality so characteristic of civilian–military relationships in Third World societies was notably underdeveloped in Thailand – although since 1992 civilian pressure for a curtailment of military influence has mounted. The military held the commanding heights for so long – from 1932 until 1973 with only a few truly civilian intervals – that it has been hard for them to forgo privileges so long enjoyed, or to appreciate the interrelationship of political and economic development. Small wonder that Prime Minister Chuan, in a reform-minded government, took the defence portfolio for himself.

But a critical mass of the military leaders *did* appreciate the significance of the new path – something that would not have happened in Ghana, where being a soldier has a more specific, less negotiable value than it does in Thailand. General Kriangsak would certainly attribute some measure of his own 'growth curve' to a long association with Americans and America, which brought substantial benefits to Thailand so long as political development could be seen as a spill-over. He also had a good working knowledge of the gap between traditional Thai society and what modernity demanded, and realized that government, let alone the army, could not bridge this gap.

The brass caught on to the need for civil society in Thailand rather more easily than they grasped the interrelation of political freedom and economic development. In the 1980s the economy was roaring but politics were still Wild West, with no fabric of alternative institutions that could challenge the unlovely mutual understanding of business-men and military men which was profiting greatly from the boom. But Anand Panyarachun, one of the greatest of Thailand's post-war statesmen, spotted the link earlier than most: in 1992, although an appointed Prime Minister without a political base, he demoted the four senior officers most closely identified with the bloody con-frontation with reform-minded students and the middle class that previous spring. This was an act of great political courage in a society where the military has deep roots and where the people have no instinctive antagonism to men on horseback. Asked for the philo-sophical sources of his actions, he replied that of the many and different swift-developing countries, those which failed to make equally rapid political strides came soon enough to economic crisis – look at Mexico.[235] In fact during his first spell as Prime Minister, after a military coup installed him as titular leader, he seized the nettle and set more reforms in motion than had been initiated in decades; in two years the government moved more legislation than in the entire period of General Prem's leadership, which spanned almost the entire 1980s.[236]

Although, as we shall see, the Thai at first used their constitutional reforms as a counterpoint to their economic problems in the midst of the economic meltdown of 1997, by 1998 there was a deep appreciation among large segments of the educated public, as well as among progressive-minded technocrats, that avoidance of further and future economic disasters depended on substantial overhaul of the polity. They had the compelling example of the Indonesian riots nearby to spur them on. Yet it must be admitted that within traditional centres of power, élite elements were not so ready to forgo their control and open up the Thai system to transparency, accountability, and popular, non-bureaucratic participation. It was going to be a long fight for leaders like Chuan and key followers like Foreign Minister Surin to accomplish their stated aims. It would never have occurred to the moral philosopher Adam Smith that getting and spending could go forward autonomously of general sound principles in the overall society.

The real weakness of democracy in Thailand has always been the thinness of commitment to democracy itself, as an idea. It is, after all, a peculiarly Western notion that grew up alongside Western social institutions that reinforced it; it is more a way of doing things, situationally specific in some ways, than an idea in itself. There is an ancient drama in Thailand, *Khun Chang-Khun Phaen,* in which Wantong, a young lady, is attracted to young and handsome Khun Phaen, but can't resist falling back, from time to time, on old and corrupt Khun Chang. Substitute Bangkok for Wantong, and democracy and military rule for Khun Phaen and Khun Chang, and one has the dilemma of Thai democracy.

How Civil Society Fosters Development

For poor countries, the development of civil society is a central engine of growth, not just a derivative consequence. Every single country in sub-Saharan Africa would be materially energized by a stronger voluntarist participatory order. As we have argued previously, development is a dynamic reciprocation of economic and non-economic factors. Our first argument, an easy one, is that at almost any level of development, civil society nourishes and underwrites its community's non-economic aspects. Where there is a developed civil society, the people have an exponentially increased opportunity to attain freedoms. Furthermore, in countries just beginning to grow, civil society helps to keep development in perspective. Poor-nation governments set on heroic industrialization are unlikely to have their minds on destitute unemployed, mercury-fouled waterways or rented judges, precisely the issues on which another voice is most needed. True, civil society, by its very nature, means there are alternative centres of power, and *that* means confrontation between those in control of policy decisions and those wanting part of the action. This is healthy.

In Africa, as Ghanaian dissident Kwesi Pratt said to one of us, 'The problem ... is that we have not been able to compete on the level of ideas.'[237] Because there has been no free speech in Africa for so long, people have not been able to discuss and decide what most urgently is to be done. Military leaders have been making decisions – although seldom about recognizable issues – and, even on those rare occasions when they have their nation's needs at heart, have only rarely had the information to be able to do what was remotely effective.

The second, more difficult, argument is that, in the beginning, civil society is an economic force in itself. In a transparent state, the claimant of rents or privileges is constrained by the lowering of the threshold of tolerance for corruption. We are not talking absolutes; there is corruption in Switzerland and England, civil societies *par excellence*. The issue here is the connection between political reform and economic betterment. In the absence of the ongoing pursuit of good government and continuing political reform, rent seekers can continue to buy access to foreign exchange, non-competitive governmental purchases, or criminal freedom from factory inspection, and there is no institutional watchdog to check up. It is in the very process of political reform that these abuses are highlighted. Witness the *reformasi* in Indonesia in 1998: political challenges led successively to economic questioning, political demands and economic demands. There was no moment, in the strangely moving run-up to Suharto's resignation, when press headlines on economic issues did not alternate with thunderings for political reform, one hinging on the other.

If one single event precipitated the whole Asian meltdown – sufficient in and of itself to have signalled the problem in time for it to be finessed – it was the bankruptcy of the Bangkok Bank of Commerce in 1996, more than a year before the crisis. Indeed, there was hardly anything conclusively economic about that phantasmagoric extremity at any point. The politicians who set up the bank – not as abuse, in the words of a major Thai political-economic player, but as outright fraud – used their positions in parliament and various ministries to create an unobstructed channel for virtually uncollateralized loans to dubious businesses and safe havens. *Everyone* in the system knew that the bank was a fraud, but no one could blow the whistle because of the enormity of the power of those protecting the bank – after all, the Prime Minister himself was known as the cash machine of Suparn Buri province.

Civil Society as the Counter to Corporate Society

The institutions of civil society are protean; the need for them is felt not only as a check upon government excess but as an obstacle to mercantile greed. Corporations, said Lord Chancellor Thurlow, are very dangerous things, lacking as they do behinds to be kicked and souls to be damned – and existing, he might have added, to make money. Given free rein, as tends to happen early in capitalist industrial development – the rather scary stage that Adam Smith called 'primitive accumulation' – the strong will force the weak (which means most players at that point in history) to go under in larger or smaller numbers. Factories are built on sacred land and pollution controls are disregarded. Children really will work fourteen hours a day amid dangerous machines, as the market is reported to dictate. Bolshevik impertinences like calls for factory legislation deserve, and are likely to be met by, the deployment of troops. Nike may well hire child labour, but we have all known executives who would hire slave labour if they could (and many governments would certainly offer it as an incentive to investment if they could get away with it). The only reason that they don't is the pressure put on them, at home and abroad, by civil society. As an ad in the *Economist* a few years back said, 'You can't get good employees for less than a dollar a day. Yes you can. The Yucatan.'

In America, as we have noted elsewhere, political office is disproportionately held by those wealthy enough to underwrite their campaigns. This is bad enough. But at least the motive in large part is civil and civic honour, not furtherance of economic objectives, and there are serious checks on such tendencies. As we wrote in the last chapter, corruption comes in many forms, some far more pernicious than others.

In Third World societies the democratic process – where it exists – all too often operates in reverse. As we have argued before, in America, money sets out to shape policies; in Thailand, and most of the Third World, political power sets out to make money. There is a case for defining a politically developed nation as one in which Burke's generalization that wealth and power are inseparable, wealth obtaining power or power wealth, is implicitly but no longer blatantly true. Thai liquor barons get concessions from the government, which consequently lowers the liquor tax, part of which will come around as further corrupt money to enrich the liquor barons with more money to bribe and support other parties. Whereas political diversification has traditionally been a product of economic diversification, in Thailand it is the reverse – next time round the beer baron gets a distilling licence.[238] Civil society is the check on this kind of corrupt feedback loop.

Civil Society: the Long-term Brake

In 1957 Simon Kuznets gave a celebrated lecture arguing that societies that were just beginning to develop would have very large income inequalities; countries that were in the middle stage of development would have much more equal income distribution; and countries that were rich would return to relatively unequal distribution. This theory has been adapted to describe environmental degradation: the countries that have no money are too poor to destroy their environments; countries that are very rich start to care about their environments; the only countries that are apt to plunder their natural resources excessively are countries like Thailand, that are in the middle. We believe that perhaps the most apt analysis is to adapt this curve to civil society. Countries like Burma, that have no civil society, are not going to grow at all. Countries that have developing civil societies, like Thailand or Botswana, are going to grow the fastest. Countries like the United States, that have very advanced civil societies, where people form interest groups that battle back and forth with each other, are not going to grow quite as fast.

It is intuitively obvious why, in its earliest stages, a civil society encourages development; in its later stages, however, there is similarly little doubt that civil society is actually a hindrance to economic growth – and, at certain points, to development in its gross sense. This is no argument for a whiff of grapeshot. Again, we're not arguing for repression, just that sometimes all good things can't go together. The central problem with a civil society stems from, and can best be understood by looking at, the 'tragedy of the commons'. Consider a field that is offered to the public for grazing. Every farmer has an incentive to let her personal cattle graze on the field even though her cattle eat up the grass, deplete the soil and make it harder and harder for every cow to survive. Every year, because of the number of cattle on the field, the quality of the soil decreases and the field can support fewer and fewer cattle. Yet, even while this happens, each individual farmer still has an incentive to send as many of her cattle as she can out there. The tragedy of the commons is that the sum of private interests is often not the public interest.

Now, move this example to the case of politics and civil society and take the example of air pollution. It is in everyone's best interest for air pollution to be eliminated, but it is in no one's best interest to take the initiative, do the research, do the lobbying and dedicate a lot of effort to fight to eliminate air pollution. The impact that one person can have is very small indeed and, even if the effect were large, eliminating air pollution really wouldn't do much good for any one person.

The result of this problem, as the late Mancur Olson has so eloquently argued,[239] is that no one in a given society is going to end up fighting for the common good (it is just not worth anyone's while); they are all going to be fighting for their own personal good. Move up one level and the interest groups that are going to form in society are the kind of interest groups that can maximize the gains to their own particular constituency. The end result, ironically, is a dog-eat-dog civil society. Olson brilliantly explained why Japan and Germany, devastated by war, could grow so rapidly, while England, encrusted by a highly developed and focused civil society, stagnated for a quarter of a century after the war.

Consider the location of hazardous waste facilities. In our society some level of hazardous waste is inevitable; at the very least, there is a certain amount of hazardous waste that we have already created and now need to store somewhere. What normally happens is that a government or administrative agency proposes a certain site. Soon thereafter, the community in the proposed site will be in uproar. They will argue, among other things, that the site is scientifically unsound; that the decision was made prematurely; that vast numbers of people will die; and so on. Often they are correct, but they always make the same points anyway.

The result of this conflict is that the decision on where to move toxic waste is generally based simply on which community will make the least fuss, or which community has the least political power and can least threaten the company or agency responsible for moving the waste. The decision is rarely based simply on the scientific evidence or on what would actually be best for the country.[240] Here a strong civil society has pushed the waste from where it should be put to where it can most easily be put.

Or consider another example – the American Association of Retired People (AARP). The AARP is one of the most organized interest groups in America, in large part because its members have more time on their hands and are willing to make the minimum sacrifices (signing petitions, sending in dues) that members of most other interest groups evade. The result is that the AARP is able to exert a considerable influence over political decisions in the USA; not surprisingly, they tend to skew political decisions in favor of the old. This is why there has been almost no effort to reform social security over the past fifty years, even though to do so would obviously be to the benefit of most of the country.

The end result of all of these factors is that as a society develops and becomes more and more free, and more and more accepting of such coalitions, growth will necessarily slow. As the interest groups continue to grow, things will slow down even more. Consider the case of Thailand. At the beginning of Thailand's modern era, when power began to be dispersed from the crown down (starting in 1932), there were only a few interest groups that were able to influence national policy – namely businesses. And small wonder, given the sixty-year growth trajectory of the Thai economy. As Thai society has progressed, these initial groups have lost power, wealth has been distributed among more groups and economic development has become still more complicated. As the number of interest groups increases, growth will continue to diminish.

It is very important at this point to make clear that we are not making an argument for totalitarianism or any sort of society where interest groups and coalitions are banned. There are three reasons for this. The first is that a free society is a good in and of itself. A society that allows us to picket a corporation planning to dump sludge in my backyard is better than a society that will throw us in jail for doing just that. Second, in a society that bans interest groups, the most likely scenario is that a few interest groups will survive and that these interest groups will be particularly hostile to the needs of the many. Even the most absolute dictators in history have proved quite willing to take bribes from large businesses.

Third, while an ideal government might arguably be a totalitarian state that had perfect information and that was only concerned about its people, this never happens. Not only have totalitarian and authoritarian governments been mainly concerned with self-preservation, but traditionally they have also proved to be the most irresponsible when it comes to accepting interest group lobbying and policies that benefit the few and hurt the many – see the history of Latin America. Furthermore, one of the problems with any sort of totalitarianism is that information flows are generally terrible: information upwards is blocked, decrees go downward on dictatorial inspiration. Perhaps the best evidence in support of this contention is that no society with a strong civil society has ever suffered a famine. As Amartya Sen has shown conclusively, famines are almost never caused by absolute food shortages but by lack of information and failures of distribution.[241] In a country with a developed civil society, there will always be a newspaper to report the potential onset and there will always be groups to help in the relief effort. And anyway, it is an absolute good that civil society empowers the disadvantaged and powerless – landless peasants, child labour, AIDS sufferers, women – all those whose interests have been neglected, abused, extorted, exploited. Even if only as a safety valve, participation by these groups is a positive good in any society.

Liberty and Economic Growth

In his 1957 essay, 'Two Concepts of Liberty', Isaiah Berlin lays out a very important distinction between 'positive' and 'negative' liberty. Positive liberty is the liberty to do certain things, to have enough to eat, to sleep late on Sundays. Negative liberty is being free from coercion, from interference. Free speech is negative liberty, as is one's freedom to stay out past midnight or to drink wine. A nation with a developed civil society is certainly one in which there is a large amount of negative liberty. Positive liberty is a critical goal of development, one that we have discussed indirectly earlier in this book, but it isn't necessary for a civil society except to a certain minimal extent (if people are starving left and right they aren't going to be able to form any sort of civil society).

One of the classic arguments that is levelled against civil society, and democracy in general, is that there is a trade-off between these two types of liberty. One must have a strong leader to set the policies right; poor nations cannot afford the luxury of political rights – so the argument goes. The commonly cited examples are Singapore and China, as nations that have grown quickly without freedom,[242] and India and Russia (during the last seven years) as nations that have offered their citizens relative freedom and stubbed their economic toes.[243]

For every extreme case, however, there is usually a counter-example. Botswana is perhaps the best – the country with the most negative liberty in Africa also has the highest economic growth rate. More importantly, most of the data support the argument that economic liberty and economic growth go hand in hand. Yes, there are outliers, but we will get to them later: the general data forcefully conclude that more civil liberty goes hand in hand with economic growth. Lee Kuan Yew can use his country as an example by offering a few anecdotes; his opponents can argue with stacks upon stacks of data.[244]

Why is this the case? After all, as that great economist Partha Dasgupta has written, rightly (as usual) we think: 'It is possible that political and civil rights would not be awarded priority in a hypo-thetical social contract written by citizens of a poor society.' Perhaps it would be right to conclude that a perfectly benign dictator, with complete access to all information and the ability to inspire people to want to work to build their nation, would be a country's ideal leader. Unfortunately, that's never the case. I'm not perfect, you're not perfect and Robert Mugabe isn't perfect – in fact some say he has become a corrupt thug. A country that has a civil society and that allows people to have ownership of the state, to feel as though they have a stake in development, is the kind of country that is likely to grow quickly. And that's the kind of state you have with democracy and political freedom; it's not the kind of state you have with a dictator.

Asian Values: Do They Exist?

Part of this question involves whether or not liberal democracy and civil society follow inevitably upon a certain level of material develop-ment. 'Give me liberty or give me wealth', the pundits wrote when the debate on 'Asian values' was at its height. Lee Kuan Yew would of course lay it down that liberal democracy and civil society are antithetical to the trajectory that Asia has and will naturally flow on. Or, at least, that liberal democracy is far from inevitable. With regard to civil society, the Senior Minister would have us change the definition completely, to a society that is civil and respecting. As he put it in a 1995 *Foreign Affairs* article, what you see in America is 'the breakdown of civil society'.[245]

On the other side of the coin people like Francis Fukuyama argue that civil society enables all citizens to satisfy three Platonic needs of the soul: 'a desiring part, a reasoning part and a part [Plato] called Thymos, or spiritedness'. To Fukuyama, all societies will inevitably move to liberal democracy, and correspondingly to civil society, in part because other forms of state organization suppress this funda-mental need.[246] Fukuyama's theory is flawed, but salient and useful.[247]

Our view, not surprisingly, is somewhere between Lee's and Fukuyama's, although it's much closer to the latter. For one thing, Asian values aren't really Asian. As Amartya Sen has demonstrated, Confucius was quite complex in the actions he prescribed for people dealing with authority. When Confucius was asked what someone should say to a leader when he had bad news, he responded, 'Tell them the truth'. As Sen has pointed out, that wouldn't really be wise in Beijing.[248]

Second, the people who are putting forward the Asian values argu-ment are far from disinterested and, while this is not an absolute litmus test, it is important. Lee Kuan Yew may well believe in Asian values, but his circle also wants to remain pre-eminent in Singapore, and he knows that by putting forth this argument the People's Action Party (PAP) can justify political repression. On the other side of the fence, leaders like Aung San Suu Kyi, who obviously have a personal interest in democracy coming to Asia, certainly disagree with Lee's thesis.

Furthermore, this debate over Asian values isn't new. Indeed, exactly the same points were made to justify tyranny in Africa in the early years after colonialism. The truth is that tyrants always want to justify their rule (and often they really believe the arguments they make). Lee Kuan Yew has been given a very large stage because his country has done things right. In response to the question whether there are African values, K. L. Busia, the one-time Prime Minister of Ghana, said:

In the last analysis, the concept of an African personality is a political myth; but for that reason it can have a strong emotional appeal and profound social consequences. There have already been extravagant abuses of the concept. It has been appealed to to justify undemocratic practices and ruthless steps toward the establishment of one-party rule, and to excuse such patent injustices as the arbitrary arrest of political figures and their imprisonment without trial.[249]

So, Asian values aren't real; they are just a justification for a form of government that has served its leaders well and, in some cases like that of Singapore, has even served the people well. If tyrants ever take over all of Europe, we will start hearing about European values, the intrinsic tendency for everyone to act like Napoleon, and so on. The notion that in Asia emphasis is placed on the group or the family rather than on the individual is just a case of mistaken centuries. So it was, too, with obvious cultural differences, in Europe prior to the Enlightenment. Civil society is gaining on tyranny and it's going to take more than the State Law and Order Restoration Council to turn it back.

CHAPTER 9

Second Chances and Momentum

Development, like life, isn't linear. It's not as though countries get going, keep going and never stop going. Things fall apart, economies collapse, civil society withers. But just as people with strong education, work ethics and support networks are apt to pick up the pieces and move on after a collapse, a country that is fundamentally sound can get it back together too. Plus, countries have one thing on us: they seldom die. David Landes, speaking specifically with reference to the consequences of colonialism, reminds us that 'in the long sweep of history, this is the heart of the matter: *down is not out'*.[250]

Nevertheless one of us, shaken then by how far down Ghana had slid in the 1970s, remembers Professor Robert West's grim reply – that 'we had no idea how much further they could go'. For Nigeria and Congo, too, and for a long train of others, his words were prophetic. Nonetheless they *do* get second chances – look at Thailand after the meltdown. But they don't get clean slates; they have to build on the pieces that have been left behind, for better or for worse. And, when it comes to Africa, it is definitely for worse. In most countries, the governments in power are unable to accumulate legitimacy, encourage innovation or preside over material improvement. Unless the whole relationship between the state – ever more a euphemism for 'the powerful of the moment' – and the people changes, a second chance only forces the need for a third chance, which will grimly require a fourth, and so on.

Perhaps the best example of this eternal regression to greater disaster is Nigeria, a country with vast natural endowments that have incited successive kleptocratic regimes to pillage, leaving it as likely to prosper as an apple seed is to take root in an empty tin can. Even though the new leaders headed by President Obasanjo are intelligent angels by comparison with their predecessors, there is still a whirlpool of ethnic conflict, ever shadowed by prodigies of corruption and rank with blood and oil. In the week before Obasanjo's inauguration, the outgoing generals sapped the state of five of its remaining eight billion dollars of reserves. In Nigeria the state is an entire baobab grove, the roots of which have burst apart the foundations of society while the insatiable trunks strangle all above-ground initiative. Even for the best-hearted leadership, the charnel house of redeemed pasts which is the history of independent Nigeria is going to be a hideous obstruction to all enterprise and honesty, let alone goodwill. The roots of the baobab shatter all coherence.

Nigeria is a special case only in the scale of its slippage. Virtually no country got it right from the start and continued to grow consistently, to develop and to learn. Every country needs at least one second chance. An inventory shows only one absolutely clear case of unbroken economic and political development: Singapore, a small island forced from the Malaysian union into independence against all anticipation, had to make an ultimately triumphant virtue of necessity. After this inauspicious and humiliating beginning, living well has proved the best of revenges. Singapore has boomed; opposition has become easier and the state less fearsome. Botswana may well have the second-best record, and a better one politically, although its growth has been on a different scale from Singapore's (but then, it's mostly desert). Japan's hundred and twenty years of success have been counterpoised by cosmic disasters – the great depression, the Second World War and the current decade-long waterlogging. The United States fought a great civil war, and reeled under two great depressions. The higher the success the more unanticipated the risks: the hard choices simply rephrase themselves, never identical and never easy. Most development theory addresses itself to how countries can launch into development and then sustain it. Far less effort has been addressed to correcting mistakes – if only because so many mistakes are the development theorists themselves? Theories, after all, inhabit a different world from countries, peoples, and us.

Removing the Albatross

The first step toward correction must be to remove, or at least muffle, the source of the original problems and to counteract the people and structures that stand in the way of transition. The albatrosses with which the country was garlanded by the previous regime must be cut loose without drowning the Ancient Mariner in the process. Getting rid of obvious evil is easy; it is more difficult to avoid killing much of the good with it. Firing squads are not delicate instruments of reform, but remain much favoured as a solution to major problems in the bitterness of a bust. Saving the Bangkok Bank, 'a Chinese unemployment company', as one of Thailand's best economists described it, 'with 30,000 employees doing the job of ten thousand', was crucial not as an act of Asian fraternity but because if the Bangkok Bank, the biggest in Southeast Asia, went down it would be like having an elephant die in your living room. 'Too big to fail' had come to a country whose finance had been handled by shroffs (money changers) only a generation before. Job satisfaction (and demonstration of financial soundness) would come with firing twenty thousand spare Chinese.

Jerry Rawlings, enthusiastically continuing Ghana's penchant for melodrama and extremity, found the simplest solution to the problem of starting anew: he shot everybody previously in power. By so doing he eliminated many an unfortunate legacy, but he also alienated a great deal of the country – less on abstract humanitarian grounds than by outraging innumerable tribal solidarities (every non-Ewe knows intensely that Rawlings is an Ewe). 'A son-of-a-bitch but *our* son-of-a-bitch' is the deepest axiom of African tribal politics, and sectional loyalties made his own longer-term objectives much harder of fulfilment. Killing in cold blood, even albatrosses, is not the ideal way to win friends or to positively influence the people: and Rawlings's subsequent terror of retribution, while an ironic force for good at the outset, has been a major check on Ghana's development.[251] By 1999, the biggest problem for Ghana's development – and for Ghana – was just getting the great whale – the now huge and even more overpowering Flight Lieutenant J. J. Rawlings – out of the castle and into retirement.

Yet however hard he tried, Rawlings was not the worst bridge burner of his generation. For Pol Pot they retired the cup. In 1978 he came into power over a country desperate for a second chance after years of bombing, ethnic massacre and general violence. Pol Pot destroyed everyone wearing spectacles, everything commercial, and sat sophisticatedly enthroned over a wilderness of skulls. Not only did he kill everyone whom the most demented suspicion could caricature into a threat, now or fifty years hence; he also proclaimed the first day of his rule to be the beginning of 'year zero'; every subsequent leadership has perforce to build upon a foundation of bones. This house divided against itself became a graveyard which somehow supported a civil war: it is not a question of whether it will stand – it fell long ago – but whether it can be rebuilt in the lifetime of anyone still holding the horrible memory.

To the severe, but by comparison idyllic miseries of Thailand, Prime Minister Chuan Leekpai has been able to impart an independent reality, or more-or-less reality: that of the IMF, the cold-eyed planetary accountant singling out the corruptions and pretences of one more financial system. But by playing off the possibility of the tough cop's getting really mad, the relatively friendly cop Chuan has been able to get a great deal of his way without burning down the barn. He has sanctioned individual delinquents,[252] but he has been able to leave the banking structure standing, mainly by enforcing long-ignored rules that were on the books and by introducing competition, with the result that it is in many respects remarkably reformed. Jail and humiliation he finds less useful than monetary assessment and the remobilization of chastened talent. The yielding willow can carry more stress, said the Elizabethans, than the rigid oak. The vitality and flexibility of constitutional and market systems is intimately bound up with the absence of rigour, mercilessness and petty consistency, and with the prevalence of endless to and fro-ing, second guessing and incomplete undertakings – expensive but heartening indicators that no powerful, but aging and brittle master vision holds sway.

In America, the process is similar. Every new administration and every new Congress sweeps in describing how it is going to revolutionize, or 'reinvent', the way government works. But it doesn't; it just tinkers on the margins, and that's a good thing too. Taxes stay pretty much the same, the same Congressional barbers shave remarkably similar shadows, military spending stays about the same. Bogus revolutionary rhetoric is all well and good in a society that doesn't need a revolution, and continuity is one of the great advantages of a country where political changes are predictable, incremental, and peaceful. A dozen geeks in Silicon Valley can have a more revolutionary effect on American society than a hundred blowhards on Capitol Hill.

But some countries suffer from just the opposite problem. Revolution is just what they require, but all they get is violent language and yet more violent (and therefore how repetitive!) change – 'same ol *déjà vu* over again', as Yogi Berra complained. It is always easy to kill someone or, to use the radical idiom, to *smash* something and proclaim it changed, as the Romans 'made a wilderness and called it peace'. While the developed world was transforming history with cybernetics and molecular biology, hundreds of millions of rage-drunk Chinese adolescents were rolling their country back down the hill of civilization in the name of Cultural Revolution.

In Zambia Frederick Chiluba, now President, campaigned against founding father Kenneth Kaunda for years, finally wrested power from him (constitutionally, to the credit of both) and has kept things pretty much the same. Kaunda is on the outside now, forcefully arguing for more revolutionary change which, of course, he is the most suitable person to bring about, but which somehow he did not implement over the decades in which his bank account grew in rough equivalence to the national debt. President Daniel arap Moi has taken this posture to a new extreme in Kenya, claiming that he is the one to change the country, even after twenty-odd years of misrule. After all, he was the one under whom the potholes sank toward the centre of the earth; surely he knows how to fill them up (sometimes even with his enemies' heads). One of Charles Taylor's campaign slogans in Liberia after he shredded the country and organized elections for 1997 was 'the devil you know is better than the one you don't know'. One Taylor supporter in Liberia said before the recent elections, 'He killed my pa, he killed my ma, and I will vote for him.'[253] This attitude is succinctly known as 'throw the rascals in'.

There is one other extremely important lesson that leaders must pay attention to when they address themselves to the source of the good: you have to consolidate political power so that what you accomplish doesn't fall back in on itself. This is what happened in the aftermath of the election that restored constitutional government, with K. L. Busia, in the early 1970s. Busia didn't have enough of a handle on the political engine of Ghana. When he cut military pay, curtailed unions and devalued the currency – all surely good moves if they could have been brought off in a political vacuum – his train was out on the open track but Acheampong was waiting to slam on the brakes. No change can come about without political control is an axiom that remains true although it has often been distorted. This is what is meant when political scientists say that the problem in the developing world is not too much power – but too *little*. It is the distinction that General Almonte, senior adviser to Philippine President Ramos, made when he called for a *strong* state, not an authoritarian one.[254]

This step is particularly important because change never comes easily; it is often the case that new governments toiling to do right by their countries cause pain in the short term through measures apt to bring benefits in the long term. This was certainly the case with the IMF in Ghana; its programme was surely the right move for the country, but it was harshly opposed by the political class and by all the people who were hurt in the short run. The same was true of the currency devaluation that Rawlings edged himself through, taking it as slowly as possible to limit political aftershocks. In Thailand the situation was the same. The danger always lurked that the policies Chuan was forced to follow to gain IMF support – indeed, the initial bail-out – would so perturb the political waters that he would be unable to win an election. General Chavalit, his predecessor, was waiting in the wings, ready to use his long-bought base in the Northeast to rally the poorest of the poor on the meretricious argument that Chuan's policies were designed to help only the rich. This slowed Chuan down and almost knocked him out, but the Thais could see far enough ahead to keep their leader in.

The next step in securing a real second chance is recognizing your mistakes and learning from them – a challenge that invariably seems greater than it should be, and is becoming far more important in this global age. When something doesn't work, in personal or national affairs, why is it so difficult to inspect the mistakes and, at the very least, try something else? There are all the usual answers: one's emotional investment in the chosen course that failed; the assumption that if one tried a little harder, with fewer reservations, it would work.

But there are two more important reasons. One is that failure serves some purpose. Success anxiety exists in states as well as people. *Any* change, for worse but even for better, changes the beneficiaries and everyone has reason to fear that. Long after it was apparent that Ghana was not only losing its cocoa sales to the Ivory Coast – its longer-term market share – but also losing its ability to grow cocoa efficiently, it continued down the same path. No one had the will to shift course. One paralyzing consideration was that when groups lose their privileges they retaliate; a second was that new things, like monsters under the bed, are almost by definition frightening.

But, monsters or not, a country has to make choices and changes if it wants to develop. Today, this is even more important as communications speed up and choices must often be made in a very short space of time. Ever since the oil crisis of 1973–4 Third World countries have been on notice that quick reaction is of the essence in averting disaster, long before one can devise a new long-term policy. Their reaction to the six-fold run-up of the price of oil between 1969 and 1974 was indeed a dry run for the economic crises of the early 1980s and late 1990s. Oil-importing states had to adapt their alliances, their spending patterns, and their development programmes rapidly or they went bankrupt and had to be bailed out. And the problems for the oil producers were in some ways more intractable because the easy route – the low road taken by Nigeria, Iran, Iraq – was so tempting.

Today the speed needed is relational to the increased pace of computers in the generational interval. There is a wholly new level of 'fast track' decision making in which learning from mistakes becomes vital. Today, a currency can plunge in hours, as the baht did, thanks to the daily trillion-dollar currency flows which not even the US Treasury can hedge against, let alone control.[255] But it has been the case throughout the period we are studying that Ghana and Thailand have had to react to international forces beyond their control. The choice has been to play King Canute – as Ghana all too often elected to do – or to adapt, to 'go with the flow' and benefit therefrom.

Change is what governments are judged by their ability to manage, and change is both positive and negative. It is not difficult to see which states learned from their experience in the 1970s, and no doubt the lessons of the 1990s will be equally clear. Wherever Thailand adjusted quickly, it won. More than $15 billion was wasted in 1997 trying to protect the baht when it was obvious – and not just with hindsight – that it was impossible. Even in 1998 after the crash there were those who seemed not to have learned the obvious lesson, but luckily they were not the ultimate decision makers. Is the opposite error, over-reaction, possible? Of course. But it's rare.

The third step is simply to get the economic fundamentals right and to be able to deal with decision making – literally *making choices*. You have to be able to learn from mistakes and change policies, but you also have to be smart enough to recognize what your mistakes were and how you can change them. This is a point so obvious that it seems redundant – yet examples in which the obvious wasn't followed overwhelm the others. A necessary, if not sufficient, condition of this process is that professional economists be elevated to a position, in whatever manner is culturally permissible, to give their advice freely and, in large measure, authoritatively. People with political skill end up in power. People who know how to run economies have to be brought in. Suharto's regime in Indonesia began to unravel when he began squeezing out the economic advisers in the early 1990s and replacing them with cronies.

This was one of the central problems with Ghana in the 1970s. Things definitely had to be changed in the early 1970s but Colonel Acheampong came in and did everything backwards. He revalued the currency upwards. He tightened control over the economy. The smart people who agreed to work for him in the beginning quickly jumped ship and watched his six years of impoverished ruin topped by another disastrous year under General Akuffo. Even in the somewhat more enlightened Rawlings days, it was a fact – at least in 1999 – that there was not a single professional economist in a position to advise the government. The head of the development board was simply a general-turned-bureaucrat.

In Brazil the junta taking power in 1964 simply turned the economy over to the brilliant economist, Delfim, and he and his team were happy to run the show for over a decade. The results were impressive. A similar model was followed in the 1970s in Chile, where a whole school of Chicago monetarists achieved even more remarkable results. Of course, economists do not always turn mud into gold; and they are certainly capable of just the reverse. But a country does need to have them around if it wants to understand what it is doing wrong, and what, perhaps, it could change to set it right. We have seen several times in preceding chapters how Ghanaian leaders from Nkrumah[256] until Rawlings systematically ignored or undermined their economic advisers and there's no doubt that this was a contributing factor to Ghana's bust.

In Thailand, it was apparent that monetary and fiscal policy were areas that politicians could benefit from almost infinitely at the expense of the state. One of the single most important strokes of policy in the success of Thailand was the granting of autonomy to the Bank of Thailand in the 1950s (something Great Britain did not do until 1997); another was elevating the post of Minister of Finance over time to a level of prestige and authority that placed anyone in that post above the swirls of politics, able to shift policy where needed. Political leaders simply decided that they could not trust themselves or their successors to resist playing with the currency, and ceded that power to the great Bank of Thailand – at least until the mid-1990s. At that point the office of Minister of Finance became a part of the governmental cash machine for politicians, with cataclysmic results.

But economic correctness is only the beginning. The great policy debate once the Chuan government had stabilized and launched its reform programme was between the powerful and rich Minister of Finance, Tarrin Nimmanahaeminda, and Supachai Panitchpakdi, Deputy Prime Minister. Tarrin had been there before and commanded a powerful position within the Democrat Party. His patronage and largesse had been extensive; but he was a banker, not an economist. Supachai, an economist, was technically higher but commanded the less influential Ministry of Commerce. Tarrin seemed wedded to a strong currency, as most finance ministers are everywhere. Supachai wanted to speed recovery with greater liquidity in the system, and considered a slightly weaker baht both easier to defend and conducive to growth. Tarrin, not a politician, was stubborn, however, and not a team player: the insightful economic advice of Supachai was discarded.

Beyond that, Chuan himself was getting a second chance. He entered Government House knowing his way around this time, and aware that he was widely considered not only the best man for the job but the only one. He did not change his 'nice guy' demeanour, but in keeping the defence portfolio he ensured that if anyone was going to play the senior officers off against each other, he would be the one. Indeed when a very high personage from Chitrlada tried to promote the candidacy of a favourite general whom Chuan considered divisive, Chuan was in a position to pass over the 'recommendation' and promote a suitable nonentity instead, thus offending the palace as little as necessary – and keeping the military in check.

More seriously, Chuan appointed Sanan Kachornprasart as Interior Minister, a powerful post with responsibility for the police, internal security, border patrol, provincial government and land distribution. Thailand always had a dozen or so people of 'real power', David Wilson argued in 1963, but they were mostly military.[257] In 1996, when one of us asked people to name the dozen holders of 'real power', Sanan's name was put forward universally – and he was then merely secretary general of the Democrat Party. He was enormously rich, enormously corrupt, and enormously, powerfully effective – until the new culture of reform in 2000 led to his fall.

The need to be able to make decisions parallels the benefit that a country gains if it disposes of relevant experience. The Japanese and German recoveries after the Second World War are the clearest and most astonishing examples of countries seizing upon their second chances. Nice guys don't have to finish last. They can appoint tough people for the tough jobs. Having done that they can focus on the larger issues of reform, salvation and strategic change. Within six months of returning to office, Chuan Leekpai was searching for ways to clip the wings of the immensely powerful bureaucracy and to mobilize civil society. That was going to take a long time and lots more changes. He and his team wanted a real transformation of Thailand.[258]

There are a couple of fundamental things that countries need to get right, things that they are most likely to get right, of course, if they appoint the right people. You need to understand what is driving the world economy. The competition for FDI is now intense and international. Potential investors simply aren't interested in the historical reasons for this or that obstacle or problem.[259] In Ghana in late 1964 World Bank president George Woods and chief investor Edgar Kaiser were expected to attend the dedication of the great VALCO aluminium smelter that was the commercial end of the Volta River Project and the Akosombo dam. Students at the university were preparing their *comme il faut* demonstration against imperialism, neo-colonialism, etc. The American ambassador called Conor Cruise O'Brien, Vice Chancellor of the university then, to express the hope that the students could be prevailed upon not to demonstrate. He declined to interfere. But then Nkrumah's very radical information minister called on the same mission. According to O'Brien, when he asked the reason for this unusual request, obviously coming from the top, the reply was, 'Edgar is here.'[260] So passions, so to speak, could indeed be controlled, but it was much too late. It was to be thirty more years before all the damage could be undone and FDI could be seriously canvassed – although not before General Rawlings, on a money-raising trip to New York in 1994, had again sent confused signals to the financial community.

Part of getting the story right is also making sure that there are free flows of information through the society. The circulation of ideas is at once a series of discrete choices by a government and a test of whether a people can search for and face the truth; it thus provides a transition to our concluding chapter in which we discuss a society's management of itself at the highest level. For the test of a society, ultimately, is whether information circulates freely. If it does, then much else follows in both economy and polity. There can be no serious justification for preventing the circulation of ideas – and in practice wherever ideas have been suppressed many other things die too. The fast-track authoritarians, like Pinochet, ultimately saw the futility of holding the lid on if they wished their economies to move past the first stage of rapid growth; this is the iron law in Anand Panyarachun's 'lesson of 1992' to which we have already alluded. All through the long last century the obviousness of this central point has been underlined – early and tenaciously by John Maynard Keynes and by others thereafter.

A country's fourth and final objective should be to keep what is strong and defining about its culture. This may sound like a nebulous goal, but it is a crucial one. If a country can hold on to its culture, then national pride has a core around which to build cohesion. One important example of this is the African and Asian emphasis on the extended family. Thais thrown out of work in 1997 floated back to their villages, where this was possible, in large numbers. When one million Ghanaian immigrants were thrown out of Nigeria in 1983 they disappeared back into their country within a matter of weeks without any international assistance. What could have been a veritable disaster, with bread lines stretching through Accra, proved nothing more than a cat's paw on the water simply because people were able to return to their families. We are not applauding the conditions that occasioned this reverse migration, but rather the cultural adaptivity that made it possible.

Arguably it is culture that has got Africans through their generation of tragedy. One is struck today by the far greater newsworthiness of chiefs in Ghana. It seems that, as government failed, traditional structures got a new lease on life.

The statistics about most African nations may be heartbreaking but there is still the family structure to back people up – though some say this is changing. According to Karl Maier, 'What centuries of slave trade and dislocation caused by colonialism failed to do – to break the backbone of African society and its central tenet of the primacy of community over that of the individual – is being accomplished in a matter of years by the onset of capitalist consumerism.'[261] Exaggeration perhaps? At least we must beware.

Second chances take time and people need to have something to fall back on. African culture has survived for thousands of years, as has Buddhist culture in Thailand. As long as these are not destroyed, and as long as they do not fade away, they are going to have a stabilizing impact and are going to allow progress to come about, even if it comes slowly.

Momentum Both Good and Bad

The final point to be made regarding second chances is that once things start to turn around, they develop momentum that pushes them further forward. Of course, the same can happen in reverse. There is, as we have often noted, a tendency for problems to spill over from one area into others. It is as true for states as for individuals. Finding seemingly unsolvable problems in one arena – and assessing the damage, the prospects, the best remedies – countries can attend simultaneously to opportunities in other areas. Alternatively, in their bitterness at one they can make the other worse: a dictator thwarted abroad can lock up more opponents at home; or, when economic results are below expectations, tighten the screws on the opposition.

We find illustrations over and over in Thailand of the first response and in Ghana of the second. Consider the drafting and passing, in 1996–7, of the sixteenth constitution of Thailand – the first one written with inputs from most segments of society, the first to assign the origin of the state's legitimacy to the people. Although considerable popular enthusiasm was mounting under the charter process, and the finest leaders of the Kingdom were in charge – Anand Panyarachun at the head – it was by no means clear that the old politicians and soldiers wouldn't riddle it of its real reforms before it could pass. No sooner had the meltdown started than many of its chief supporters doubled the pressure for its passage. The catastrophe looked – and largely was – the product of the old order and there was no better time, and no better reason, for changes to be made.

Thailand's latest constitution has been generally lauded as a participatory constitution following a drafting process that involved many members of the community and public hearings throughout the country prior to its adoption. It has been a success and it certainly sets a precedent. But, as Vitit Mutabhorn wrote in the *Bangkok Post*, it wouldn't have come about if things hadn't been in flux and if there hadn't been momentum pushing virtuous reform.[262] For there is a bottom line underlying the process of evolution of this new constitution for Thailand.

> Were it not for the economic whirlpool, the new constitution might not have been born. It was this magnetic mess which mobilized the public to *seek the passage of the new constitution as a political cure for economic ills*, granted that these ills were greatly the consequence of the nexus between political misdeeds and economic mishaps. Those politicians who had previously rejected this constitution ultimately yielded to its adoption as they did not want to be seen as countering the public sentiment or losing their credibility.[263]

This same momentum may also be what eventually gives Ghana the kick forward that it needs. Ghana started doing things right in the 1980s, and once a country has started to get things moving in the right direction they can continue to move that way. Consider private investment. Traditionally Ghana has done nothing to win the trust of private investment. It also has done nothing to convince the public that government support for private investment, on the rare occasions that it does occur, is good for the people. Now that the government of Ghana is starting to support private investment for the right reasons, however, the odds are that the ball will continue to roll in the right direction. Once a few companies are in, it will be easier for others to enter. Then, if private investment works for the economy, people will begin to trust it. And so on.

On another level, as Ghana's economy begins to grow, domestic demand will increase. People will have more money that they will want to spend. As they spend more money, the producers of the goods that are being bought will have more money, which they too will spend or save. If they spend it, the money will go right back into the same cycle. If they save it, banks will lend it out to companies. After Thailand began to move to an export-based economy in 1985, Thais not only earned the revenue from the exports, but also prospered because of the multiplier effect.

There is, of course, also the positive impact of the growth of one's neighbours, and Africa as a whole may be heading in the right direction. As the continent grows, demand for Ghanas products will increase, cross-continental information sharing will increase and continental competition will increase. As Ghana gets richer, Ivory Coast grumbles and gets ready to kickstart its own economy.

Africa needs a second chance. It needs to escape the failures of the past forty years. And Asia needs a second chance to escape the failures paid for in the meltdown. It can happen, if the right people make the right decisions.

CHAPTER 10

The Great Society

Writing a generation ago in praise of one 'essential characteristic of a great society', Walter Lippmann noted:

> It is not monolithic and cannot be planned or directed centrally. It is too complex for that.... Its needs are too varied, and there are no men who have the minds, even if they are assisted by computers, capable of grasping all the data and all the variables which are needed for the central planning and direction of a great society.[264]

Lippmann was evoking the vision of two centuries of classic liberalism that we now jejunely and inadequately style civil society.

Almost in spite of itself, Thailand, a country of deference, seemed to sense how human beings could live with greater scope in an order that worked to multiply individual powers by one another, not simply to add them. Even its sternest military leaders consciously conceded vast tracts of authority where many another huddle of brass hats has asserted itself as a matter of manhood. To the long and bloodchilling history of other militaries in finance and economics – ordering currencies not to depreciate – we may contrast the amazing arms-length relationship of most of the marshals to the Bank of Thailand, up until the eve of the great meltdown. Alas, not all were clean, but enough had been.

The distending mango of wealth and well-being that has been – and to a solid degree remains – the history of the last thirty years of Thai society has not crushed the role of any of the great interests that made up this Third World country of a generation ago. The resources of palace, parliament and corporation have all gained absolutely, while contracting relatively (but towards a greater legitimacy and security) within the growth coordinates of the country's newly industrial, reasonably stable democracy. Whether army and temple have gained, in the end, is more problematic and raises substantial questions for the future.

In Ghana, the question still has not got beyond Humpty Dumpty's 'Who shall be the master?', and the wearyingly repetitive zombie substitution of force for enterprise has corroded even the weathered interests that survive forty years of effortful self-destruction. With wealth, Thailand became a vastly more differentiated society; Ghana simply has yet to grasp the point and we must wait to see if Rawlings himself has. Ghana's second chance hinges on that question.

To be 'great' a society need not be large, if its statecraft is exemplary or if the polity, by which we mean far more than the state, stands for something. Ghana certainly set out to do so in its first decade. At different times Tunisia, Vietnam, Botswana, the Czech Republic, Israel, Barbados and Taiwan have distinguished themselves, small as they were, because they achieved much in the economic, diplomatic, political or military dimensions of statecraft. More generally, it was in combinations of these arms of statecraft. But, however reckoned, certain pretty inescapable dos and don'ts emerge from a study of the two countries, in the context of the Third World as a whole.

A Sense of Proportion

Small states tend vastly to overrate their importance in the great capitals, or miss where they can exercise influence. It is difficult to get it right but it doesn't hurt to try. Ghana's sense of importance was almost pathological. Its early independence and much that happened before, perhaps even the ingredients of its national character and culture, predisposed it to a gross miscalculation of where it stood. Old eyes foresaw. David Williams, who knew West Africa in the independence generation better than any other outsider, asked the sympathetic last British governor what Ghana would really amount to; this was during the independence celebrations when the clichés about Ghana as a beacon were flying fast, from few so generously as from the Governor, Sir Charles Noble Arden Clark. 'Well, after it quiets down,' he answered, 'Ghana will be a good little "cocoa" republic.'[265] Richard Wright said wearily, as early as 1954 in *Black Power,* that the Gold Coast African 'feels that he is at the centre of the universe and a conversation about world affairs is likely to elicit silence'.

Thailand had the long-developed and nuanced sense of where power sat and from whence threats emanated. Obviously it had an agenda with the old European colonial powers – and they had scores to settle with Thailand – but, well beyond that, Bangkok began playing Washington with skill from an early stage. Its fast-track young diplomats were switched from Oxford to American schools.[266] Senior diplomats like Thanat Khoman and his protégé Bira Kasemsri were given long enough leashes to explore avenues of influence whenever they were in America. They had a highly developed sense of the balance of power as well; Thanom and Thanat were chomping at the bit to begin playing a China card long before Kissinger did, but knew full well Thailand couldn't until it was doing so in tandem with the United States.

True, Thailand was almost a real player in the international game of nations, and had a real stake, at the peak of the Cold War, while Ghana was almost a merely symbolic one.[267] That is to say, the Americans believed that Thailand might well be the first boulder in a landslide, a likely consequence of Vietnamese unification in the 1960s; whereas Ghana was seen as a bellwether, an annoyance, a voice, but too small to affect the global power balance. Ironically, the meltdown showed that Thailand had become a real and serious player in the game of nations, so much had its greater economic import and stake increased its international influence and prestige: this only emerged fully when it was seen how far the ripples of its problems would travel.

Nonetheless, influence follows upon a nation's identifying its strongest cards and then keeping its attention focused in the long struggle to play them, with as few distractions as possible, in something like the right sequence. So long as Nkrumah merely veered toward the Soviet Union, he could keep the West vigilant, interested,

and self-interestedly generous: but that was when there was only one
Ghana. The history, for instance, of Dahomey-Benin's endeavour to
play the Marxist-Leninist powerhouse is pure Evelyn Waugh, with
screen revision credits to Jeanne Kirkpatrick. Once Nkrumah had laid
his hand face up, with every card a commissar or comrade, there was
nothing for the West to do, some said, but ignore him and wait for the
inevitable.

Nkrumah's decision also had the less visible effect of emboldening
enemies who no longer had Western goodies to gain through him. The
Osagyefo gravely overestimated how much his Soviet patrons – he
never could see that it was impossible for them to contemplate
themselves in the equality of an alliance – could and would do for him
(beyond the usual Lenin Peace Prize and some industrial projects no
worse thought out than those willed on the Ukraine or Estonia). The
East German attempt to wire Accra for espionage turned into the
predictably agreeable farce that Nkrumah's very canny Ghanaian
intelligence chief, Eric Otoo, so hilariously recalls – yielding not very
interesting or useful conspiracies to find the most attractive bed-
mates.[268] But these were the initial *bêtises*. Ghana played its hand – by
now its finger – with diminishing finesse. When no less than Mrs
Charles Black – better remembered as Shirley Temple – arrived as
American ambassador, President Acheampong treated her not with
the chief's courtesy to a herald, but with the villager's condescension
to a woman – sometimes, indeed, downright insultingly, especially
when he was stoned.[269]

In sum, the instances where small or medium-sized states can
genuinely stand up to international forces are few, and such opportunities as there are occur more readily in the political realm than in
the economic. Vietnam accurately assessed America's staying power
and, with its larger stake in the outcome, steeled itself to endure
mutilation, to stand firm and prevail. Immediately thereafter its
attempt to turn this triumph of will into victory in the marketplace
proved as disastrous as the other in its terrible way had been
successful. A decade after the tanks rolled into Saigon, the country was
unified, socialist and destitute. Nevertheless, unlike North Korea,
Vietnam had the adaptive capability to change course fast enough to
catch and ride the tides of the century's end. Although in the late 1990s
it would stall again on a no-growth plateau, it had plainly developed

the ability to preserve its essential structures while surfing the worldwide waves it could not keep from its doors.

Accepting Responsibility – Dealing with the Past

Another requisite for moving forward is avoiding the assignment of blame. In politics as in life there are blamers and there are those who move on, looking to the future whoever was to blame. For a generation Africa was a continent of blamers. Everything was 'their' fault; 'they' were the Americans, the neo-colonial system, the world pricing structure, the previous government or some other ethnic group. In 1994 the United States Institute of Peace held a conference on Africa, drawing participants from all over the world. Many of those attending found it remarkable, indeed refreshing and astonishingly original, that the African participants declined to blame all their continent's current failings on those paying for their visit; they even, indeed, imputed responsibility to their own governments, past and present, and suggested that the frantic imperative to blame outsiders was a main taproot of the current distress. Back home, African leaders were beginning to strike the same note. President Rawlings, receiving his neighbour President Eyadema of Togo, noted that 'Africa's political history has been punctuated with so much conflict and ... if the continent had enjoyed long periods of peace and stability, its progress would have been faster.' Indeed, said he,

> 'More often we blame external forces for some of our shortcomings, but we should also be taking some of the blame', and went on to express the hope that the present crop of leaders would bestow a legacy of peace and stability on their people. 'If this is not done,' he said, 'the dreams of the founding fathers of the Organization of African Unity ... and other ... groupings would go unfulfilled.'[270]

Self-esteem

Countries have to know who and what they are: this is more than the question of identity, as it goes into the question of self-esteem. Interestingly, Ghana and Thailand were going through the quest for their identity in the late 1990s in some similar ways. In Ghana one detected a systematic attempt to find in the nation's modern roots things of value amidst the disaster that had engulfed almost everyone. But the search became more creative and richer as evidence raised the hope that Ghana had truly turned the corner. The venerable *West Africa* ran a series of articles on Kwame Nkrumah which, at least between the lines, suggested a reevaluation of him: it saw him not as the mentor of the remaining radicals who might wish to scuttle IMF discipline, but as the founder of the nation who had fought tribalism and pressed for pride in Africanness. One might object that the pickings were few, but on a continent where most leaders for a generation had got everything wrong, it was noteworthy that the Ghanaian leader had at least foreseen the disaster that would befall his continent if it did not learn how to work together. Even Julius Nyerere – who had mocked Nkrumah at the 1964 OAU summit for calling for unity only so long as it came under him, and for destroying every practical chance of it – saw fit to attend Ghana's fortieth birthday celebrations and pay homage to this remarkable visionary who had died in exile twenty-five years earlier.

In Southeast Asia the financial crisis had if anything sped up the search for true 'Asian values' – not the self-serving arguments we have already found discarded, which were simple rationalizations for strong-man rule such as we saw in Africa in the 1960s. Rather, as Kishore Mahbubani puts it, this was 'not only or even primarily a search for political values'. Rather, he said:

> They represent a complex set of motives and aspirations in Asian minds: a desire to reconnect with their historical past after this connection had been ruptured by colonial rule and the subsequent domination of the globe by a Western *Weltanschauung*; an effort to find the right balance in bringing up their young so that they are open to the new technologically interconnected global universe and yet rooted in and conscious of the cultures of their ancestors; an effort to define their own personal, social, and national identities in a way that enhances their sense of self-esteem in a world in which their immediate ancestors had subconsciously accepted the fact they were lesser beings in a Western universe.[271]

When All Else Fails...

When everything is failing a society must have internal structures, including well-integrated élites, to pose the right questions. The first question is whether size counts. Ghana failed here and Thailand got it right. Might Ghana just have been too small, too easily dominated by a single dictator? In part, yes. But culture is more important than size. Smaller societies than Ghana had élites that could deal with problems effectively: the Caribbean countries, whose peoples hailed mostly from West Africa, are obvious examples, fairly wealthy ones at that. Botswana, as always, has something to teach other small African countries.

But consider that the toughest dictator in Thai history, the remarkable Sarit Thannarat, sent the defeated Ratchakru group and its financiers and supporters into exile. General Chatichai, highest son of Ratchakru, went to Argentina as an embassy 'adviser', became the greatest horseman in diplomatic circles, and was soon the ambassador. He became a popular prime minister in 1988 and, when he died in May 1998, the nation almost closed down to honour him. 'The End of an Era', the press said everywhere – forgetting that the crowds had cheered General Suchinda when he threw Chatichai out in 1991. The head of the Bangkok Bank was similarly packed off to Hong Kong in 1957, where he developed his China channels and helped to create what is now the third largest economy in the world: the vast financial network of the overseas Chinese. In the process the Bangkok Bank became the largest bank in Southeast Asia, with $60 billion of assets at one point.

When Flight Lieutenant Rawlings came to power, he lined up the three living former heads of state his country had produced at an army base and shot them down, along with some other competent army officers who might have known too much – like the very fine General Kotei. All the protests from around the world were to no avail. And the three judges who had pronounced him guilty of his first misdemeanour were murdered in mysterious circumstances. Small wonder that it was difficult to envisage that Rawlings would honor his own constitution by standing down in 2000. Out of office, there would be no protection from the ghosts – and their descendants – whom he had cold-bloodedly murdered. In a rambling and odd speech, given while running a high fever on the anniversary of his takeover, Rawlings defied logic and bragged, 'I have no regrets' – which probably indicated just how many nightmares he had.[272] Nkrumah, not much kinder, had allowed his mentor J. B. Danquah to die in chains. He imprisoned his college classmate, latterly his foreign minister, Ako Adjei, on the flimsiest evidence. Societies without compassion at the top are unlikely to become successful beacons to the world.

What does a society do when its gears stop meshing? In the first place, if fear dominates the political marketplace, it does little or nothing, unless a courageous colonel, like Kotoka, is willing to risk his life to strike. In the gentler atmosphere of Bangkok, the élite talk, learn and listen. In the early 1970s, economists discussed the problems of political unresponsiveness – and people listened.

After the meltdown, Thailand behaved adaptively, intelligently and courageously. 'We were the first down and we are going to be the first up,' Surin, the foreign minister, told us.[273] Instead of headstrong defiance of the IMF as in Indonesia – at first even the students were with Suharto on this – there was a determination to take the medicine quickly and get the tragedy behind them, the lessons learned. This is not to say that anything was 'swept under the rug'. There were systematic examinations of what had gone wrong throughout the commanding heights of the polity. The Nakul Report, for example, on the technical failures at the Bank of Thailand in July 1997 which precipitated the baht's collapse became required reading and the most discussed document of the year upon its clandestine circulation in April 1998.

Where were the traditional leaders of Ghana when things began going wrong? The Asantehene when Nkrumah consolidated power lacked the sophistication to buck him or his cohorts – and Nkrumah went after him. His successor, Otumfuo Opoku Ware II, already a distinguished businessman and diplomat, was the strongest Ashanti king in a century, and came just in time – as national politics and national health declined – to fill the void where a state was intended to be. But it was too late for him to play a national role beyond Ashanti, though he did much to resurrect civil society in the region. His son, who held an American PhD on the Organization of African Unity, had a pan-African and national view, and was made Oheneba, or premier of the Ashanti people. He became an intellectual and political leader of great substance in the republic. In 1999 it seemed as if the chiefs had again become the backbone of the society.

Although we repeat that Ghana and Thailand were at the same level of economic development in 1957, in Ghana there was nowhere to go when things turned sour. Ghana had talent to burn, but its high-flyers left for major posts in the UN and Commonwealth secretariats, and in numerous other international institutions.

Thailand was just sufficiently differentiated – its civil societal institutions that much more secure, its second-level leaders that much more confident – not to be cowed by strong leadership, which anyway was bringing the Kingdom rapid economic results. From 1957, the new civil authority gave the King a role, which he ultimately used to displace his own political power as he burnished the throne. There is little to be said about modern Thailand without reference to the role of the King, although only recently has this been getting its (Western) scholarly due. Analysts from purportedly meritocratic democracies like to pretend that such awesome influence could not possibly issue from a throne; if they bothered to analyze they would discover that the power did not in fact emanate from the throne but from this particular monarch's lifetime development of his political base. Analysis of Thailand for almost a generation has been a deconstruction of *Hamlet Prince of Denmark* without attention to the role of the Prince.

Time and Luck

It's sometimes tempting to think that Thailand was lucky: a fertile basin, a fortunate geography, and a gentle national personality that the world admired. 'Amazing Thailand', as its tourism slogan put it in 1998. And that Ghana, conversely, was unlucky: it had to bear the ideological cross of its first leadership, the folly of its second; the oil all drifted down the Bight of Benin to Nigeria; Ghana was already all at sea when the African crisis impinged.

But destiny is not so determined. Instead we have shown how people made decisions that steered affairs of state the way they wished them to go. A few African leaders have got it right and their number is beginning to grow. President Rawlings was not the likeliest candidate to accept the dictates of the IMF. Ghana had been going downhill for so long that, given the fear he inspired, he could have kept it on that course a while longer. The models abound: Haiti, Guinea and Nigeria under Abacha. In Thailand, the King, government ministers like Thanat Khoman, diplomats like Anand Panyarachun and Bira Kasemsri, industrialists like Amaret Sila-on and bankers like Banthoon Lamsan all worked together to make Thailand great: it was back on that path when this book was completed. Trickle-down economics don't work in economics but they do in culture and effort. When men and women at the top are open and dedicated to the country, it is likely that millions of countrymen will be too.

A final lesson may come to Thailand by way of Ghana, and through them to all of the Third World. Overall, it seems, it takes at least as long to reform as it does to make the problems in the first place. That would help to explain why, seventeen years after its structural adjustment programme was introduced, Ghana was still creeping along at so slow a pace. Indeed, there was real backsliding in 1999–2000: as a result of end-of-term corruption, the Cedi plummeted against the dollar. If we assume that the worst of the Thai practices which brought the meltdown began in the early 1990s, then it would not be unreasonable to expect the Kingdom to be growing rapidly again by about 2002 – a five-year hiatus. Maybe it will take longer. Great traumas, to the state as to the person, always govern much of subsequent behaviour and operations, until new experiences and new victories have effaced, indeed replaced, the old miseries.

Thailand, whose prospects seemed so quaint and modest in the 1950s, had joined the big leagues by the millennium, overtaking many European economies. It could begin to press upon some of the big ones in the new millennium. Ghana, whose prospects were so trumpeted at that earlier time, was still struggling merely to get back on its feet: if it is lucky it will soon at least be back at the original starting post. Little of this happened by chance. The decisions that made it so were made at identifiable times by real people with names which need to be remembered, for better and for worse.

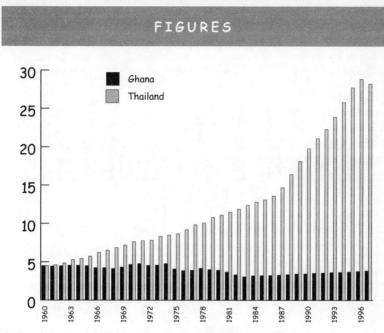

GNP per capita, 1960–96: Ghana and Thailand compared

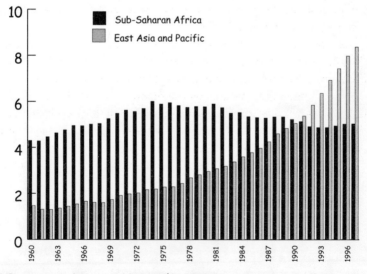

GNP per capita (constant 1995 US$), 1960–96: Sub-Saharan Africa and East Asia compared

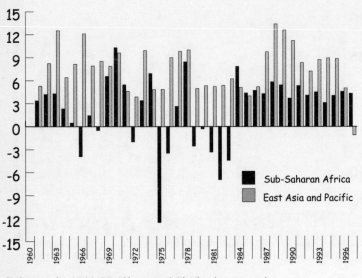

GNP growth, 1961–97: Ghana and Thailand compared

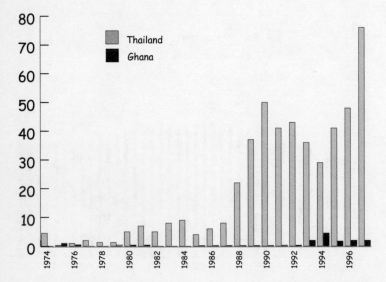

Foreign direct investment, net inflows (current US$), 1974–96: Ghana and Thailand compared

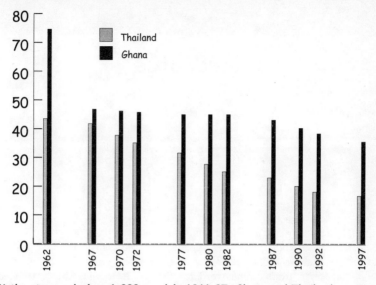

Birth rate, crude (per 1,000 people), 1961–97: Ghana and Thailand compared

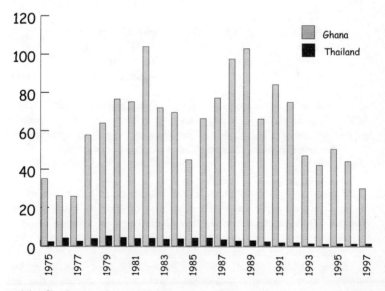

Aid (as % of gross domestic investment), 1974–1997: Ghana and Thailand compared

Endnotes

1 The Thai word for 'foreigner', presumably a corruption of '*francais*'.

2 Kwame Nkrumah, *I Speak of Freedom: a Statement of African Ideology* (New York: Praeger, 1961), p. 111.

3 'Asia' is a troublesome word for writers. Is Russia part of it? Geographically, yes. Ethically and culturally, no. In this manuscript we frequently use 'Asia' to refer to the countries in Oceanic Asia which have been able to develop their economies rapidly: the so-called tigers.

4 Kwame Nkrumah, *Ghana: an Autobiography* (London: Nelson, 1957), p. 34.

5 Kwame Nkrumah, *I Speak of Freedom*.

6 Jeffrey Herbst, *The Politics of Reform in Ghana* (Los Angeles: University of California Press), p. 14.

7 'Talk of the Times', *Washington Times*, 29 March 1998, p. A2.

8 Fred Riggs and W. Scott Thompson, *Thailand: the Modernization of a Bureaucratic Polity* (Honolulu: East-West Center, 1966); Norman Jacobs, *Modernization without Development: Thailand as an Asian Case Study* (New York: Praeger, 1971).

9 See Pasuk, Sung sisdh and Nualnoi, *Guns Girls Gambling Ganja: Thailand's Illegal Economy and Public Policy* (Bangkok: 1998). See also Bello, Walden, Shea Cunningham and Li Kheng Poh, *Siamese Tragedy: Development and Disintegration in Modern Thailand* (New York: Zed Books, 1998).

10 Sinith Sittirak, *Daughters of Development* (London and New York: Zed Books, 1998), p. vii.

11 As a good example of the bad side of development, consider smoking. In Ghana, fewer people smoke than in most developing countries, and women never smoke in public. The Ghanaian interpretation of traditional and Christian values opposes smoking and the population hasn't been inundated, or perhaps bought off, enough by cigarette advertisers peddling the destructive and lucrative message that smoking is both cool and sophisticated. If Ghana develops like Thailand, surely this will change and cigarettes will line the streets in Accra just as they do in Bangkok. Traditionalists oppose this; cigarette companies are salivating.

12 It is difficult in the extreme to thumbnail the Thai monarchy: one risks being declared *persona non grata* for the faintest slight. See, however, William Stevenson, *Revolutionary King* (London: Constable, 1999); see also Rayne Kruger, *The Devil's Discus* (London: Cassell, 1964), one of the best books about Thailand and the definitive one about the the the death of Rama VIII – but proscribed in the kingdom. The topic is coming into the mainstream.

13 Tanzania, at one point, had a tax rate of 100 per cent on all income above $35,000.

14 See W. Scott Thompson, *Unequal Partners: Philippine and Thai Relations with the United States, 1965–76* (Lexington, MA: Lexington Books, 1976), for case studies of the giving and receiving of aid, and the kinds of influence bought at both ends. This study credits Thailand with a remarkable ability to use aid for its own purposes – usually benign.

15 While, of course, accepting – and mismanaging – vast amounts of foreign aid from virtually every aid-giving state.

16 Kwame Nkrumah, *Ghana: an Autobiography*, p. 398.

17 We must also note here, of course, that non-metaphorical baobabs are ecologically important keystone species and do provide a home for other species.

18 Jean-François Bayart, *The State in Africa: the Politics of the Belly* (London: Longman, 1994), p. 233.

19 *The Story of Mahajanaka*, translated by H.M. Bhumibol Adulyadej, King of Thailand (Bangkok: Ammarin Printing, 1996).

20 Even a country like Somalia which virtually died recently, can rejuvenate itself. See *The Economist* (August, 1999).

21 Samuel Huntington, *Political Order and Changing Societies* (New Haven: Yale University Press, 1968).

22 This is not, of course, to say that similarities don't exist across Asia (remember, though, that Asia's largest state is Russia). Indeed, the 'East Asian Miracle', to use the title of a widely read World Bank study (1993), created commonalities for the region that the 1997–8 meltdown has only underlined, including the now frequently discussed 'Asean style' (ASEAN is the Association of Southeast Asian Nations, an organization founded by Thai Foreign Minister Thanat Khoman and his then counterparts in the Philippines, Malaysia, Indonesia and Singapore, and now embracing every Southeast Asian nation).

23 If the God of geography had wanted to simplify political science a bit, she surely would have moved Burma into central Africa or just swapped it with Botswana.

24 There is a school of thought that argues that all cultures are equal and have contributed equally in their own ways. We disagree. It seems clear that Chinua Achebe has contributed more to the world than an average petty thief. And, if that's the case, one can extrapolate to the level of an entire culture and argue that one culture has contributed more than

another (by virtue of there being more Achebes and fewer petty thieves). The question is terribly complex and a potential landmine, but should not be shunned just for those reasons.

25 Of all the nations that have suffered because of the arbitrary borders that were given to them by the colonialists at the end of the nineteenth century, a strong case can be made for Nigeria having suffered the most.

26 Lord Lugard, *The Dual Mandate in British Tropical Africa* (London: Archon, 1965), p. 1.

27 Basil Davidson, *Black Man's Burden: Africa and the Curse of the Nation State* (New York: Times Books; Oxford: James Currey, 1992).

28 It also removed the curse of a European-sounding name with 'Coast' in it, a name given by unliked traders which was a standing provocation to the inland Ashanti. Here was a genuine bitterness inherited from colonialism.

29 Indeed, until recently observers of Thailand complained of the lack of an intelligentsia, finding only 'literati' – though with the development of a critical mass of highly educated graduates this was changing. But the Thai tendency to live at the surface, as opposed to the tendency of some societies to probe deeply, is widely noted. See Mont Redmond, *Wondering into Thai Culture* (Bangkok: Redmondian Insight Enterprises, 1998). For the manner in which the survivals of a rudimentary civilization can nonetheless be fought over, see Peter Jackson's insightful essay, 'Thai Buddhist Identity: Debates on the Traiphum Phra Ruang', in Craig Reynolds, ed., *National Identity and Its Defenders: Thailand 1939–1989* (Clayton Victoria: Centre of Southeast Asia Studies, Monash University, 1991).

30 Karl Maier, *Into the House of the Ancestors: Inside the New Africa* (New York: Wiley, 1998) p. 16.

31 Gunnar Myrdal, *Asian Drama: an Inquiry into the Poverty of Nations* (New York: Twentieth Century Fund, 1968).

32 Indeed, in China the government was taking a series of steps that arguably inflicted more damage on its civilization than any government had ever meted out to any people.

33 Jeffrey Sachs, 'Nature, Nurture and Growth', *Economist*, 14 June 1997, p. 19.

34 'The Sea', Special Section in *Economist*, 29 May 1998, p. 3.

35 Thomas Sowell, *Conquests and Cultures: an International History* (New York: Basic Bangkok Books, 1998), p. 107.

36 Sachs, 'Nature, Nurture and Growth', p. 19.

37 Sowell, *Conquests and Cultures*, p. 107.

38 *Ibid.*, p. 108.

39 Reminding us that like does not guarantee getting on with like.

40 Following the anti-Chinese riots of 1969 the New Economic Policy was agreed, by which the indigenous Malay were assured of an increased share of the future growth of the nation – with weighted access to the universities and professions.

41 On which the best work still is R.E. Robinson and J. Gallagher, *Africa and*

the Victorians – the Official Mind of Imperialism (London: Macmillan, 1963).

42 See 'State Identity Creation', in Reynolds, *National Identity and Its Defenders*, p. 72.

43 Bayart, *The State in Africa: the Politics of the Belly*, p. 41.

44 Interview, Accra, August 1998.

45 The Sardauna of Sokoto, hitherto the most powerful man in Nigeria. *Ibid.*, p. 41.

46 The relationship between sports and civil society is an interesting one that we shall explore later on in the book. It's also a relationship that certainly isn't confined to Africa. In fact, there's an old joke with a certain amount of truth in it that 'Nebraska is a huge flat rectangle unified by loyalty to the Cornhuskers football team'.

47 Interviews, Kumasi, February 1998.

48 David Lamb, *The Africans* (New York: Random House, 1983), p. 12.

49 Maier, *Into the House of the Ancestors*, p. 161.

50 *Ibid.*, p. 163.

51 The Gold Coast then, of course: the land that Nkrumah renamed Ghana.

52 Cited in P. Pasuk and C. Baker, *Thailand: Economy and Politics* (London: Oxford University Press, 1997), p. 400.

53 See Edward Luttwak's controversial article, 'Give War a Chance', *Foreign Affairs*, July–August 1999, in which he argues that most efforts to suppress conflict over natural and inherent issues are misguided and even prolong conflict in some cases. 'It might be best for all parties to let minor wars burn themselves out,' he says (p. 37).

54 Wilks, *Asante in the Nineteenth Century. The Structure and Evolution of a Political Order* (Cambridge: Cambridge University Press, 1975), pp. 308–9; quoted in Bayart, *The State in Africa: the Politics of the Belly*, p. 2.

55 The Kingdom has suffered in one major way, however: the build-up of the sex trade was kick-started by US soldiers taking their 'R & R' in Thailand.

56 Interview, Bangkok, 1996.

57 Interview, Bangkok, 1996.

58 One of the present authors first learned who Nkrumah was from an adulatory passage in one of Maya Angelou's memoirs.

59 See Kenneth Weisbrode and W. Scott Thompson, *The Rise and Fall of Third World States*, forthcoming.

60 Dennis Austin, *Politics in Ghana, 1946–1960* (Oxford: Oxford University Press, 1964), p. vii.

61 Chinua Achebe, *The Trouble with Nigeria* (Enugu: Fourth Dimension Publishing), p. 3, cited in George Ayittey, *Africa in Chaos* (New York: St Martin's Press, 1998), p. 29.

62 According to Amos Perlmutter, who was present.

63 Sékou Touré of Guinea, close associate of Kwame Nkrumah, was the only leader of a Francophone African state to reject continued relationships with France when offered the choice in 1958. After Nkrumah was over-

thrown in a coup in 1966, Touré invited him to Guinea to become 'Co-President'. Nkrumah lived the rest of his life in Conakry.

64 Sowell, *Conquests and Cultures*, p. 173.

65 Interview, Washington DC, 30 July 1998.

66 Nkrumah, *I Speak of Freedom*, p. 196.

67 Keith Kyle, 'Dr Nkrumah's New Man', *Spectator*, 4 September 1964.

68 'Beyond African Dictatorship: the Crisis of the One-Party State', *Encounter*, p. 18.

69 Gilchrist Olympio, 'Domestic Institutional Crisis and Poverty in Black Africa', paper delivered to the Committee on African Studies, Harvard University, 28 April 1981.

70 Interview, Accra, August 1998.

71 Interview, Accra, August 1998.

72 As we will discuss later in a section on current politics in Ghana, there is a feeling among many people there that the problem wasn't that Nkrumah got the country off to a bad start, but rather that he was overthrown before he could make everything right. As Kojo Botsio, one of the men who worked with Nkrumah and one of Ghana's founding fathers, said in an interview with one of us: 'If Kwame's plans had been followed through, Ghana would be like Thailand' (interview, Accra, August 1998).

73 He practised sound economics, and was a man of culture and character. But for a sterner view, see Samuel Decalo, *Coups and Army Rule in Africa: Studies in Military Style* (New Haven: Yale University Press, 1978),pp. 96–8.

74 Interviews, Ougadougou and Harare, March 1998.

75 Ironically, one of the reasons that Bill Clinton was so idolized when he toured Africa in the spring of 1998 is that many Africans see him as an exemplar of the democratic process. Clinton had been practising constitutional politics, and preparing to be President, for most of his life, and they respect such steady commitment. However many the faults imputed to Clinton in his own country, he never staged a coup and he is certainly a politician by profession. 'The patience of politics' is a dull, slightly sleazy quality until one encounters its absence.

76 See Christos A. Frangonikolopoulos, 'Tanzanian Foreign Policy: the Proportions of Autonomy', *Round Table*, 307 (1988).

77 Christopher Clapham, *Africa and the International System: the Politics of State Survival* (New York: Cambridge University Press, 1996) , p. 187.

78 'Rawlings: My Time Is Up', *Ghanaian Times*, 16 August 1998.

79 Interview, Accra, August 1998.

80 Interview, Accra, August 1998.

81 Bayart, *The State in Africa: the Politics of the Belly*, p. xiii.

82 A. F. Mullins Jr, *Born Arming: Development and Military Power in New States* (Stanford: 1987), pp. 9–12.

83 Youri Petchinkine, *Ghana: in Search of Stability* (Westport, CT: Praeger, 1993), p. 60.

84 *Ibid.*, p. 89.

85 Nana Akufo-Addo, 'The Stolen Verdict', private paper held by authors.

86 Interview, Accra, August 1998.

87 Cited in W. Scott Thompson, *The Philippines in Crisis – Development and Security in the Aquino Era* (St Martin's Press, 1992), p. 48.

88 See Sulak, 'The Crisis of Siamese Identity', in Reynolds, *National Identity and its Defenders*, pp. 47–50.

89 The title reveals his direct descendance from the great fifth reign. Titles descend from royalty for five generations, each time a notch lower, until they become a mere *na Ayutthya* in perpetuity within the family. Otherwise, given the scores of kingly wives and princely children, the court would have become unmanageably large within a few generations. Titles are applied rigorously in Thailand.

90 Interview, February 1996.

91 See the *Far Eastern Economic Review*'s interview with him, in which it does appear that, at least in appearances, titles *do* count. Michael Vatikiotis and Faith Keenan, 'Banking: Princely Tradition – Thai Central Banker Mixes Reform and Nationalism', 3 June 1999.

92 A small taxi-cab.

93 Interview with MR Chatumongol, 17 February 1996.

94 Thailand has no natural frontier on its eastern border, but Thai prosperity had made traffic in the capital a formidable obstacle by the 1970s.

95 Jeremias van Vliet, *The Short History of the Kings of Thailand*, translated by Leonard Andaya, originally compiled in 1640 (Bangkok: Siam Society, 1975), p. 83.

96 *Ibid.*, p. 81.

97 Sulak Sivaraksa, 'The Crisis of Siamese Identity', p. 51. Sulak is not to be trusted here, however. It is strenuously to be doubted that the royal dialect – only about thirty per cent overlapping with modern Thai – was abandoned, even at the monarchy's nadir. The author encountered aides to the King at Chitrlada whose families had been in service to the King since the *third* reign, or a century and a half! Surely the major problem for Rama VIII – who died in mysterious circumstances soon after his return to Bangkok from a youth spent in Switzerland – was dealing with the fact that, despite the monarchy's near-total political eclipse, he was still a Godhead.

98 Field Marshal Thanom Kittikachorn told us that his cabinets got much useful guidance from the King on agricultural policy, for example. This was an area the King took most seriously, even establishing research and demonstration fields within the grounds of Chitrlada Palace – which thus looks to the outsider, driving around its walls and *klongs*, more of a well-landscaped field station than a royal enclosure.

99 The King was passionately concerned about the possibility of a Yugoslav-like situation in Burma, and the effect it would have on Thai security. He even translated works on Tito into Thai to make his point.

100 See the forthcoming study by W. Scott Thompson, 'Zeitgeist: Philippine and Thai Roads to NIChood', in which the King's role is examined at greater length.

101 Especially when the controversial Crown Prince succeeds to the throne. A frequently cited prophecy is that the Chakri line would not last to the tenth reign. Some have used this as an additional justification to argue for the ascendance of the Princess Royal as reigning monarch – in the hope that gender would befuddle the prophecy. Those more scientifically inclined might suppose that, with the great expansion of the Thai economy, the monarchy might – after the succession – come to fill less psychic space in the Thai mind and *imaginaire*.

102 Academics at the time told stories – without evidence – of thousands of bodies being dumped by helicopter over the Burmese border. There certainly were several dozen deaths and up to a hundred casualties. Tienanmen numbered at least ten thousand, according to Roderick MacFarquar. Also audience Chitrlada Palace, February 1997, HM King Bhumibol Adulyadej.

103 The reverence shown for the current monarch should not preclude incisive political analysis, or the realization that the King himself is capable of such.

104 It is necessary to note, however, that as the Thai king aged, he began to fall into the usual and predictable confusion between reality and the supernatural qualities commonly ascribed to him. At the time of writing, these still remained of a sort to which the élite could make subtle and restrained reference, but which had not attained operational significance. The fact that Thai in recent years have reverted to nineteenth-century style obeisance, at least in private audience, we take to signify the amplitude of the reverence he is accorded personally – if the distinction can in fact be made.

105 Donald G. McNeil, 'Zimbabweans (Minus the President) Brace for a Crisis', *New York Times*, 5 July 1998, p. A3. See also Bayart, *The State in Africa: the Politics of the Belly*, Chapter 2, 'The Unequal State: "Little Men" and "Big Men"'.

106 Andrei Gromyko, on a visit to Accra during which he discussed economic matters with Ayeh-Kumi, Nkrumah's very capitalist friend and the richest Ghanaian, was quoted as saying, 'You Ghanaians are not socialists.' W. Scott Thompson, notes, 1966.

107 The resurgence of Nkrumah's influence – although this has one salutary effect in building national self-esteem – is one sign; see the three-part series in *West Africa*, 4157–9 (July 1998), 'How Nkrumah was "Betrayed"', by A. B. Assensoh, written to mark the twenty-fifth anniversary of his death. Indeed, the article refers to Nkrumah in a headline by the sycophantic title *Osagyefo*. A generation of Ghanaian student papers, in classes taught by one of the authors, convinces one of this lingering influence.

108 Kofi Busia, *Africa in Search of Democracy* (New York: Praeger, 1967), p. 118.

109 On this point see Daniel Pipes, 'The Third World Peoples of Soviet Central Asia', in W. Scott Thompson, ed., *The Third World* (San Francisco: Institute of Contemporary Studies, 1978). See also Richard Pipes, *The Formation of the Soviet Union: Communism and Nationalism, 1917–1923* (Cambridge, MA: Harvard University Press, 1964, 1997), with respect to the Soviet acceptance of – and fight for – the Tsarist inheritance in the 1920s.

110 See W. Scott Thompson, *Ghana's Foreign Policy: Diplomacy, Ideology, and the New State* (Princeton, NJ: Princeton University Press, 1969)

111 During a conference at the National Defense University in Washington in 1976, a Nigerian stopped the dithering among Americans about international trends, saying that 'for five hundred years we have had to put our finger to the winds to see which way it is blowing, for survival. Right now it is plainly blowing from the East'.

112 One of the authors attended a conference on sanctions against South Africa in London as early as 1967.

113 Interview by W. Scott Thompson, Accra, 1966, cited in *Ghana's Foreign Policy*, p. 100.

114 See his revealing autobiography, remarkably entitled *Ghana* and cited above.

115 W. Scott Thompson, *Ghana's Foreign Policy*, p. 399.

116 Indeed, the older author recalls with intensity awakening that February morning of 1966 to the sound of gunfire in Accra, to turn on the radio and hear a coup leader announcing their success with the words: 'The myth of Kwame Nkrumah is broken forever.'

117 The NLC even put out several versions of a slick study of Nkrumah's attempts to subvert Africa, so obvious in its provenance that it irritated British intelligence, who saw it as 'made in Washington' – or, more likely, in Langley, Virginia. The sophistication of the NLC was not great, however; they briefly imprisoned one of the present authors to drive home a point to the diplomatic community – who, they then discovered, had immunity.

118 'School buildings were well maintained,' a memoir of Accra said of the 1940s, 'unlike the present where most are largely in a decrepit state.' Sam Clegg, 'Accra: Down the Years,' *West Africa,* 1–15 March 1998, p. 315. One of the present writers, on a 1999 visit to Accra, was appalled by the same comparison with thirty years earlier: the poor were just the same though more numerous; the rich were the same but now there were more of them to drain the poor; and still nothing in between. Only a few new business headquarters gave a sheen to Accra – for the most part it had just slipped downhill over a generation.

119 Clapham, *Africa and the International System*, p. 134.

120 See Han Fook Kwang, Warren Fernandez and Sumiko Tan, *Lee Kuan Yew, the Man and His Ideas* (Singapore: Times Editions, 1998).

121 Clapham, *Africa and the International System*, p. 111.

122 Cited in W. Scott Thompson, *Ghana's Foreign Policy*, p. 353. Tanganyika and Zanzibar united in 1964, becoming Tanzania in 1965.

123 Kwame Nkrumah, *Dark Days in Ghana* (New York: International Publishers, 1968), p. 14.

124 Touré's Guinea is a prime example of the failure of African nations' relations with the Communist world. The tales of snowploughs delivered to Conakry we cannot verify, but we did see more toilets sequestered in a graveyard than there were likely to be bathrooms in the country for a long time, this in 1964.

125 Benedict Anderson, 'From Miracle to Crash', *London Review of Books*, 17 April 1998.

126 Interview, Manila, January 1996. Subsequently he became governor of the Central Bank.

127 It wasn't entirely; many of the 'promoters' who made the 1932 coup admired Japan and saw it as a model. Truly, however, Thailand was the only sovereign entity in the region able to negotiate its own deal with Tokyo. In any event, resistance was futile.

128 In any case the declaration would have been greeted with a large ho-hum: but MR Seni's omission was of great importance in setting legal precedent.

129 See Darmp Sukontasap, 'The Third World and the UN Security Council: the Thai Experience 1985–86,' PhD dissertation, Fletcher School of Law and Diplomacy, 1992.

130 The Rockefeller family, through its foundations, has played an important catalytic role in Thailand, especially in the medical area. ML Birabongse Kasemsri developed a friendship with David Rockefeller while serving at the United Nations, an extraordinary achievement for a Third World diplomat in that period.

131 True, in 1999 the goal of an African union, to be achieved in two years, resurfaced at an OAU meeting. No one thought it realistic, but it reveals how needed some sort of strategic vision was for the despairing continent – and how visionary Nkrumah had been. See Samir Gharbi, Ridha Kéfi 'OAU: Les États-unis d'Afrique: Faut-il y Croire?' *Jeune Afrique*, 2019 (21–27 September 1999).

132 Bayart, *The State in Africa: the Politics of the Belly*, p. 79.

133 Interviews, Manila, Washington.

134 We are using the real population ratio. According to a UN source, the Gabonese President at the time leveraged the estimate of his population to up its status at least two-fold. This is another insight into the politics of the aid game.

135 See George Tanham, *Trial in Thailand* (New York: Crane Russak, 1974).

136 It is revealing that, despite a diplomatic debacle between the US and Thailand just after the end of the Vietnam War, as a consequence of which American bases on Thai territory were closed down, the American and

Thai military forces continued their close cooperation: only years later was it generally realized that the two allies routinely held joint military exercises, of course bolstering Thai confidence as Vietnam expanded, but also providing the US with trumps in the region.

137 In fact, the Third World, which became the 'developing world' in the past twenty years, was increasingly being divided, conceptually, into 'emerging markets' (or 'emerging market states') and, of course, 'Africa', the exception to most of the rules of progress across the old Third World.

138 James Fallows, *Looking at the Sun: the Rise of the New East Asian Economic and Political System* (New York: Vintage, 1994), p. 4.

139 Sweden was the first example.

140 Partha Dasgupta, *An Inquiry into Wellbeing and Destitution* (New York: Oxford University Press, 1993), p. 430.

141 United Nations Development Programme, *Human Development Report* (Oxford: Oxford University Press, 1993), pp. 156–7.

142 Admittedly there is the same problem in the rich world. The lower down the income level one goes, the greater the percentage of junk food, the less the amount of fresh fruits, vegetables, fibrous breads, etc. Nutrition has plummeted among the lowest-income levels in the US, where staples like black-eyed peas, soya beans and the like that were commonplace in the past (and sustained relatively high levels of nutrition) have been replaced by Coke, potato chips, etc.

143 Dasgupta, *An Inquiry into Wellbeing and Destitution*, p. 92, citing World Bank (1991).

144 Lawrence Altman, 'Parts of Africa showing HIV in 1 in 4 Adults', *New York Times*, 24 June 1998, p. A1. Ghana, *A Country Study* (Washington: Library of Congress, 1994), p. 115.

145 Ghana, *A Country Study*, p. 115.

146 Dasgupta, *An Inquiry into Wellbeing and Destitution*, p. 541.

147 See J. von Braun, 'Effects of Technological Change in Agriculture on Food Consumption and Nutrition: Rice in a West African Setting,' *World Development*, Vol. 16 (1989), pp. 1083–98; and M. Garcia, 'Resource Allocation and Household Welfare: a Study of Personal Income and Food Consumption, Nutrition and Health in the Philippines', PhD thesis, Institute of Social Studies, The Hague, 1990.

148 See J. Hoddinot and L. Haddad, 'Household Expenditure, Child Anthropometric Status and Intrahousehold Division of Income: Evidence from the Ivory Coast', Research Program in Development Studies, Woodrow Wilson School Discussion Paper 155 (1991).

149 Ghana, *A Country Study*, p. 73.

150 Interview, Washington, September 1999.

151 This is why the chief variable in Ted Robert Gurr's classic study, *Why Men Rebel* (Princeton, NJ: Princeton University Press, Center for International Studies, 1970) is relative deprivation.

152 World Bank: *World Development Indicators* (Washington DC: World Bank, 1999)

153 We are not denying the momentum toward globalization, but are merely saying that, at the moment, the state remains the defining source of legitimacy and the agency of justice. For an insightful essay on the changing role of the individual in an increasingly global economy, see Jean-Marie Guéhenno's 'The Impact of Globalisation on Strategy', *Survival* (Winter 1998–9).

154 The exception is so rare that we have to go back to the Swiss decision not to hold on to Mulhouse in the post-Napoleonic settlements, given that franco-phone city's location outside the federation's logical strategic frontiers.

155 Narat Pinunsottikul to authors, 31 August 1999.

156 David Landes, *The Wealth and Poverty of Nations: Why Some Are Rich and Some Are Poor* (New York: W. W. Norton, 1998), p. 412, pp. 418–21.

157 Sowell, *Conquests and Cultures*, p. 378.

158 Interview, Accra, August 1998.

159 Pasuk Phongpaichit and Chris Baker, *Thailand's Boom* (Bangkok: Silkworm Books, 1996), p. 210.

160 There are some tangential environmental benefits to poverty. In Ghana, if you buy a glass bottle of Malta, you must pay 20 per cent extra for the privilege of keeping the bottle, effectively mandating recycling. The other somewhat counter-intuitive advantage that Ghana has is that the state is so expansive, and there are so many different levels of bureaucracy, that it is difficult to get around the system and cut trees. Plans must be cleared with innumerable officials and, since all the land in Ghana is 'entrusted in the President on behalf of the chiefs' you have to go through both tribal and national bureaucracies. And it is possible that President Rawlings may really have the personal commitment to environmental protection with which many Ghanaians credit him.

161 See James Fain, 'Survey Shows "Green Gap" Is a Factor of the Generation Gap,' *The Nation*, 11 February 1996, p. B. 8.

162 'Learning from the Ozone Experience', in Lester Brown *et al.*, *State of the World* (Phyllis, 1997) p. 167.

163 Martha Nussbaum, 'Aristotelian Social Democracy', in R. Bruce Douglas, Gerald M. Mara and Henry S. Richardson, eds, *Liberalism and the Good* (New York and London: Routledge, 1990), p. 274.

164 Interview, Nasser Adam, 13 August 1998, Legon.

165 Amartya Sen, *Resources, Values and Development* (Cambridge MA: Harvard University Press, 1984), p. 34.

166 GDP is GNP less factor income from abroad plus factor payments to the rest of the world. The difference is trivial in the United States but can be significant for a country like Saudi Arabia that imports a lot of foreign labour services. The total GDP of a country is equal to the sum of every citizen's *per capita* income.

167 As George Gilder has argued perceptively, a country isn't 'rich' because it has depletable resources which it sells; it only becomes rich when it has the productive means to replace and sustain what it has. By that argument Saudi Arabia is *not* a rich country. See G. Gilder, *Wealth and Poverty* (New York: Basic Books, 1981).

168 See Martha Nussbaum, 'Aristotelian Social Democracy', pp. 203–52 .

169 Of course, if environmental degradation was included in the measurement of wealth, this deforestation would have hurt, not helped Brazil in the eyes of the World Bank.

170 Interview, Green Earth, 13 August 1998, Accra.

171 Morris D. Morris, *Measuring the World's Poor. The Physical Quality of Life Index* (New York: Pergamon Press for the Overseas Development Council, 1979).

172 Sulak Sivaraska, *Siam in Crisis* (Bangkok: Thai Inter-Religious Commission for Development, 1990), p. 171.

173 World Bank: *Development Indicators* CD-Rom (Washington: World Bank, 1999).

174 World Bank, *ibid.* Note that this is done in constant international dollars, not in purchasing power parity (PPP). In PPP, the numbers for 1996 are the far more realistic $1,360 and $5,070 respectively.

175 Interview, 14 August 1998, Accra.

176 Interview, 16 August 1998, Accra.

177 When we say 'African' we are referring to the economies south of the Sahara. When we say 'Asian' we are referring to the countries that are normally lumped together as part of Asia's boom.

178 Pranay Gupte, 'In Ghana, Little Zeal for New Regime', *New York Times*, 20 January 1982, p. A3.

179 Kwame Nkrumah, *Dark Days in Ghana* (London: Pnaf Publishers, 1969), p. 95.

180 This is probably the best argument against free trade. See Stephan Haggard, *Paths from Periphery: The Politics of Growth in the Newly Industrializing Countries* (Ithaca: Cornell University Press, 1990). In the Korean case, there was the powerful motivation to keep Japan out; had a way been devised to welcome foreign investment without permitting Japanese, Korean policy might well have been much more open, a point we owe to Ambassador Kim Kwang-won. It is the strangest case of 'they all look alike' that we have ever encountered – but then, GATT made them all look alike.

181 World Bank, 'Removing Price Controls in Ghana', in Gerald M. Meier and William F. Steel (eds), *Industrial Adjustment in Sub-Saharan Africa* (New York: Oxford University Press, 1989), pp. 180–2.

182 World Bank, *Private Capital Flows to Developing Countries: the Road to Financial Integration* (Washington, DC: World Bank, 1997), p. 9.

183 *Ibid.*

184 We are unsure of who came up with this notion first; it is often credited to old Japanese economists. See Frank Gibney, 'Pacific Basin Shapes Next Trade World', *The Los Angeles Times*, 17 May 1987, Part 5, p. 1.

185 Note, though, that this was a small sum compared with Japanese investments in America and elsewhere in the developed world. The Japanese knew that they must spread their investments over Asia if they were to have solvent customers.

186 See Chapters 6 and 11–14 in W. Scott Thompson (ed.), *The Third World*, first edition.

187 And, of course, the nationalized firms themselves.

188 W. Scott Thompson, *Ghana's Foreign Policy*, p. 390.

189 Nkrumah would, of course, reply that he didn't control the press, whereas the role for investment was laid out in the national plans. The disclaimer regarding a press that routinely referred to him as 'His Messianic Dedication' and 'Osagyefo,' or Saviour, was less than plausible. Recalcitrant editors were locked up.

190 Pasuk and Baker, *Thailand's Boom*, pp. 127–8.

191 *Ibid.*, p. 127.

192 See Mel McNulty, 'The Collapse of Zaïre: Implosion, Revolution or External Sabotage?' in *Journal of Modern African Studies*, 37, 1 (1999).

193 World Bank, *Adjustment in Africa* (Washington, DC: World Bank), p. 90.

194 Herbst, *The Politics of Reform*, p. 41.

195 Napoleon Abdullai, 'The Revolution and the IMF', *Daily Graphic*, 7 September 1982 (cited in Herbst, *The Politics of Reform*, p. 41).

196 Agricultural land available is defined as 'the land used as cropland and permanent pasture. Cropland includes land under temporary and permanent crops, temporary meadows, market and kitchen gardens, and land temporarily fallow. Permanent pasture is land used for five or more years for forage crops, either cultivated or growing wild.' World Bank, *Development Indicators*, CD-Rom (Washington, DC: World Bank, 1999).

197 World Bank, *Development Indicators* CD-Rom (Washington, DC: World Bank, 1999).

198 World Bank, *Thailand's Macroeconomic Miracle*, p. 78.

199 Michele Wong, 'Bumper Bean Crop Expected', *Financial Times*, 9 July 1996, p. 9.

200 World Bank: *Development Indicators* (Washington: World Bank, 1999).

201 Malcolm Gillis, Dwight Perkins, Michael Roemer and Donald Snodgrass, *Economics of Development* (W.W. Norton, 1996), 4th edn, p. 254.

202 Arthur Alexander, 'Japan's Economy in the 20th Century', Japan Economic Institute of America Report, 21 January 2000.

203 Joseph Kahn, 'Folk Hero Strips Teflon from Thailand's Corrupt', *New York Times*, 26 April 1998.

204 According to Professor Smita Notosusanto, there was reason to fear a worsening of corruption even prior to Madame's death: from 1993 Suharto

began replacing professional economists around the presidency with political hacks and cronies.

205 See the remarkable account in the *Wall Street Journal* by Peter Waldman, Marcus Brauchli and Jay Solomon, 'Fortune Hunting: Decades in Power Enriched the Suhartos, But It's All Relative', 30 December 1998. 'Given – and having taken – many opportunities,' they write, 'to profit from a nation steeped in treasure from forests to oil to gold, the Suhartos blew a remarkable number of the corporate schemes they touched. Far from having a fortune that some political rivals have estimated at $40 billion or more, the Suhartos appear to have at most a tenth that.'

206 Melchor, executive secretary of the government and author of most of the reforms, denied a request by Mrs Marcos to preempt a fully booked Philippine Airlines jet to transport herself and her friends to New York. She demanded – and got – his head. He became Philippines ambassador to the Asian Development Bank.

207 John Reader, *Africa: a Biography of the Continent* (New York: Random House, 1997), p. 670.

208 See *New York Times*, 9 September 1999, for a very optimistic report on the changes Obasanjo was able to bring about in his first three months. These, however, were the easy changes that came simply from stopping the backward slide of Abacha; at the time of writing it was not at all clear that the country could escape the old ways – or that Obasanjo was blameless enough to take the harder steps to remedy the old ills.

209 'Corruption Flourished in Reign of Abacha', James Rupert, *Washington Post*, 9 June 1998.

210 *Ibid.*

211 It is important to note that, without the Swiss, and the ease with which they have allowed kleptocrats to dump their winnings into secret bank accounts, corruption in the Third World would not be as rampant as it is today. Happily, the Swiss are changing their ways – in response to the hard data on Marcos corruption, and Philippine pressures. But it is still the case, as a major politician told us in Ghana in 1999, that 'every politician here has an account in Switzerland'.

212 Paraphrasing Professor Bayard.

213 Pasuk Phongpaichit and Sungsidh Piriyarangsan, *Corruption and Democracy in Thailand* (Bangkok: Silkworm Books, 1996), p. 23.

214 Though many would put Anand Panyarachun in this pantheon, he was in office too briefly to have the sort of impact Lee has had in Singapore and throughout the region.

215 Pasuk Phongpaichit and Sungsidh Piriyarangsan, *Corruption and Democracy in Thailand*, p. 41.

216 They were of the blood – as 'MR' denotes (Mom Rajawong, great-grandson of a king); more pertinently, they had a successful brother who funded their political, cultural, and media activities.

217 Shortly before taking office as Prime Minister he had submitted an MA thesis at a public university which, as it turned out, bore too close a resemblance to a government report submitted by one of his closest aides, soon to be a minister at Government House; it was even replete with French phrases – a language unknown to Banharn, but the one in which the aide had been educated. In Thailand, foreign birth requires a higher level of education for entry to high office. Banharn thus apparently faked birth certificates in order to ensure that his school diploma sufficed.

218 Even the benefits of cheap electricity created a false sense of sufficiency: by the 1990s there had been no effort to develop additional energy sources, with the result that Accra was frequently blacked out – not a sound basis on which to attract foreign investment.

219 Interview, Bangkok, 1998.

220 See 'A Global War against Bribery, *Economist*, 16 January 1999.

221 Pasuk Phongpaichit and Sungsidh Piriyarangsan, *Corruption and Democracy in Thailand*, pp. 80–1.

222 Mahbubani, Kishore, *Can Asians Think?* (Singapore: Times Books International, 1989) p. 189.

223 Jean L. Arato and Andrew Cohen, *Civil Society and Political Theory* (New York, 1994), p. x.

224 Vaclav Havel, *The Power of the Powerless: Citizens against the State in Central and Eastern Europe* (Almonk, NY: M. E. Sharpe, 1985), p. 31.

225 'Increasingly, the monarchy was becoming involved in an array of self-governing, civil institutions, from the Foundling Hospital to the Royal Academy, essential to the creating of a republican society…. Well before the French Revolution, the King had shown himself to be sensitive to civic and social needs.' Frank Prochaska, 'The Saneness of George III', review of Marilyn Morris, *The British Monarchy and the French Revolution*, *Times Literary Supplement*, 17 April 1998, p. 11.

226 This point was driven home to one of us when deciding recently whether to attend graduate school in the United States or in England.

227 Pasuk and Baker, *Thailand's Boom*, p. 173.

228 Chai-anan Samudavanija, 'Economic Growth and State Alliance in Thailand', in W. Scott Thompson and Kenneth M. Jensen (eds), *Rapid Economic Growth, Conflict and Peace in Southeast Asia*, p. 179.

229 Sulak Sivaraska, *Siam in Crisis* (Bangkok: Thai Inter-Religious Commission for Development, 1980), p. 167.

230 This bill, the Preventive Detention Act, gave Nkrumah the power to throw anyone he wanted in jail for whatever reason that he wanted, to the outrage of civil libertarians around the world. But the argument for 'African values', so akin to that twenty years later on behalf of 'Asian values', had begun.

231 To be fair, some of history's heroes are heroes precisely because they saw that mankind wasn't fulfilling its potential and stood for something

different. Vaclav Havel and Martin Luther King, Jr come quickly to mind. Of course, neither Havel nor King insisted on being called Osagyefo, and neither put themselves before the rest of the nation.

232 We draw here on Petchinkine, *Ghana: in Search of Stability*, pp. 72–5.

233 Interviews, intermittent, 1969–80. Interestingly, he 'commissioned' one of the present authors, two weeks before his coup, to inquire systematically of academics and of the more thoughtful members of the press their solutions to the existing impasse, and to report his findings to him. We found a universal clamour for a Kriangsak coup – which of course might well have been prompted by the certainty of knowledge that such was the desired response. But it was too emphatic and specific. Kriangsak's motives for this inquiry, to be sure, included – in a very Thai way – ensuring that his American friends knew what he was up to, and approved.

234 Though a young Turk, by an authoritative account, facilitated his decision by putting a gun at his head – literally.

235 Interview, W. Scott Thompson, Government House, Bangkok, August 1992.

236 Interview, W. Scott Thompson, with the Hon. Amaret Sila-on, Minister of Commerce in the first Anand government, 8 May 1998, Bangkok.

237 Interview, Accra, August 1998.

238 Thompson and Jensen (eds), *Rapid Economic Growth,* Chapter 1.

239 Mancur Olson, *The Rise and Decline of Nations* (New Haven: Yale University Press, 1982).

240 Toxic waste disposal sites are usually located in poor communities (where the land has less economic and political value) and those dominated by people of colour (where there is generally less political power, even holding wealth constant).

241 Amartya Sen, *Poverty and Famines* (Oxford: Clarendon Press, 1981).

242 Although there is a great gap between them. Singapore's PAP came to power in hard-fought but free elections and stayed there because it delivered on election promises and thus won further elections. The PRC emerged out of a predecessor's failure and remained in power, unelected.

243 See Robert Kaplan, 'Sometimes, Autocracy Breeds Freedom', *New York Times,* 28 June 1998 , p. 17.

244 The best study is by Partha Dasgupta, who regressed every single developing nation's rate of economic growth against political and civil liberties (as well as against changes in literacy, life expectancy and infant mortality rate). When he ran the numbers through his computer, he found that both political freedom and civil liberties bore a statistically significant relationship to a country's economic growth. P. Dasgupta, *An Inquiry into Well-Being and Destitution*, pp. 116–21.

245 Fareed Zakaria, 'Culture is Destiny: a Conversation with Lee Kuan Yew', *Foreign Affairs*, March 1994 , p. 109.

246 Francis Fukuyama, *The End of History and the Last Man* (New York: The Free Press, 1992), p. 168.

247 In some ways, the failure of Fukuyama's thesis is the same as the central failure of Marxism: its inability to recognize the variety of life (a particularly ironic failure on Fukuyama's part). Fukuyama, like Marx, ignores such factors as race and nationalism, assuming that everything boils down to the desire for a liberal society, just as Marx argued that everything boils down to class. In his original formulation, in any event, he left out three fourths of the world.

248 Amartya Sen, 'Human Rights and Asian Values', *New Republic*, 14 July 1997.

249 Kofi Busia, *The Challenge of Africa*, p. 44.

250 Landes, *The Wealth and Poverty of Nations*, p. 433, emphasis added.

251 Rawlings might not have been so afraid of failure economically had he not feared retribution so much: this was probably one of the main reasons why he called in the IMF. Now, however, when it would clearly be in Ghana's best interest for Rawlings to step aside, few are sure that he will.

252 'Chuan is clean', everyone agrees: he lives alone in his modest house. But asked to compare corruption at the top in his government compared with its predecessor, a man in a position to know said, 'Under Banharn, there was perhaps one of 49 ministers who was not corrupt. Under Chuan, there are ten.' Interview, Bangkok, 3 May 1999.

253 Karen Lange, 'In Liberia the People Choose an Awful Hope for Peace', *Washington Post*, 10 August 1997, p. C4.

254 See his essay, 'The Philippine Framework for Policy Reform', in W. Villacorta and W. Scott Thompson (eds), *The Philippine Road to NIChood* (Manila: De la Salle University Press, 1996).

255 Unless, of course, the market perceives that there is political substance in efforts to protect a currency – as when Washington moved to protect the yen in the summer of 1998. Even then, the effect was short-term. See Nicholas Thompson, 'Hard Trade', *Washington Monthly*, June 1999.

256 One of us asked the chief economic adviser under Nkrumah, E. N. Omaboe, how he got away with publishing in the annual economic surveys such candid criticism of the regime's economic policies. He would have gone to jail had many of his statements been in the press. 'But no one reads the *Economic Survey* in Ghana,' he said. 'Only in England and the United States.'

257 David Wilson, *Politics in Thailand* (Cornell University Press, 1967), p. 60.

258 We are grateful to Dr Surin Pitsuwon, foreign minister and adviser to Prime Minister Chuan, for taking the time in both 1998 and 1999 to discuss political reform with us in Bangkok.

259 'If you don't have the rule of law,' Harvard professor Huang Yasheng points out, 'capital leaves.' 'Predicting the Future of China', *Time*, 19 July 1999.

260 W. Scott Thompson, *Ghana's Foreign Policy*, p. 395.

261 Maier, *Into the House of the Ancestors*, p. 28.
262 'Towards a Democratic Charter', 10 June 1998.
263 *Ibid.*, emphasis added.
264 'On the Importance of Being Free', *Encounter*, 1965, p. 89.
265 W. Scott Thompson, notes, 1966.
266 The first PhD in the Thai Foreign Service, to Owart Suthiwart-Narueput, was awarded by the Fletcher School of Law and Diplomacy in 1951. Numerous others followed, including ML Ambassador Birabongse Kasemsri. There was an equally brilliant group in more recent days; Bunyaraks Ninsananda got his in 1971 and returned to the civil service thereafter.
267 The gradations are important. On a trip to China in 1981, one of the authors asked the then senior American what 'China and America talked about ... what are our areas of mutual concern?' The answer was immediate: 'The American-Chinese condominium over Thailand.'
268 Interview, Accra, 1966.
269 Interview, Ambassador Shirley Temple Black, 1976.
270 Pan-African News Service (PANA), 23 May 1998.
271 'Can Asians Think', *The National Interest*, Summer 1998, p. 35.
272 See *The Dispatch*, Accra, 4–10 January 1999. 'He was very ill with malaria and yet "stubbornly" tried for over two hours, to present an address which was sometimes incoherent, unfocused and irrelevant.' Ben Ephson, the writer and editor – a lawyer by training – wrote such reportage with great care to avoid libel suits.
273 Interview, Saranrom Palace, 12 May 1998.

Index